👁 INSIGHT GUIDES MUSEUMS AND GALLERIES OF NEW YORK CITY

Editorial

Editor
John Gattuso
Design
Klaus Geisler
Picture Editor
Hilary Genin
Picture Research
Susannah Stone
Editorial Director
Brian Bell

Distribution

United States
Langenscheidt Publishers, Inc.
46–35 54th Road, Maspeth, NY 11378
Fax: (718) 784-0640

Canada
Prologue Inc.
1650 Lionel Bertrand Blvd., Boisbriand
Québec, Canada J7H 1N7
Tel: (450) 434-0306. Fax: (450) 434-2627

UK & Ireland
GeoCenter International Ltd
The Viables Centre, Harrow Way
Basingstoke, Hants RG22 4BJ
Fax: (44) 1256-817988

Worldwide
**Apa Publications GmbH & Co.
Verlag KG (Singapore branch)**
38 Joo Koon Road, Singapore 628990
Tel: (65) 6865-1600. Fax: (65) 6861-6438

Printing

Insight Print Services (Pte) Ltd
38 Joo Koon Road, Singapore 628990
Tel: (65) 6865-1600. Fax: (65) 6861-6438

©2002 Apa Publications GmbH & Co.
Verlag KG (Singapore branch)
All Rights Reserved

First Edition 2002

ABOUT THIS BOOK

So you want to "do" New York's museums? A laudable ambition, but where in the world do you start? There are more than 75 museums of note in the metropolitan area and scores of galleries. They range from world-class institutions that sprawl across several city blocks to highly specialized collections that occupy no more than a snug gallery or two.

The tendency among most travelers is to make a beeline to one of the Big Five – the Metropolitan, MoMA, Guggenheim, Whitney, Museum of Natural History – but even this abbreviated list leaves you with more options than you could possibly manage in a single visit. Art or science? Dinosaurs or Dalí? Mummies or Monet? And what of the dozens of lesser-known museums, most of which, if located in a smaller city, would be star attractions in their own right? It's enough to make your head spin.

That's why we created this book. We recognize that visitors who turn up at a major museum, pick up a leaflet at the entrance and aim to do it in a couple of hours will rapidly find themselves exhausted and con-fused. To get the most out of a visit, it's essential to prepare in advance, and this book provides the information you need to set your priorities. It also explains, in introductory features, how New York became one of the world centers of art and culture, and why it's one of the best museum towns on the planet. And for the latest museum news, you can check the special updates page of our website: www.insightguides.com.

The writing team

This book was produced by John Gattuso of Stone Creek Publications in Milford, New Jersey. He is a veteran of more than a dozen Insight Guides and editor of Discovery Travel Adventures, a series of illustrated guidebooks for travelers with special interests. In addition to his editorial duties, he covered the history of the New York art scene and the American Museum of Natural History.

The principal writers are William G. Scheller and Edward A. Jardim. Scheller, a travel journalist who writes often for *National Geographic Traveler* and *Islands* magazines, covered the early history of New York art and the city's architectural heritage as well as writing profiles of more than 40 museums. Jardim has been a newspaperman in the metropolitan area for over 40 years. He covered 18 museums, including the Met, Guggenheim and MoMA, and co-wrote much of the history section. Artist and writer Daniel Rothbart covered about a dozen venues. He has exhibited widely in the U.S. and Europe and is associate editor of *NYArts Magazine*. Divya Symmers, who wrote about the gallery scene and several museums, contributed to Insight's New York City guide and frequently attends gallery openings. Michael Castagna, a former Stone Creek editor, is a free-lance writer living in New Jersey.

OPPOSITE:
The central
atrium of the
Guggenheim
Museum.

BELOW: Taking
a break at a
SoHo café.

The Dyckman Farmhouse Museum preserves a slice of 18th-century life.

A silk-screen Marilyn by Andy Warhol, pied piper of New York's Pop Art scene.

Fossil nautilus from the American Museum of Natural History.

Child in Sunlight by Willard Metcalf, from the Florence Griswold Museum.

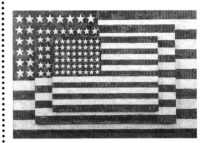

Three Flags, by Jasper Johns, from the Whitney Museum of American Art.

Iron spur from the American Craft Museum.

The dramatic setbacks and spire of the Empire State Building.

FOLLOWING PAGES: Detail from Dance on the Battery in the Presence of Peter Stuyvesant, 1838, Asher B. Durand, from the Museum of the City of New York; Poker Night (from A Streetcar Named Desire), 1948, Thomas Hart Benton, from the Whitney Museum of American Art; Pershing Square Bridge, 1993, Bascove, from the Museum of the City of New York.

WHY MUSEUMS MATTER

Gathered from near and far and in between, New York's varied
collections of great treasures await the public and its age-old
fascination with the artifacts of cultural and natural history

The Greeks had a name for it – *mouseion*, "seat of the Muses." We know it by its Latin nomenclature: museum. And just as the ancients had their different Muses – Clio for history, Urania for astronomy, Terpsichore for song and dance – so there are different types of museums, a rich assortment of them in New York and environs: Fine arts, performing arts, crafts, historical, science and natural history, military, business, communications and all the rest.

Evidence of museum-like practice in one form or another has been identified as far back as the 6th century BC. In not so ancient times, there were places with collections of precious objects and what were called "curiosities." They were few in number and reserved for the upper social strata, church people, connoisseurs, and generally not available to ordinary people. That all changed by the 19th century. Now there are museums by the thousands just in the United States alone, the greater number of which were only established in the second half of the 20th century. And they're visited every year by millions of ordinary folks.

What's the big attraction? Aside from being supposedly convenient places for meeting lovers and other strangers, museums cater to our curiosity about mankind's cultural history – who we are and how we got this way, perhaps even where we're heading. Along with this basic sense of inquiry is the impulse to acquire – to collect, sort out, classify and preserve. This is what museums do, for our edification and moral uplift, gathering the artifacts, precious objects and leftovers of earlier times to give us a glimpse of the way we were.

Soul of a city

These mementos include the good, the bad and the ugly – as in memorials to the European Holocaust or exhibitions on American slavery. The purpose of such stark reminders is not just to teach us a lesson, either, but to help forge bonds of reconciliation within society. More and more, museums have been taking on such social responsibilities, and in an age when terrorism can muscle aside informed debate, there's never been a greater need.

Though New York's museums were hard hit by a slump in tourism after the 2001 terrorist attacks, they have never been more appreciated by the public or felt a stronger sense of mission. In the dark days after the horror, the city's museums served as sanctuaries – quiet, contemplative places to seek the solace of great art and the companionship of those who appreciate it. "It's comforting to come back and see everything still here," said a visitor at the Metropolitan Museum of Art a few days after the World Trade Center fell. "All this beauty … and the good that people do." At a time when the arts were often criticized for being out of touch with the concerns of ordinary people, museums and galleries never seemed more relevant. Though the shadow of a hateful and destructive act laid heavily on the city, the power of the imagination to create beauty and order, to express every nuance of anxiety and joy, to recall the people and events that came before us, and to awaken at the most profound level our common humanity, remained undaunted.

As Philippe de Montebello, director of the Metropolitan Museum of Art, put it shortly after the tragedy: "Hospitals are open … to fix the body. We're here to fix the soul."

ABOVE: *Liz,* 1965, Andy Warhol.

OPPOSITE: *Prometheus,* 1934, Paul Manship, at Rockefeller Center.

NEW YORK RENAISSANCE

By the late 19th century, the city had been transformed from a colonial backwater to the seat of a fledgling empire, whose artists created work suitable for the "princes" of the Gilded Age

Despite its eventual status as the capital of American art, New York City was not an important locus in the early development of painting and sculpture in the colonies of British North America. That role fell to the two larger and more prominent cities of the colonial era, Boston and Philadelphia. Both of those places were quicker than New York to give rise to a mercantile elite, the class on whom artists of that era relied for patronage. New York produced no John Singleton Copley, chronicler of the 18th-century Boston aristocracy, or Charles Willson Peale, who painted Philadelphia's nabobs and gave that city (and the nation) its first real museum.

Having been a colony of the Netherlands during the first 60 years of its existence, New York was to some extent the beneficiary of the 17th-century Dutch aesthetic in painting – that frank, atmospheric and quite plastic realism that characterizes some of the greatest work produced by European artists of any era. Needless to say, no Rembrandt or Vermeer landed at the docks of

New Amsterdam, palette and brush in hand. But as a portrait of Peter Stuyvesant in the New-York Historical Society shows, a certain Dutch painterly competence was in evidence even in the earliest work produced in the colony. Heirs to this tradition, although in an even more naive vein, were the "Patroon painters" who fanned out from New Amsterdam throughout the Hudson River Valley to limn the landed gentry of New Netherlands.

Aside from Boston's Copley, who put in a six-month residence in New York in 1771, the principal painters associated with the city during the late 18th century are John Mare, Thomas McIlworth, Abraham Delanoy and John Durand. Typical of this group's portraiture work is Durand's *Richard Crossfield*, painted about 1769 and now in the collection of the Metropolitan Museum of Art. Though not without a certain naive charm in his expression, Durand's subject is posed with the stiffness and lack of natural articulation more characteristic of the itinerant folk limners of 50 years earlier than of the sophisticated postures of Copley's patrons (by way of comparison, look at the Bostonian's 1767 *Nicholas Boylston*, in the collections of Harvard University).

Oddly enough, for a famously expansive city, two of the most prominent painters in New York during the closing decades of the 18th century seem to have been miniaturists. John Ramage, a Dublin-trained Bostonian who worked in New York from 1777 to 1794, produced a series of highly competent portraits set in handsomely chased gold frames of his own design and execution – but none of these exquisite ovals was more than 2 inches (5 cm) in length. Another miniaturist was British émigré Archibald Robinson, who with his brother Alexander established the Columbian Academy of Painting in New York City in 1792. Between the mid-1700s and his retirement in 1795, Archibald Robinson supplemented his work as a miniaturist with larger-format watercolor and pen-and-ink renditions of landscapes and city scenes. His ink and color wash *New York from Long Island* (ca. 1795) not only serves to document the city's skyline in an era when church steeples and ships' masts were the only features to rise substantially above the harbor. It also reveals a growing sophistication in depth perception through the contrast of dark, detailed foreground elements with a sketchier, light-filled distance that almost prefigures the luminist harborscapes of a half-century later.

Wall Street, Half Past Two O'clock, 1857, James Cafferty and Charles Rosenberg, from the Museum of the City of New York.

Governor Peter Stuyvesant, attributed to Henri Couturier, from the New-York Historical Society.

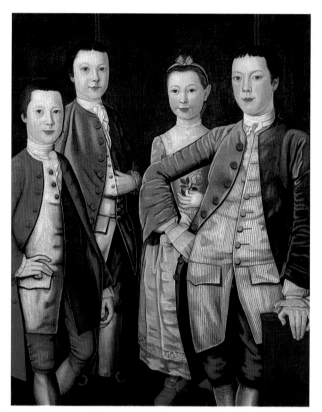

The Rapalje Children, 1768, John Durand, from the New-York Historical Society.

Hudson River School

New York artists of the early 19th century tended largely towards European-inspired academic subjects and technique, as the influence of such institutions as the New York Academy of the Fine Arts (1802) and National Academy of Design (cofounded by painter and telegraph inventor Samuel F. B. Morse in 1826) began to make their influence felt. Annual art exhibitions became a fixture of the New York calendar in 1827 and largely attracted derivative local talent. But the city was soon to serve as the launching ground for the first great native American art movement, the Hudson River School.

Thomas Cole, the school's English-born progenitor, emigrated to America in 1818 and established his studio in Manhattan in 1825. In the following year, he collaborated with Samuel F. B. Morse and architect Ithiel Town in founding the National Academy of Design. Concentrating on the landscapes favored by his wealthy patrons, to whom he was introduced by Academy President John Trumbull, Cole ranged north from the city on painting trips throughout the Hudson Valley and Catskill Mountains. The result was a new page in art history, the celebration of sublime and unsullied vistas and the appreciation of nature for its own sake, rather than merely as background for human activity and the built environment. During the next two decades, painters such as Asher B. Durand, John Kensett, Albert Bierstadt and – most spectacularly – Frederic Edwin Church would also base themselves in or near New York City, as they apotheosized the landscapes that lay just north of the metropolis. Eventually, of course, the relatively tame subject matter of New York's exurbia gave way to such Hudson River School subjects as the Rocky Mountains (Bierstadt's *Donner Lake from the Summit*, at the New-York Historical Society) and South America (Church's *Heart of the Andes*, at the Metropolitan Museum of Art).

Ironically, the emphasis upon wild, romantic nature that these painters popularized helped forestall the eventual acceptance of urban themes – other than portraiture of city gentry and genteel interior scenes – as fit for serious painters. Even as "genre painting" based upon everyday pursuits gained favor during the mid-19th century, the characters and situations portrayed tended to be drawn from rural and small-town life, as in the work of William Sidney Mount and George Caleb Bingham, rather than from the workaday world of the city. The clamor and vigor of New York's streets, and the muscular lineaments of its bridges and buildings, would have to wait for the next century – and for painters named Sloan, Bellows, Henri, Marin and Hopper.

The Gilded Age

This is not to say that the New York City of the late 19th century was a place that art passed by. But the painting and sculpture produced in New York during the Gilded Age – the earlier part of the 40-year span which followed the Civil War – was generally heavily influenced by European academicism and, as with all derivative art, lacked vigor and freshness of expression. The stunting of taste and artistic imagination at such a time should hardly seem surprising. New York in the immediate postwar era was a city whose middle and upper classes, in large part, were new to prosperity and inclined to purchase their aesthetic notions along with the fine and decorative artworks with which they furnished their parlors and public spaces. The tried-and-true European academic tradition was bound to have a particular appeal for the nouveaux riche, who had in earlier years hardly given art much thought at all. Many of them, when young and not yet rich, had no doubt been exposed to little in the way of art beyond Currier & Ives prints (those sentimental narratives were the products of a New York lithography studio), and, in a more serious vein, Winslow Homer's Civil War illustrations for *Harper's Weekly*.

But respect for the academic tradition, and in particular homage to the ideals and examples of the Renaissance, did produce a generation of highly competent if not visionary artists in the New York of the closing decades of the 19th century. Ohioan Kenyon Cox, trained in Paris, spent the latter part of his career in New York; he executed a great many public murals in a neoclassical vein as well as a number of academic portraits. New York City native John La Farge was a muralist of greater capability, a subtler colorist than Cox and a man far less prone to fall into the almost wooden formality that was Cox's interpretation of classicism. La Farge's 1887 *Rhinelander Altarpiece* in the Church of the Ascension (Fifth Avenue and Tenth Street) is considered by many to be his finest work. It depicts the Ascension of Christ with a warmth

DUNCAN PHYFE

New York in the late 18th and early 19th centuries was a more fertile ground for the decorative arts than for painting and sculpture. Cabinetmaking attained a high degree of refinement during this era, and none of its practitioners surpassed Duncan Phyfe.

Working in maple, rosewood and Caribbean mahoganies, Phyfe excelled in the Sheraton, Adam, and Hepplewhite designs that were so well suited to the restrained Federal mode. Beautifully proportioned, with slim, subtly curved arms and legs, Phyfe's work typically featured acanthus, oak leaf, and parallel rows of reeding as ornamentation.

In the 1820s, Phyfe turned to the more ponderous Empire style, with its blocky classical motifs. By the time he retired in 1846, he had even begun to venture into Rococo Revival designs. But that style, which gave us the overall voluptuousness of mid-Victorian furniture, was brought to its pinnacle by another New York craftsman, John Henry Belter. In the trajectory from early Duncan Phyfe to 1850s Belter, we can see spare elegance evolve into an almost grotesque showiness.

Winter on the Skating Pond in Central Park, by the lithography firm Currier & Ives, self-described "Publishers of Cheap and Popular Pictures."

The Berry Pickers, 1768, by John Durand, a notable New York painter of the late 18th century.

of color that redeems the formal symmetry of the composition – a symmetry reflected in an architectural surround designed by the renowned Stanford White.

In addition to his work as a muralist, John La Farge indulged in pure decoration, perhaps best represented by his abstract designs for the interior of a commission located outside New York, H. H. Richardson's Trinity Church in Boston. But La Farge's forays into decorative art had a solid New York foundation in his collaboration with the era's greatest artisan in stained glass, Louis Comfort Tiffany. Tiffany's New York studio was responsible for a vast amount of the window glass, as well as occasional objects such as lamps and vases, that came to characterize another aspect of fin-de-siècle American taste – neither classical nor Renaissance-inspired, but lushly romantic, possessed of a vaguely Oriental mystical character, and so preciously voluptuous that the obvious influence of the English Arts and Crafts movement could easily be seen segueing into Art Nouveau.

In sculpture, the preeminent figure in the New York of the late 19th century was Augustus Saint-Gaudens, Irish-born and Paris-trained, who honed his skills as a young man while working as a cameo cutter in the city. Saint-Gaudens' best known New York monuments are his 1881 *Farragut Monument*, honoring Civil War Admiral David Farragut, in Madison Square Park, and the *General Sherman Monument* at Fifth Avenue and 59th Street, an equestrian statue of William Tecumseh Sherman in gilded bronze, with a winged Nike, goddess of victory, striding before him. Unveiled in 1903, the Sherman statue not only serves as the capstone of the neo-Renaissance in New York, but also seems to usher in the city's imperial epoch, the century in which it became a world colossus.

A vision of things to come

And yet the close of the 19th century in New York City was not all Renaissance grandeur and lush stained glass. Any summary of artistic accomplishment in that place and time should take account of the career of Albert Pinkham Ryder, a New Englander who spent much of his life as a near recluse in a shabby, junk-strewn New York apartment. Ryder's small canvases were moody, mystical, almost dreamlike; they were infused with the moonlight he seemed to prefer to the frank light of day. His *Moonlight Marine* (ca. 1880) is an eerie, bitonal antithesis to the bright luminist seascapes of a generation before; his *The Race Track, or Death on a Pale Horse* (ca. 1896), a depiction of a galloping horse with a ghastly, scythe-brandishing mount, is a vision out of Poe by way of Hieronymus Bosch – only without Bosch's color and clutter.

"The artist should not sacrifice his ideals to a landlord and a costly studio," Ryder once remarked. "A rain-tight roof, frugal living, a box of colors, and God's sunlight through clear windows keeps the soul attuned and the body vigorous for one's daily work." Apropos of his own tastes, Ryder might have substituted moonlight for sunlight. But otherwise, his point was to be well taken. During the decades following his 1917 death there would be plenty of New York artists whose sense of art as personal vision would keep them from ever having to consider such a sacrifice of ideals. The days of the academy and of Renaissance-redux were over; an era of rough, personal and highly individualistic expression lay ahead.

Kindred Spirits, 1849, by Asher B. Durand, depicts poet and editor William Cullen Bryant and painter Thomas Cole in the Catskill Mountains.

THE ASHCAN AND THE ARMORY

Spirited urban realists took the city by storm at the start of the 20th century, only to be upstaged by a groundbreaking exhibit of modern art

New York at the turn of the 20th century was a city in the throes of convulsive change. Taking in more than 2,000 immigrants a day, it had become the largest and most diverse metropolis in the Republic and a launching pad for a great outpouring of industrial energy. Skyscrapers and bridges soared overhead. Subway trains clattered below. Electricity lit up the night. And people flocked to new kinds of entertainment like nickelodeons and moving pictures.

It was a heady time to be an artist. New York was a city of extremes – a rowdy, chaotic, polyglot place where sumptuous uptown mansions contrasted sharply with the squalid tenements of the Lower East Side. Streets brimmed with exotic people and ideas, a reformist spirit was in the air, and Victorian ideals of sex roles and morality were being called into question. Social transformations unleashed by the Industrial Revolution had forged an amorphous though distinctly modern culture, and New York City was on the cutting edge.

OPPOSITE: *Picture Shop Window*, 1907, John Sloan, from the Newark Museum.

Challenging the academy

As the city grew in prominence, it attracted artists from around the country, many of them eager to challenge the influence of the established schools of painting. The dominant presence in the visual arts during this period was the National Academy of Design, a mostly conservative organization that catered to the decorative needs of the well-to-do, whose taste leaned heavily toward classical imagery, formal portraiture, and the tried and true Old Masters.

BELOW: *Ballet Girls* by Everett Shinn, a member of the New York realists known as The Eight.

This was anathema to young artists keen on developing an indigenous American vision. To them, pictures of winged goddesses and society matrons were all well and good for representing the "eternal verities," but they were utterly divorced from the realities of everyday life and out of step with the robust and audacious spirit of industrial capitalism – the very system that gave rise to the art-buying class.

It was this desire for art with an authentic American verve that motivated the first serious challenge to the academy's authority and the first of two exhibits that turned the art world on its ear. At the center of the fracas was a group of artists led by Robert Henri, a painter and gifted teacher whose magnetic personality and iconoclastic nature made him an ideal candidate to lead a rebellion.

Henri had studied in Philadelphia at the Pennsylvania Academy of the Fine Arts, where he was trained in the realist tradition of Thomas Eakins and his protégé Thomas Anschutz. Eakins was one of the few painters of his day to encourage artists to capture the truth of the world around them. He was unrelenting in his attention to detail, demanded that his pupils engage in rigorous anatomical study (he was later expelled from the Academy of the Fine Arts for removing the loincloth from a male model in the presence of female students), and urged them to "study their own country and portray its life and types."

Robert Henri's *Salome*, 1909, raised eyebrows among critics accustomed to classical themes and genteel subject matter.

That's exactly what Henri did. After traveling in Europe, he settled in New York and turned his attention to portraying the "spirit of the people of today." He exulted in the clang and clamor of city life, especially in the working-class neighborhoods of lower Manhattan. Let the academicians fuss over their classical allegories. As Henri saw it, such work lacked vigor and spirit. He was enthralled by the world of ordinary people and the little dramas of everyday life. In the place of society matrons, he painted dancing girls and street urchins. Instead of dreamy Arcadias, he rendered crowded city streets in all their grit and humanity.

He attacked the canvas with equal vigor, applying paint in rapid, spontaneous brush strokes. Immediacy was the thing, getting the image down on canvas before the feeling passed. "Do it all in one sitting," he instructed his students. "In one minute if you can."

His enthusiasm was contagious. Henri was "a catalyst, an enthusiast ... a born preacher ... [with] the pioneer's contempt for cant and aestheticism," as he was fondly remembered by John Sloan, one of several students who followed him from Philadelphia to New York. Like Sloan, many of his pupils had worked as illustrators for the Philadelphia press and honed their abilities to quickly record the details of urban life. As artists, they scoured the tenements, saloons, alleys and markets, giving shape – in Walt Whitman's words – to the "endless and noisy chorus" of "million-footed Manhattan."

The Apostles of Ugliness

Henri's showdown with the establishment came in 1908, when he organized an exhibition of eight dissident artists – most urban realists like himself – in response to what he regarded as the academy's exclusionary policies. It was a generally good-natured revolt, although the press sensationalized the story as the "New York Art War," describing Henri and his comrades as the "Eight Rebels," "a revolutionary black gang," and "the Apostles of Ugliness." The public was hooked and came to the show in droves. Henri's vision was vindicated, and several members of The Eight – as the group came to be known – formed the core of what was later and more accurately dubbed the Ashcan School, referring to the scenes of everyday life depicted in their naturalistic paintings.

While Henri excelled at portraits – the frank sexuality of his *Salome*, a full-length rendering of a dancer known as Mademoiselle Voclezca, caused quite a stir – his colleagues and students concentrated on other aspects of city life. "Guts! Guts! Life! Life! That's my technique," said George Luks. He injected a dose of machismo into such pictures as *The Wrestlers* (1905), in which a pair of bare-chested men are locked in a knot of straining muscle – Darwinian struggle at its most elemental. The same intensity is evident in slum scenes like *Hester Street* (1905), produced in a loose and impulsive style that accentuates the sense of teeming humanity. The crowd recedes to the horizon – people as far as the eye can see; the Lower East Side was the most densely populated place on earth.

Even more explosive and brutal than Luks' wrestlers are the paintings of boxers produced by the much younger George Bellows, who, though not a founding member of the Ashcan School, was one of the most successful. The strongest of the bunch is *Stag at Sharkey's* (1907), which depicts a pair of fighters pummeling each other at a quasi-legal "boxing club" just across the street from Bellows' downtown flat. The boxers are the only figures illuminated in the painting. Their faces are bloodied, heads butting, bodies arched against the force of the blows. Spectators surround the ring in a sea of dark faces, leering and cartoonish.

Human contact of a different sort is the subject of Bellows' *Cliff Dwellers* (1913), a scene of urban congestion in which tenement dwellers gaze down on a street thronged with pedestrians. Even the sparsely populated *Pennsylvania Station Excavation* (1909) seethes with a kind of raw, primeval energy. The picture shows an enormous crater dug for the construction of the city's main rail terminal, a few spectators watching from the rim. The pit smolders like a volcano, an allusion to the geologic scale of the forces reshaping the city.

John Sloan, on the other hand, had a keen eye for the quiet, telling moment – women peering into a shop window, children building a snowman in a back alley, men hanging out at McSorley's Ale House, a venerable all-male tavern where the artist liked to drink. In *Sunday, Women Drying Their Hair* (1912), for example, three young women sun themselves on a tenement rooftop. They are hearty, buxom, apparently happy. Perhaps they are shop girls, a new class of women whose economic independence was breaking down Victorian notions of female gentility. Though Sloan was politically active (he served on the editorial board of the *Masses* and was a Socialist candidate for office), his paintings were largely apolitical. Indeed, his depictions of poverty seem at times picturesque, as if the poor were somehow more in harmony with the vital energy of the metropolis.

Other Ashcan painters found the pulse points of the city where people gathered for public entertainment. Everett Shinn created some of the group's most stark images of slum life early

George Bellows' *Stag at Sharkey's*, 1907, captures the explosive violence of an illicit boxing match at a downtown saloon owned by former prizefighter Tom Sharkey.

in his career. Then, influenced by Degas, he became absorbed with painting theater scenes and later worked as an art director in Hollywood. William Glackens set his sights somewhat higher on the socioeconomic scale, depicting fashionable restaurants, cafés, music halls and other middle-class amusements – yet another facet of American culture coming into its own after the turn of the 20th century.

Early modernism

While Henri was championing the cause of realism, an even more potent challenge to the academy was coalescing around another charismatic figure, the photographer Alfred Stieglitz. Born in New Jersey of German-Jewish parents, Stieglitz grew up in New York City and was introduced to photography while an engineering student in Germany. He returned to New York in 1890 and soon made a name for himself as an art photographer as well as an organizer and promoter.

In 1902, he co-founded a group he called the Photo-Secessionists and later launched a journal, *Camera Work*, to chronicle the group's work and ideas. In 1905 he and fellow photographer Edward Steichen opened a small gallery at 291 Fifth Avenue. It was a tiny, modest place, but under Stieglitz's forward-thinking if often autocratic direction the Little Galleries of the Photo-Secession would become one of the most influential galleries in New York.

It's not entirely clear why Stieglitz chose the name Photo-Secessionists or what he thought the group was seceding from. Many members shot in the Pictorialist style, characterized by moody, soft-focus pictures that were intended to evoke a vague sense of magic and the meta-physical. An image that recurs in much of the group's work, for instance, is a woman, usually naked or in robes, gazing into a mysterious glass orb.

Hester Street, 1905, George Luks, from the Brooklyn Museum of Art.

Stieglitz himself didn't go in for this sort of self-conscious spirituality, nor did he have much use for crystal balls. Although much of his work before 1910 had a gauzy, low-contrast look, it was relatively hard-edged compared to the woozy mysticism of some of his colleagues. He even-tually eschewed the practice of manipulating the lens or printing process in order to create a

blurred, painterly effect, preferring, as he said, to shoot "straight."

More important, however, was his choice of subject. Like the Ashcan painters, Stieglitz was exhilarated by city life, and he turned his camera on the sky-scrapers, streetcars and rail yards that embodied the power – both positive and negative – of industrial America. Recalling his famous 1903 photograph of the Fuller (or Flatiron) Building – the very symbol of the nation's technological prowess at the time – he said the wedge-shaped structure appeared to be moving toward him "like the bow of a monster steamer – a picture of a raw America still in the making."

But unlike Henri and the urban realists, who were trying to create a distinctly American aesthetic, Stieglitz believed that art transcended national boundaries, and he was eager to fling open the doors of American culture to foreign influences, particularly those of the modern artists of the Paris salons. It was this role as a bridge to the European modernists even more than his photographic work that made Stieglitz a pivotal figure in the history of American art in the 20th century.

Alfred Stieglitz abandoned soft-focus techniques in *The Steerage*, 1907, a picture of immigrants returning to Europe.

In its first three years, the Little Galleries of the Photo-Secession– better known as the 291 – showed only American photographers. That changed in 1908 after Edward Steichen gave up his New York studio and moved to Paris, where he worked informally as Stieglitz's scout. It was on Steichen's recommendation that Stieglitz mounted his first exhibition devoted to a European artist – watercolors by Auguste Rodin – followed a few months later by a show of drawings and lithographs by Henri Matisse. The New York critics couldn't believe their eyes. They had never seen this level of abstraction and howled with derision. After seeing Rodin's work, William Merritt Chase, a popular American Impressionist, vowed never to set foot in 291 again.

Stieglitz, characteristically, was undeterred, and a string of important shows followed, including exhibitions of the work of Picasso, Cézanne and Toulouse-Lautrec. Stieglitz was equally enthusiastic, if not more so, about "progressive" American painters like John Marin, Alfred Maurer, Max Weber, Arthur Dove and Marsden Hartley, and was famously unstinting in support of their work. As Arthur Dove later put it, "I do not think I could have existed as a painter without [Stieglitz's] super-encouragement and the battle he has fought day by day for 25 years. He is without doubt the one who has done the most for art in America."

Breaking away

Modernism didn't arrive in New York as a cohesive movement but as a multiplicity of "isms"– Post-Impressionism, Fauvism, Cubism, and later Dadaism and Futurism – each with porous boundaries and a shifting roster of acolytes. What tied the artists together was a desire to break away from the conventions of representational art. They ditched the old rules of perspective, color and composition in order to, in Stieglitz's words, "work out their own vision." Their attitudes were reinforced by scientific discoveries that seemed to question the solidity of the "real" world and the reliability of perception. Darwin, Freud and quantum physics had undercut the certainties

Cityscape, a watercolor by John Marin, reflects New York's vitality in the early 20th century.

of the 19th century. Apprehending "reality" – whatever that was – became a far more slippery prospect than it was a generation earlier, and modernists reacted by abandoning intellect for intuition and depicting the world as they perceived it behind the veil of physical appearance.

The American modernists who showed at 291 during these formative years represented a wide range of personal vision. There were painters like Alfred Maurer and John Marin, both deeply influenced by the bold, expressive colors of Matisse and the Fauvists. Maurer later adopted a Cubist style. Some of his strongest images are portraits, usually of two or more people with merged facial features. He never achieved critical or commercial success and killed himself in 1932 after the death of his father, a Currier & Ives illustrator who despised modern art. Marin returned to New York in 1910 shortly after his show at the 291 and, like Stieglitz, turned his attention to the city itself, producing watercolors in which buildings, streets and bridges – set askew with strokes of color – are animated with a restless, urban energy.

Few painters exerted more influence on Stieglitz during this early period than Max Weber, who lived in a small room behind the gallery in 1910 after returning from Paris. Weber was responsible for enlightening Stieglitz on a variety of topics, including the importance of Paul Cézanne, whose work Stieglitz exhibited the following year. Weber may have been the only artist in New York more difficult to get along with than Stieglitz himself, and the two men parted company over the pricing of Weber's paintings at his only 291 show.

Unlike Weber, Marsden Hartley got his first taste of modern art in New York at Stieglitz's gallery before traveling to Paris and then Berlin, where he was smitten with the city's homosexual subculture and pre-war pageantry. He developed an idiosyncratic, collage-like style evident in such paintings as *Portrait of a German Officer* (1914), in which he assembled images of military insignia, banners and uniforms to memorialize his lover, a German officer killed in the early days of World War I.

Other early American modernists such as Arthur Dove and, a bit later, Georgia O'Keeffe sought inspiration in the natural landscape, transcribing organic forms of "Sky, Sea, Mountain, Plain" into flowing masses of color. Dove was fascinated by synesthesia – the experience of color as sound – and one can almost hear bass tones resonating through the sea air in his *Fog Horns* (1929). O'Keeffe, who became well-known for her sensuous

STIEGLITZ AND O'KEEFFE

After learning in 1916 that Alfred Stieglitz was exhibiting her drawings without her permission, Georgia O'Keeffe demanded their removal. It was a fitting beginning for one of the art world's most tempestuous but fruitful relationships.

Stieglitz was soon as fascinated with O'Keeffe as he was with her work. By 1918 he and the young artist were lovers; they married in 1925, after Stieglitz divorced his wife. For the next two decades, the relationship between the maturing artist and the much older photographer was a source of both inspiration and exasperation for both.

"They are as if I saw a part of myself," Stieglitz wrote of O'Keeffe's drawings in the early days of their liaison. Soon O'Keeffe's own self would become a core part of Stieglitz's opus, as she posed for hundreds of photographs. But it was never an easy relationship: Stieglitz needed people, O'Keeffe needed solitude. Beginning in 1929, answering that need and stung by her husband's infidelities, the painter began to spend part of each year in New Mexico, where the elemental shapes and clear light of the desert increasingly informed her work. But she was with Stieglitz when he died in 1946, at age 82. As she had written to a friend, "I like that I can make him feel that I have hold of his hand to steady him as he goes on."

close-ups of flowers, tried her hand at cityscapes as well, repeatedly painting the view from the Shelton Hotel apartment she shared with Stieglitz, and, most notably, the soaring mass of the Radiator Building, which she rendered as a black shaft illuminated by brightly lit windows, a column of light cleaving the night sky nearby.

The big show

Stieglitz was instrumental in laying the groundwork for modern art in New York, but even his efforts were dwarfed by the power of a single event, the Armory Show of 1913, to redefine American visual arts. The person most responsible for assembling that landmark exhibit was Arthur Davies, a Symbolist artist with conservative connections whose work, at first glance, had little in common with modern sensibilities. Davies had been appointed president of the Association of American Painters and Sculptors, a group formed in 1912 to put together a sweeping exhibit of contemporary art. Originally the plan was to include only a few European works, but Davies convinced the group to broaden the scope of the show and, with his colleague Walter Kuhn, set out on a whirlwind scouting tour of Europe.

In all, the group amassed nearly 1,300 works representing more than 300 artists, about two-thirds Americans, covering a patchwork of styles ranging from Ashcan to French Impressionist, Fauvist and Cubist. The show, formally named the *International Exhibition of Modern Art*, opened on February 17, 1913, at the armory of the New York National Guard's 69th Regiment. Drawing the biggest crowds, and the most vitriolic criticism, were the European modernists – Gauguin, Cézanne, Picasso, Braque, Léger and, most notoriously, at least as far as the press was concerned, Marcel Duchamp. His inscrutable *Nude Descending a Staircase, No. 2* (1912) was ridiculed by one reviewer as an "explosion in a shingle factory."

The louder the critics protested, the more curious the public became. When the show closed in New York after four weeks, more than 75,000 people had attended, and thousands more saw it in Boston and Chicago, where students from the Art Institute were so outraged that they burned several artists in effigy. But an entire generation of artists, collectors and critics had been given a glimpse of the future. The Modernist seed had been planted in American soil and would be nourished in coming years by the flood of European artists into New York at the onset of World War I.

LEFT: *Painting, Number 5,* 1914–15, Marsden Hartley, from the Whitney Museum of American Art.

RIGHT: *Purple Petunias,* 1925, Georgia O'Keeffe, from the Newark Museum.

OF MEN AND MACHINES

The stock market crash of 1929 put an end to the Jazz Age, prompting
New York artists to abandon abstraction in favor of socially relevant art

"**A**merica is just as Goddamned good as Europe." Blasphemous, right? Yes, also brash and boosterish. But what else might you expect from Henry McBride, longtime art critic and know-it-all for the *New York Sun*, whose life span stretched nearly from the days of Abraham Lincoln to those of John F. Kennedy? Still, what he was saying, or writing, had a point.

McBride was sending a message that American culture in the 1920s was alive and well, and able to compete with the best the Old World had to offer. Fatigued by war, artists and intellectuals on both sides of the Atlantic looked to the New World for fresh ideas and inspiration. What attracted them was the vibrancy of American society – its industry and technology, jazzy music and glamorous movies. No other city embodied those qualities with more gusto than New York.

Even before World War I, artists had seized upon the city as a symbol of America's industrial prowess. A case in point was the painter Joseph Stella, a southern Italian immigrant who came to New York in 1896 and was promptly smitten. Hello Gotham, goodbye Mezzogiorno. Stella fell in with Alfred Stieglitz's circle of modern artists, basked in Coney Island's garish lights, and took special delight in the Brooklyn Bridge. To him the span was more than a monumental work of engineering. It was "a shrine containing all the efforts of the new civilization of America." In later years he recalled, with Whitmanesque ardor, walking the bridge and drinking in its towered expanse, "deeply moved, as if on the threshold of a new religion or in the presence of new divinity."

Stella painted the bridge many times but perhaps never more exuberantly than in *The Brooklyn Bridge (The Bridge)*, the final canvas in a five-panel tribute to his adopted city (*The Voice of the City of New York Interpreted*, 1920–22). Here the bridge's Gothic arches, enmeshed in a web of steel cables, frame a distant view of shimmering white skyscrapers – Manhattan as the Promised Land. It's no accident that the work is presented in a polyptych format typical of Italian altarpieces, or that its luminous colors recall stained-glass windows. In Stella's view, technology was a new religion, the bridge a sacred icon.

OPPOSITE: Detail from *Coney Island*, 1936, Reginald Marsh. The popular New York beach was one of the artist's favorite subjects.

BELOW: *Shopper*, 1928, by Kenneth Hayes Miller, who portrayed ordinary people around his 14th Street studio.

The short, happy life of Dada

Lighter and more satiric in their approach were the émigrés Francis Picabia and Marcel Duchamp, central figures in the brief but influential New York Dada movement. Both artists viewed technology as a key metaphor of modern society. "The machine," Picabia observed in 1915, "has become more than a mere adjunct of life. It is really part of human life, perhaps the very soul." This was shortly before his showing of a series of "object portraits" in which drawings of machines stood in for actual people. The best-known, *Ici, c'est ici Stieglitz (Here, This Is Stieglitz*, 1915), represented the photographer as a folding camera with a broken (and unmistakably flaccid) bellows. A series of machine images followed, many of which look like engineering diagrams with suggestive labels that equate lovemaking to the workings of various pistons, cogs and cylinders.

The same sort of loopy, sardonic humor is evident in Marcel Duchamp's masterpiece *The Bride Stripped Bare by Her Bachelors, Even* (1915–23), an enigmatic assemblage of oil, wire, lead foil and "dust" on a couple

of glass panes. The whole thing registers as a sexual allegory involving "love gasoline," "desire motors" and a weird mechanical apparatus. Absurdity is part and parcel of the experience, shocking at the time, meant to subvert the viewer's expectations. Even more notorious in this regard was Duchamp's *Fountain* (1917) – a porcelain urinal that he submitted to a supposedly open show by the Society of Independent Artists. The piece was promptly rejected, though Duchamp's appropriation of manufactured goods for artistic purposes – he called such works "readymades" – presaged by some 40 years the use of "found objects" by artists like Jasper Johns and Robert Rauschenberg.

Working in the same vein was Duchamp's friend Man Ray, who created found-object sculptures like *New York* (1917), a bundle of chrome strips held tight with a C-clamp. But in the end, the realities of New York life proved too absurd to sustain the Dadaist vision. Man Ray said, famously, "All New York is Dada, and will not tolerate a rival." He went back to Paris in 1921, like Duchamp before him.

Equally prescient was the work of Stuart Davis, a student of Robert Henri before being awakened to modernism at the Armory Show. "I paint what I see in America," Davis said, and what he saw in the early 1920s was the seepage of consumer culture – advertising, packaging, household products – into every aspect of American life. His best-known efforts during this period are pictures of cigarette boxes (*Lucky Strike*, 1921) and a mouthwash bottle (*Odol*, 1924), rendered in a bold, flattened, Cubist style. Consumer products wouldn't figure prominently in American art again until Andy Warhol's Coke bottles and soup cans of the 1960s.

ARTISTS OF THE HARLEM RENAISSANCE

New York in the 1920s was home to the Harlem Renaissance, a remarkable burst of creativity focused on a neighborhood that in the preceding two decades had become the capital of Black America. Today associated primarily with the advent of jazz and the flowering of literary talents such as Langston Hughes, Jean Toomer and Zora Neale Hurston, the Harlem Renaissance has often been neglected as a matrix which nurtured the visual arts.

Among significant visual artists of the Harlem Renaissance were Meta Vaux Warrick Fuller, a sculptor who had studied under Rodin in Paris and who mined traditional African themes in works that ranged from realism to Expressionism in style, and Palmer Hayden, a painter who likewise plumbed the African experience but who made vigorous use of Black American folklore in his "John Henry" series. Aaron Douglas painted in two markedly divergent styles: in his illustrations for poet James Weldon Johnson's book *God's Trombones: Seven Negro Sermons in Verse* he employed subtle tones and a stylized geometry, but he could render prosaic urban scenes in a realism suggestive of a softer-edged Edward Hopper. William H. Johnson was another protean figure, capable of evolving his style from an academic naturalism to a stark primitivism whose whimsy occasionally earned the painter criticism from African-Americans who felt his work bordered on caricature.

Parade for Repeal, 1934, Ben Shahn's commentary on the folly of Prohibition, at the Museum of the City of New York.

Early Sunday Morning, 1930, by Edward Hopper, whose work conveys the loneliness and isolation of urban life.

Studies in precision

If Joseph Stella responded to industrial technology with feelings of religious awe, and the Dadaists with subversive playfulness, then the work of artists like Charles Sheeler and Charles Demuth was about using "The Machine" to restore a classical sense of order. Drawing on technology as both metaphor and subject, they rendered images of factories, warehouses, bridges and other works of industrial architecture in a flat, mechanical style with little evidence of expressive gesture. Sheeler called it Precisionism, and its resemblance to photo-realism was no coincidence. He was a photographer as well as a painter, and the two media were in constant dialogue.

People and nature are virtually absent from paintings like Sheeler's *American Landscape* (1930) and Demuth's Cubist-influenced *My Egypt* (1927; *see page 104*), except when needed for scale or background. In their place are man-made structures – smokestacks, turbines, rail yards – cool, static, devoid of sentiment. Beneath the surface, however, many of Sheeler's Precisionist works belie a deep passion for order and an almost naive faith in the power of rational and efficient management to remedy social ills. In a moment of zealotry, Sheeler declared his faith: "Our factories are our substitute for religious expression," he said, echoing Calvin Coolidge's classically bourgeois epigram: "The man who builds a factory builds a temple. The man who works there worships there."

Although Precisionism never coalesced into a formal movement, the style reverberated through the work of painters Elsie Driggs (*see page 206*), Louis Lozowick and Ralston Crawford, as well as photographers Margaret Bourke-White, Paul Strand and Lewis Hine (*see page 79*), and one still sees its influence in slick "product shots" and other types of modern advertising.

Hopper: Painter of melancholy

Faith in technology, industry and the rejuvenating power of urban life were hardly universal. A variety of intellectuals and artists raised concerns about the dehumanization of the assembly-line worker and the stress and alienation caused by life in congested, industrial cities.

In the visual arts, no one captured the loneliness and desolation of town life more poignantly than Edward Hopper. A student of Ashcan painter Robert Henri, Hopper imbued his work with a profound sense of melancholy and loss. His figures are often depicted alone – passive, dejected, bored – or, if shown together, strangely disengaged, unable to connect or communicate.

In *Second Story Sunlight*, 1960 (*see page 107*), for example, two people lounge on a balcony – a pleasant enough scene until you notice how disconnected they are. One reads the paper; the other gazes absently away. Stark light accentuates the odd flatness of the house but illuminates nothing about the two figures. The general impression is of emptiness and boredom. Even street scenes like *Early Sunday Morning* (1930) convey a sense of sadness. The effect is created by

what's absent as much as by what's present. Though the buildings were well known to Hopper (he lived nearby in Greenwich Village), he chose to omit identifying details. They could be anywhere. And where are the people? We see only darkened windows that reveal nothing of the lives within.

The view from 14th Street

Hopper's dark vision took on even more poignancy after the stock market crash of 1929 and the onset of the Great Depression. Disillusioned by the failure of industrialism, many artists searched for redemption in the values of common people and the routines of everyday life. Known as the American Scene, the movement focused on rural tableaus evoking the virtues of family, hard work and individuality. But there was also an urban wing in New York dedicated to portraying ordinary people and scenes of daily life.

The pivotal figure was Kenneth Hayes Miller, a painter who depicted the shoppers – usually sturdy middle-class matrons – around his 14th Street studio. Miller's women sometimes have a sad, faraway look in their eyes, but the images are mostly dignified, with a formal quality he modeled on Renaissance portraiture. The overall impression is of normalcy and contentment, tinged with nostalgia for the simple pleasures of domestic life.

One of Miller's best-known students, Reginald Marsh, once complained that the people his mentor encouraged him to paint were ugly.

The Great White Way Leaving the Subway, 1920–22, from Joseph Stella's five-panel tribute to New York City (Newark Museum).

Miller's reply: "They *are* ugly; they are people. Buy a pair of field glasses." It was a lesson Marsh took to heart. His pictures are detailed visions of urban life teeming with Bowery bums, strutting gigolos and blonde bombshells in a restless, jitterbug style. One of his favorite subjects was Coney Island, packed with the flesh and foibles of urban denizens enjoying a day at the beach.

Another of Miller's well-known students, Isabel Bishop, took a more empathetic approach, catching the neighborhood's students and shop girls in moments of quiet rapport. Her subjects usually appear relaxed, comfortable, at ease, though many are shown in motion, between home and office, perhaps. Her work is distinguished by the nuances of interaction – a subtle gesture, a telling expression – and a muted and "filmy" application of color and fine, etchy draftsmanship.

The voice of protest

For many New York artists, however, it wasn't enough merely to observe the urban scene. They wanted to use their work as an instrument of social change. "Yes, paint America, but with your eyes open," said Moses Soyer. "Do not glorify Main Street. Paint it as it is – mean, dirty, avaricious."

Soyer was a Social Realist, like brothers Isaac and Raphael and such others as Ben Shahn and Philip Evergood. Associated with radical left-wing journals like the *New Masses*, these artists addressed the issues of racial injustice, chronic poverty, lynching and workers' rights. The Soyers were particularly adept at conveying the hopelessness and boredom of the unemployed in works such as *The Mission* (Raphael Soyer, ca. 1935) and *Employment Agency* (Isaac Soyer, 1937). Ben Shahn, on the other hand, attacked the legal system with the series *The Passion of Sacco and Vanzetti* (1931–32), chronicling the trial and execution of the Italian anarchists, as well as projects devoted to prison reform, the labor movement and the folly of Prohibition.

The Communist sympathies of some Social Realists roused the government's suspicion and put them in direct opposition to American Scene painters like Thomas Hart Benton and John Steuart Curry, who worked in the Midwest and largely depicted rural life. Benton – the most outspoken and influential of the group – had spent more than 20 years in New York before returning to Missouri in 1935 angry about what he regarded as the moral bankruptcy of the urban art scene. Left behind in the city were two of his most significant murals – *America Today*, commissioned by the New School for Social Research, and *The Arts of Life in America*, for the Whitney Museum of American Art.

Art as civic project

Meanwhile, artists of all political stripes benefited from an unprecedented outpouring of governmental largesse. Inspired in part by the success of Diego Rivera and the Mexican school of mural painting, President Franklin D. Roosevelt in 1933 approved the creation of the Public Works of Art Project, which funded over 3,500 artists to create murals, sculptures, easel paintings and other works for public buildings. The program lasted only six months but was soon followed by the Federal Art Project and the Treasury Department's Section of Painting and Sculpture; both ran to 1943.

In a curious turn of events, Rivera himself came to New York to execute a major commission. Well-known for his Marxist leanings, the artist was nonetheless hired in 1933 by the Rockefeller family to create murals for the lobby of the RCA Building at Rockefeller Center – a virtual monument to the power and glory of American Capitalism.

It didn't take long for the project to turn sour, as Rivera and his assistants sketched the outlines of marching workers, mechanized warfare, and the Kremlin. But the straw that broke the capitalist's back was the likeness of the Bolshevik leader himself, Vladimir Ilyich Lenin, peering out from a group of grim-faced proletarians. Objecting, Nelson Rockefeller asked that the offending portrait be altered. Rivera refused; better that the piece be destroyed than its integrity compromised, as he saw it. The artist was paid in full and ushered out. The unfinished mural was shrouded in canvas during the building's opening ceremony and, six months later, reduced to rubble.

City Activities with Subway from the *America Today* murals, 1930, Thomas Hart Benton.

THE NEW YORK SCHOOL AND BEYOND

A major American art movement took root in the city after World War II as the art world's center of gravity shifted from Paris to New York

With the outbreak of World War II, the influence of Paris on modern art declined, to the benefit of New York City. It was time for those long-absent Americans in Paris to return home, and with them came an influx of European artists. "The probability is that the future of painting lies in America," art dealer Sam Kootz wrote, presciently, in a letter to the *New York Times* in 1941, "and all you have to do, boys and girls, is get a new approach, do some delving for a change – God knows you've [had] time to rest."

In fact, the "new approach" that Kootz was looking for was already taking shape among a loose affiliation of painters in Greenwich Village. They weren't a particularly cohesive group. Their styles tended to be as idiosyncratic as the artists themselves, and it wasn't until the early 1950s that they were given a name – the Abstract Expressionists or, more generally, the New York School.

What united them initially was a dissatisfaction with their immediate predecessors. Although many had apprenticed under the WPA in the 1930s, they rejected regionalism and social realism, which they regarded as provincial and tainted by nationalistic overtones. Nor were they satisfied with geometric abstraction, which they felt was academic and emotionally detached.

What they wanted was a mode of expression that sprang from the most elemental urges and emotions – anxiety, terror, rage, ecstasy – the only legitimate response, in their view, to a world devastated by a great depression and global war. They were deeply influenced in this regard by surrealist painters like André Masson and Matta, who had fled to New York at the start of the war. The surrealists believed that artists could gain access to the subconscious with a method known as automatism – a form of free association. Taking their cue from the émigrés, to varying degrees, were painters such as William Baziotes, Robert Motherwell and Mark Rothko. Destined to be the most famous, however, was an intensely gifted and troubled young man named Jackson Pollock.

Jack the Dripper

A hard-drinking, rugged American type out of Cody, Wyoming, Pollock had studied with Thomas Hart Benton at the Art Students League in New York. Like many of his colleagues in these early days, he was influenced by the Jungian notion of the "collective unconscious" – a repository of myths and archetypes thought to reside at the most primordial level of the human psyche. Much of Pollock's work from this period involves themes and images from classical mythology wrapped in a welter of expressive scrawls and "linear arabesques."

In 1943, at the age of 31, Pollock met Peggy Guggenheim, an heiress and art collector with a passion for "difficult art." She helped further young Jack's career as well as the careers of Baziotes, Motherwell and Rothko, and they soon won praise from the influential art critics Clement Greenberg and Harold Rosenberg, who later coined the term "action painting" to emphasize the importance of spontaneous gesture in creating their work.

Hardly any paintings were sold at first. The public could only gaze in incredulous dismay at the perverse arrangements of color, lines and shapes on canvas. It must have seemed to some like a

ABOVE: *Pistol*, 1964, Roy Lichtenstein.

OPPOSITE: Detail from *Twenty Marilyns*, 1962, Andy Warhol.

Circumcision, 1946, Jackson Pollock, from the Solomon R. Guggenheim Museum.

replay of Armory Show craziness. Pollock's old mentor, Thomas Hart Benton, escaping back to the sane and sober American heartland, scorned the Expressionists as "an intellectually diseased lot."

Then, in 1947, Pollock made a breakthrough, producing in four short years some of the best known – and perhaps the most ridiculed – pictures in the history of modern art. These are his famous "drip paintings," created by flinging, spattering and pouring oil onto large canvases affixed to the studio floor. The results, in works like *Number 1, 1950 (Lavender Mist)* and *Autumn Rhythm* (1950) are turbulent skeins of paint that loop and swirl with tumultuous energy, suggesting, in the opinion of one critic, "the traces of subatomic particles on the plate of an electron microscope." In Pollock's view, the paintings weren't illustrations of an object or idea but an enactment of subconscious urges in an improvisatory "dance" with paint and canvas. "I'm not aware of what I'm doing," he said of his technique. "It is only after a sort of 'get acquainted' period that I see what I have been about … [T]he painting has a life of its own. I try to let it come through."

An article in *Life* magazine in 1949 effectively declaring Pollock America's greatest living painter brought him instant celebrity. Success did little to mitigate a lifelong struggle with alcoholism and depression, however, and by the early 1950s he had returned to brush painting, creating images similar to those of a decade earlier. He died in an automobile accident in 1956 at the age of 44.

Looking back years later, Willem de Kooning credited Pollock with "breaking the ice" for other members of the New York School. "Every so often," de Kooning wrote, "a painter has to destroy painting. Cézanne did it. Picasso did it with cubism. Then Pollock did it. He busted our idea of a picture all to hell. Then there could be new paintings again."

De Kooning may have been overly generous with his praise, because he too was breaking new ground, as were other action painters such as Robert Motherwell and Pollock's wife, Lee Krasner. Among the most powerful images to come out of this period, in fact, were de Kooning's own "women" – a series of grimacing, grotesque figures with enormous eyes and protruding teeth emerging from smears and streaks of garish color. They are images rendered, as de Kooning said, "with anxiousness and dedication to fright maybe, or ecstasy."

The essence of color

While Pollock and de Kooning were developing a visual language of energy and anxiety, Mark Rothko, a leading figure among the "color-field painters," was concerned with an evocation of the "sublime." Like Pollock, Rothko drew upon myth and totem to dredge up the primordial roots of the human psyche – "the eternal symbols upon which we must fall back to express basic psychological ideas," he explained in a radio interview. "They are the symbols of man's primitive fears and motivations, no matter in which land or what time, changing only in detail but never in substance."

The images were gradually simplified until, by the late 1940s, he had hit on the format that would occupy him for the rest of his life – luminous rectangles arranged vertically against a colored background, evoking in variations of tone and contrast an infinite range of mood and atmosphere. Rothko wanted large expanses of color to envelop the viewer, and he often created huge canvases and insisted that they be shown in such a way that the viewer encountered them at close quarters. The intention was spiritual, believing as he did that fields of luminous, gently modulated color could induce a transcendent state of mind in those who experienced them.

Untitled (Red Painting), ca. 1953, Robert Rauschenberg, from the Solomon R. Guggenheim Museum.

Objects of affection

Even as the Abstract Expressionists were reaching the height of their fame and influence, a small group of New York artists were moving in a different direction. Chief among them were Robert Rauschenberg and Jasper Johns, friends working in neighboring studios who, in a manner of speaking, steered art away from the murky depths of the human psyche into a world populated – brimming, in fact – with the artifacts of consumer culture: manufactured goods, second-hand junk, newspapers, photographs, and signs and symbols of every sort.

Where Pollock plumbed the subconscious for his raw material, Rauschenberg prowled the streets, junk shops and news-stands. Rauschenberg's signature style was the making of "combines" – assemblages of objects spattered and swiped with paint, like his infamous *Monogram* (1955–59), which features a stuffed goat ringed with an automobile tire, or *Bed* (1955), a quilt with lurid splotches of pigment. By the early 1960s Rauschenberg stopped making combines and concentrated instead on photographic images, which he silk-screened onto large canvases, then finished with drips and spatters of paint.

Similar in some respects, though stylistically cooler and more controlled, was Jasper Johns, who chose to recycle and "recontextualize" icons rather than material objects, including, in 1956, one of the most potent symbols of all: the American flag, a favorite and recurring subject. Johns had an uncanny knack for altering familiar images just enough to make the viewer question what he was about. He also had a fondness for reworking images and icons that are used to take measurements or provide orientation – numbers, maps, rulers, firing-range targets – urging viewers perhaps to question their own conceptual maps and yardsticks.

Implicit in the work of Rauschenberg and Johns was a breakdown of boundaries. Art could be made of anything and by just

Title Unknown (Purple, Green and Red), Mark Rothko.

about anybody – or so it seemed to hostile critics. As Rauschenberg put it: "Painting relates to both art and life … I try to work in the gap between the two." He and Johns set the stage for what art historian Sandro Bocola called "the most spectacular artistic transformation of the postwar era – the Pop Art revolution."

Clothespins and other crap

The term "Pop Art" was coined in Britain in 1958, and for many its spirit must have evoked that of Marcel Duchamp, chief Dadaist and first of the postmodernists. Among the first American Pop artists were Roy Lichtenstein, Andy Warhol and Claes Oldenburg, all distancing themselves from the heroic themes and seriousness of the Abstract Expressionists. "I am for an art that embroils itself with everyday crap," said Oldenburg, who began making oversized sculptures of such mundane items as baked potatoes, electric plugs, hamburgers, clothespins, lipstick and electric fans in the 1960s – some taking the form of droopy vinyl objects resembling half-melted ice cream, others monumental steel or fiberglass structures, like the famous *Clothespin* (1976) in downtown Philadelphia.

The focus of the Pop Art makers was consumer culture and the mass media. Lichtenstein's comic-book paintings (*see page 102*), with their simulated Benday dots, stripes and heavy black outlines, parodied Abstract Expressionism (*see page 107*), Cubism and other vaunted schools of art. But the real Pied Piper of Pop was Andy Warhol, who seemed somehow to both attract and repel public interest. Warhol came from blue-collar stock in Pittsburgh, where he was born in 1928. Drawn inevitably to the New York scene, he settled there and succeeded in wrenching art from a mass-market culture, a McLuhanesque world in which the medium is itself the message. In his reflexively ironic vision, he crafted silk-screened representations of Coca-Cola bottles, each one exactly like the next, and did numerous takes on Elizabeth Taylor, Elvis Presley, Marilyn Monroe and Marlon Brando, soup cans and electric chairs. They spewed forth from his "Factory" on East 47th Street like so many commodities, like the commodity that art itself had become.

Mass appeal

Warhol was prophetic about the direction in which cultural history was heading, the phenomenon of mass media, the impact on the realm of art. By the late 1960s, art styles were veering off in multiple directions, all generally falling within the ubiquitous classification of "postmodern." In rapid-fire fashion came Optical Art, Minimalism, Conceptual Art, Performance Art, Land Art and more. There were highly charged forays into feminist ideology and identity politics as well as a nationwide debate over censorship and public funding sparked by the "homoerotic" work of Robert Mapplethorpe and Andres Serrano's notorious *Piss Christ*, a photograph of a crucifix in a jar of the artist's urine.

Driving this fragmentation, at least in part, were economic forces that, by the early 1980s, had whipped the New York art market into a feeding frenzy. The gallery scene – ensconced in SoHo since the mid-1970s – went into overdrive, hyping artists like so many media celebrities (à la Jean-Michel Basquiat) in an effort to discover, or manufacture, the "next big thing." Venture capitalists got into the art game, too, and the cost of masterpieces soared to unimaginable prices – like $82.5

million for van Gogh's *Portrait of Dr. Gachet* at Christie's in 1990. Museums were also motivated by the blockbuster mentality, measuring success – in the words of conservative critic Roger Kimball – "by the take at the box office rather than at the bar of aesthetic discrimination."

As the "greed-is-good" economy of the 1980s slowed down, the SoHo scene gradually ran out of steam. Artists and gallery owners – victims of their own success – moved on to greener pastures (and cheaper rents) elsewhere in the city, and there's now a thriving concentration of galleries around 22nd Street in Chelsea.

Museums, of course, continue to be a vital force in New York's cultural life. Although the terrorist attacks of September 11, 2001, were a blow emotionally and financially, the city's museums responded with a determination to meet the needs of shocked and grieving visitors. Rarely did the tonic of great art and quiet spaces seem more welcome or relevant. The opening of the American Folk Art Museum in a major new building on West 53rd Street just a few months after the tragedy was a hopeful note, as was the resumption of plans to expand the Museum of Modern Art. Other museums are on the move as well – the Isamu Noguchi Garden and Museum, the Museum for African Art and more. As with all aspects of life in hurry-hurry New York, change is the only constant and a sure sign of cultural vitality.

ART AND POLITICS

It's nice to get public funds, but there are strings attached. When the Brooklyn Museum of Art brought over from London in 1999 a group showing by young artists collectively known as the "Brit Pack," trouble erupted. One painting in the provocative *Sensation* exhibit particularly annoyed New York Mayor Rudy Giuliani. It was Chris Ofili's rendering of the Virgin Mary, a black Madonna that combined elephant dung dabbed at her breasts and cutouts from porn magazines. Giuliani, who at the time happened to be campaigning for election to the U.S. Senate, labeled the show "sick stuff" offensive to Catholics and threatened to shut off the spigot that provided the museum with a helpful $7.2 million a year. The usual round of legal threats and protests followed, including one memorable episode in which a man arrested for throwing dung at the museum claimed to be "just expressing himself creatively." In the end, mayor and museum agreed to disagree. Lawsuits were dropped and funding was restored, though the question of censorship and decency remains as sensitive as ever.

Three Flags, ca. 1958, Jasper Johns, from the Whitney Museum of Art.

GRAND CENTRAL
TERMINAL

New York City Architecture

From humble Dutch farmhouses to soaring Art Deco skyscrapers, the
city encompasses a wide range of architectural styles

"Around this fort a progeny of little Dutch-built houses, with tiled roofs and weathercocks, soon sprang up, nestling themselves under its walls for protection." So wrote Washington Irving, describing the appearance of New York in its earliest incarnation, a scruffy colonial settlement on the southern tip of Manhattan Island.

What were those "little Dutch-built houses" like in that long-ago village of New Amsterdam? If there had existed a landmarks commission during the 18th and 19th centuries – not to mention a fire department capable of containing the blazes that made short work of what little was spared by generations of developers – we might have a better idea of the architecture of Dutch Manhattan and its environs. But since historic preservation is but a recent phenomenon, we can only surmise what Peter Stuyvesant's 17th-century town looked like by turning to examples of the architecture of the period that have survived in the Netherlands. Early Manhattan had similar step-gabled brick buildings, although wood construction and simple sloping roofs would have been far more common than in the Dutch homeland.

Below: Lee Lawrie's 1937 *Atlas* stands before the entrance to the International Building at Rockefeller Center.

Colonial survivors

Although the last of Manhattan's 17th-century structures has long since disappeared, there are several survivors in the outer boroughs, all modest farmhouses and one-time village residences. The oldest building in New York City is the Pieter Claesen Wyckoff house, which stands at Clarendon Road and Ralph Avenue in the Flatlands section of Brooklyn. This is a modest, one-and-a-half-story cottage dating to 1652, or possibly earlier; some architectural historians have suggested that the oldest portion may have been built by the Dutch Governor Wouter van Twiller before 1641. The building's most telling characteristic is an overhanging roof that ends in a "ski jump" curve. Along with the gambrel style, this was a typical roof treatment among early Dutch colonists.

The Bowne House, at 37-01 Bowne Street in Flushing, Queens, is a late-17th-century farmhouse in the English vernacular style. The oldest part of the house was built by John Bowne, a Quaker dissident, in 1661. Additions were made in 1680 and 1691, after the English takeover of New Amsterdam. Despite the raising of the roof and the addition of a wing in 1830, the house retains a steep-gabled, late medieval English appearance.

The borough of Richmond, better known as Staten Island, was the last portion of New York City to be intensively developed. The flood tide of suburbanization didn't reach the island until after the completion of the Verrazano-Narrows Bridge in 1964, and consequently a greater portion of historic buildings were preserved there than in the other boroughs. A significant cluster of these makes up Richmondtown Restoration, where the stout little two-story Voorlezer's House, 59 Arthur Kill Road, dates to 1695 and is believed to be the oldest elementary school building in the United States (a *voorlezer* was a schoolteacher and lay leader of religious services). Unaware of the house's great age, a passerby might fail to give it a second thought – its foursquare practicality seems to foreshadow half of the two-story "colonial" homes in the United States.

Residential architecture in 18th-century New York still showed substantial Dutch influence, particularly where the setting was rural. An example is Manhattan's last surviving 18th-century

Opposite: Sculpture by Jules-Alexis Coutan crowns the facade of Grand Central Terminal, a triumph of Beaux-Arts style.

farmhouse, the Dyckman Farmhouse (*see page 167*), at Broadway and 204th Street. Built about 1784, the wood-and-stone structure has a gambrel roof that sweeps out over a porch, and Dutch doors at the front and rear.

Georgian and Federal styles

Town and city architecture in 18th-century New York followed the Georgian pattern. Georgian is a classically-inspired style often executed in brick, with simple, elegant proportions dependent on the basic rectangle, ornate treatment of doorways (often with flanking columns), and steep hipped or gable-ended roofs. Although it is essentially a 1907 reconstruction of a 1719 building, lower Manhattan's Fraunces Tavern (Pearl and Broad streets, *see page 149*) – site of George Washington's farewell to his officers in 1783 – is a good example of the style. Built as the home of wealthy merchant Stephen De Lancey, the house became a tavern in 1763. Although little more than its west wall is original, its balustrade-topped hipped roof, tall chimneys, and trim little shed-roofed dormers have been re-created to accurately convey the formality of the Georgian mode.

The Federal style, essentially a lightening and simplification of Georgian elements, predominated from the 1790s to 1820s. In the city, Federal architecture came to be associated with the new vogue for row houses, particularly in Greenwich Village and adjacent neighborhoods (Nos. 83, 85 and 116 Sullivan Street and No. 131 Charles Street are noteworthy). But perhaps the finest example of Federal-era domestic architecture in New York is an expansive house, just the sort of building that seems hardly likely to have survived into the 21st century in such a space-hungry hive as Manhattan. It is Gracie Mansion, the official residence of the mayor of New York.

Well-to-do merchant Archibald Gracie built his country villa at what is now East End Avenue and East 88th Street between 1799 and 1810. While it is not known for certain whether the mansion was designed by Washington, D.C. planner Pierre L'Enfant, as tradition maintains, there can be no doubt about the building's impeccable Federal pedigree – note the Chinese Chippendale railing surrounding the low hipped roof, the trim colonnade supporting the first-floor veranda, and the elegant sidelights and semicircular lunette that set off the front door. After a long stint as premises for the Museum of the City of New York, Gracie Mansion became the mayor's residence in 1942.

City Hall, designed by the French architect Joseph Mangin, embodies the refined and graceful style of Federal architecture.

Mayor Fiorello LaGuardia chose the house after rejecting the since-demolished Schwab mansion on Riverside Drive, a 75-room French château that caused the unprepossessing LaGuardia to gasp, "What! Me in that ?"

Down at the other end of Manhattan, the mayor's workplace – City Hall – is also an expression of the Federal aesthetic, as interpreted by French architect Joseph Mangin in 1802. As we might expect in a public building, City Hall is more assertively neoclassical than Archibald Gracie's private home, although it exhibits a restraint and a cool elegance characteristic of its period.

Reviving the past

During the early 19th century, American architects began to seek inspiration from Greece and Rome. Greek Revival architecture – highlighted by stately columns capped with Parthenon-style pediments, corner pilasters and broad triangular gables – projected dignity and trim practicality. With its noble proportions and cool, reasonable facades, Greek Revival seemed the perfect stylistic expression for the new republic. Wall Street's 1842 Federal Hall is an outstanding example, so is the 1840 St. Peter's Church at Barclay and Church Streets.

As with Federal, the style was readily adaptable to row houses. Many of the Greenwich Village row houses near Washington Square boast Greek Revival elements, and the colonnaded row at 428-434 Lafayette Street, just south of the Square, sums up much of the movement's classicist ambitions.

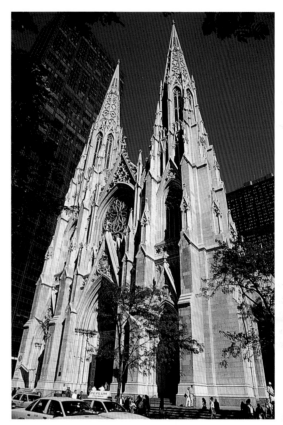

The twin Gothic spires of St. Patrick's Cathedral soar above busy Fifth Avenue.

As the 19th century advanced, other revival styles followed. Two of the most important were Gothic and Italianate. The former had its most notable New York City exponents in Richard Upjohn, architect of the 1846 Trinity Church at Broadway and Wall Street; and James Renwick, Jr., who followed his 1845 Grace Church (Broadway at 10th Street) with his masterpiece, St. Patrick's Cathedral (1858-79; spires completed 1888), on Fifth Avenue between 50th and 51st streets.

Victorian extravagance

High Victorian architecture is perhaps best represented in New York City by a structure once considered too ugly to bother preserving – about which the *New York Times* critic Ada Louise Huxtable said, "If they can save that, they can save anything." This is the 1877 Jefferson Market Courthouse (Sixth Avenue at West 10th Street), a Ruskinian Gothic pile that was voted the fifth most beautiful building in America in an 1880s architects' poll. It is nothing if not busy, with polychrome brickwork, peaked stained-glass windows, and finial-capped gables, all topped with a clock tower that would have pleased Ludwig II of Bavaria. It was saved after years of disuse, and converted into a library branch in the 1960s.

While neo-Gothic architecture represented the romantic stylistic impulse, the mode that carried the classical tradition through the mid-19th century was Italianate. Italianate is the prevailing style of that most typical of New York City dwellings, the brownstone row house. Look for flat roofs, round-headed windows, and projecting cornices supported by ornate brackets.

The French Second Empire style, easily identifiable in small-town residential guise as the mansard-roofed "haunted house" mode of architecture, survives in space-conscious New York

mainly in a few public buildings. One example is the 1867 Metropolitan Savings Bank, later a Ukrainian church, at 9 E. 7th Street. With its quoins, cornices and dormered mansard roof, this building is all about texture and three-dimensionality, typical Second Empire traits.

Much of New York's most extravagant Victorian architecture is long gone, having been exemplified by mansions that grew too expensive even for plutocrats to maintain. Along Fifth Avenue between 51st and 58th streets stood a collection of Vanderbilt extravaganzas. William K. built an immense château, and his son put up another right next door. Cornelius II's castle was an ersatz Loire chateau. And they were all outdone by steel mogul Charles Schwab, whose château on Riverside Drive – the one that raised Fiorello LaGuardia's common-man hackles – took up an entire city block between 73rd and 74th streets.

More practical examples of French Renaissance architecture include a famous hotel and an equally famous apartment building. The 1907 Plaza, at Fifth Avenue and Central Park South, was designed by Henry J. Hardenburgh, who 23 years earlier had completed the then-remote Dakota (Central Park West at W. 72nd Street), built when the idea of apartment living was a questionable novelty among New York's well-to-do.

Public monuments

Architects of public and commercial buildings of the turn of the century were much enamored of the

The 22-story Flatiron Building was the world's tallest building when it was completed in 1902.

Beaux-Arts style, a French import that drew heavily on classical, Renaissance and Baroque traditions to create a formal, monumental look in which sculpture – and sculpted architectural elements – play an important part. The city's greatest examples are Richard Morris Hunt's 1902 Metropolitan Museum of Art (Fifth Avenue at 82nd Street), Carrère & Hastings' 1911 New York Public Library (Fifth Avenue at 42nd Street), and Warren and Wetmore's 1913 Grand Central Terminal (42nd Street at Vanderbilt Avenue). The style is also well represented in the 1904 Ansonia Hotel (now residential) at Broadway and W. 73rd Street. This structure's heavy fireproof construction, incidentally, made its apartments so soundproof that it became home to generations of musicians.

One of the grandest New York structures of a century ago owes more to a direct interpretation of Roman classicism than to later embellishments on the style. This was McKim, Mead & White's much-lamented Pennsylvania Station, the 1910 temple to transportation modeled on Rome's Baths of Caracalla. It was demolished in the 1960s and replaced with a characterless Madison Square Garden and subterranean Penn Station.

The sky's the limit

Beginning in the early 20th century, residential architecture became far less important than public and commercial building in New York. Private houses virtually disappeared from architects' drawing boards, and new apartment buildings grew less and less distinguished. If an architect set out to make a grand statement, it was likely to be in the form of a skyscraper.

The skyscraper was invented by Midwestern architects, particularly the Chicago firm of Burnham

& Root. But it was in space-hungry New York that the steel frame, curtain wall and elevator – the three elements that made tall buildings possible – were employed to the most dramatic effect.

The term "skyscraper" properly applies to a tall building freed from the constraints of all-masonry construction and allowed to rise unfettered by the requirements of load-bearing walls. Its support derives from its steel skeleton, and the term "curtain wall" refers to walls that are mere coverings for the frame. If masonry walls alone had to support the load of a building much more than ten stories in height, they would have to be so thick that interior space would be negligible. Steel can do the job in far less space. Naturally, elevators are necessary to make tall buildings something more than enormous pieces of exercise equipment – a fact brought home to New Yorkers during the great power blackouts of 1965 and 1977.

Throughout the 1890s, a great many steel-framed buildings were constructed in New York. People called them skyscrapers, but the first real attempt to break from the eight- and ten-story pack was Daniel Burnham's 1902 Flatiron Building. Rising 22 stories in the shape of its triangular knife-edge lot (its form suggests an old-fashioned clothes iron) at Broadway and Fifth Avenue, the Flatiron owes its aesthetic appeal not only to its freestanding height and classical styling, but to the appearance it gives of sailing up Broadway. It was, in fact, compared to a "monster steamer" by Alfred Stieglitz, who in 1903 made what remains the finest photograph of the building.

A trio of new towers soon proved that steel framing and electric elevators were capable of soaring far higher than 22 stories, although their architects remained committed to historical styles. Ernest Flagg capped the tower of his 612-foot (186-meter) Singer Building (1908, since demolished) with a mansard roof. A year later, Napoleon LeBrun gave the Metropolitan Life Insurance Company (Madison Avenue at E. 23rd Street) a 700-foot (210-meter) tower that replicated the

LEFT: Pennsylvania Station, McKim, Mead & White's neoclassical masterpiece, was leveled in the 1960s.

BELOW: Designed by Stanford White and dedicated in 1895, the Washington Arch stands in Washington Square Park.

Campanile of St. Mark's in Venice – at more than twice the campanile's height. Finally, Cass Gilbert handed the tallest-building title to retail tycoon F. W. Woolworth, also with an historicist twist. The 1913 Woolworth Building (Broadway at Park Place) soars 792 feet (241 meters), and is so unabashedly Gothic that it was heralded as a "cathedral of commerce."

Get back, Jack

The most important 20th-century influence upon the appearance of New York and its signature skyline was a political rather than an artistic development. With new technologies enabling builders to achieve previously unheard-of heights, planners feared that the city's streets would soon become grim, lightless canyon floors, hemmed in by skyscraper walls. In 1916, they addressed the problem with a zoning ordinance that limited the height to which a street-level facade was permitted to rise by a formula based upon the width of the street, and allowed towers of unlimited height to rise only over one-quarter of the area of a building's plot. This led to the architectural concept called the "setback," which – along with the economic boom and civic confidence of the 1920s – brought about the classic era of New York high-rise construction.

Along with setback zoning and the easy money of the Roaring Twenties came Art Deco, a style that seemed to have been made for skyscrapers. Nowhere are the two better paired than in the Chrysler Building (Lexington Avenue and E. 42nd Street), William Van Alen's 1930 masterpiece. The 1,048-foot (319-meter) structure, which employs automotive motifs such as gargoyles inspired by radiator caps, reaches a pinnacle composed of narrowing crowns topped with a rapier-like spire. The whole business is an immense piece of Art Deco jewelry.

The 1,250-foot (381-meter) Empire State Building (Shreve, Lamb & Harmon; Fifth Avenue and 33rd Street), which took the "world's tallest" title from the Chrysler in 1931, toned down the Art Deco vocabulary but still managed, with its sleek capstone tower (originally intended as a mooring mast for dirigibles!) and soaring lobby, to incorporate the geometry of aspiration that was a hallmark of the style.

Raymond Hood's 1934 RCA Building, centerpiece of Rockefeller Center, was a more muted version of the genre, and in some ways presaged the slablike skyscrapers to come. Other fine Raymond Hood Art Deco-era buildings include American Radiator (1924; 40 W. 40th Street); McGraw-Hill (1930; 330 W. 42nd Street); and Daily News (1930; 220 E. 42nd Street).

Behind the glass curtain

During the postwar era, the spare-lined International style ruled the day. The style's greatest New York monuments are the 1952 Lever House (390 Park Avenue), by Skidmore, Owings & Merrill, and Mies van der Rohe's 1958 Seagram Building (375 Park Avenue), both of which illustrate the grace with which glass curtain walls can rise from an open plaza. Most New York architects of

More than 10 million bricks and 180 miles of steel beams were used in the construction of the Empire State Building.

IRON AGE

In the rapidly expanding New York of the late 1840s, builders had to provide commercial space as quickly and inexpensively as possible. There was no electricity, of course, so it was necessary for windows to admit a maximum amount of light. With rear walls often facing gloomy alleys, the only place sunlight could enter was through voluminous front windows.

The answer to these requirements was provided by an iron-foundry owner named James Bogardus, who began casting building facades in modular pieces and assembling them on site. Although some early cast-iron facades carried part of the load from the floor joists, the technique quickly evolved into one in which loads were borne by wooden beams and brick side walls or on cast-iron columns. With facades thus liberated from the need to carry weight, there was more room for windows. And since casting iron requires far less time and labor than sculpting stone, facades could be quite ornate.

The cast-iron trend lasted into the 1870s, when steel-frame construction was introduced. In one corner of Manhattan, though, the old iron facades continued to dominate streetscapes long after their once-colorful paint had flaked away. This was SoHo, where the 1960s saw light manufacturing gradually replaced by artists looking for cheap space. Recognition of the buildings' historical importance followed, and a 26-block area was designated the SoHo Cast-Iron Historic District.

the 1950s and '60s handled the International style with far less aplomb, giving the city scores of anonymous glass boxes.

Standing above the crowd – quite literally – were the 1,350-foot (412-meter) Twin Towers of the World Trade Center (1976). The critical response to the towers was mixed at first. Some thought the structures were too intrusive and lacked character, others felt the windswept plaza sterile and uninviting. But aesthetic objections were soon outweighed by the towers' symbolic potency. The World Trade Center became a New York icon on a par with the Statue of Liberty or the Empire State Building – a status only enhanced by a terrorist bombing in 1993 and tragically confirmed by the towers' destruction on September 11, 2001.

Some of the city's modern structures fall outside the realm of classification by style. Frank Lloyd Wright's only New York City building is the 1956 Guggenheim Museum. Working at the end of his 70-year career, Wright designed the flowerpot-shaped Guggenheim to provide an upwardly-spiraling exhibition gallery with no formal division of stories. It is one of New York's most idiosyncratic architectural works, perhaps equaled in that regard only by Eero Saarinen's great swooping bird of a

G U G G E N H E I M

TWA terminal (1959) at Kennedy International Airport, a facility that has grown so prodigiously that Saarinen's great statement on the romance of air travel now seems almost pathetically quaint.

In the late 1970s, "postmodern" architects returned to historical references. There were no Gothic cathedrals this time – rather, the Philip Johnson-designed AT&T Building (1984, now the Sony Building), with a broken-pediment top said to resemble a piece of Chippendale furniture, and a rash of post-International towers fought each other for predominance on the skyline.

If there is a post-postmodern look, it may well belong to Times Square's 2000 Bertelsmann Building. It is a skyscraper with its steel underclothes showing, and with commerce – in the form of lower-floor tenants' neon signs – shouting at the street with no attempt at concealment via Roman columns, Beaux-Arts bullseye windows, or the cool glass facades of Miesian minimalism.

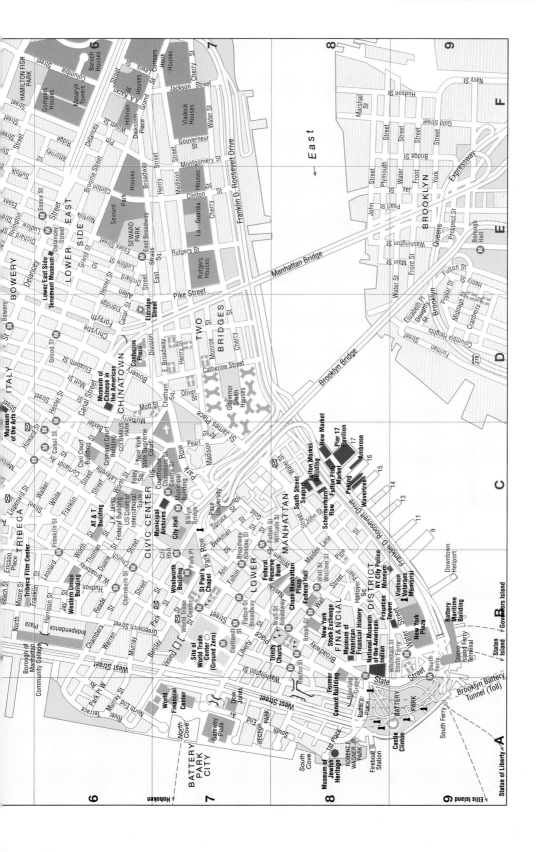

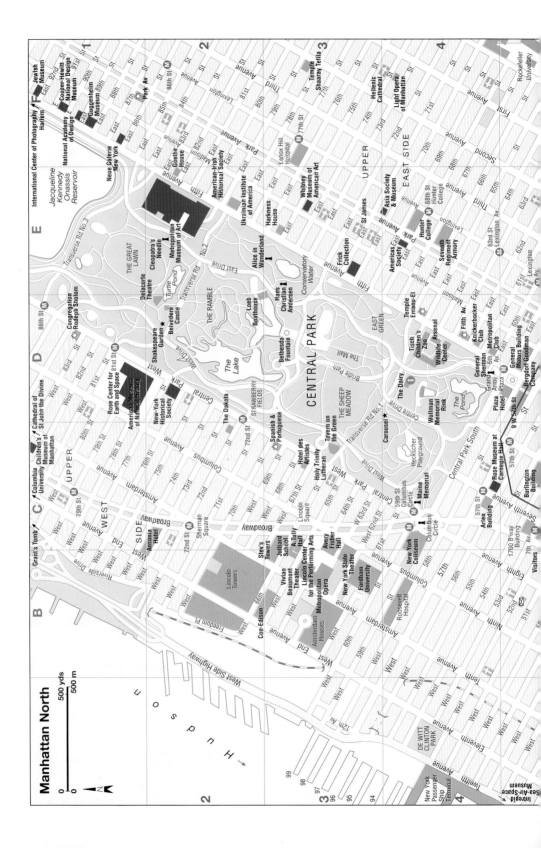

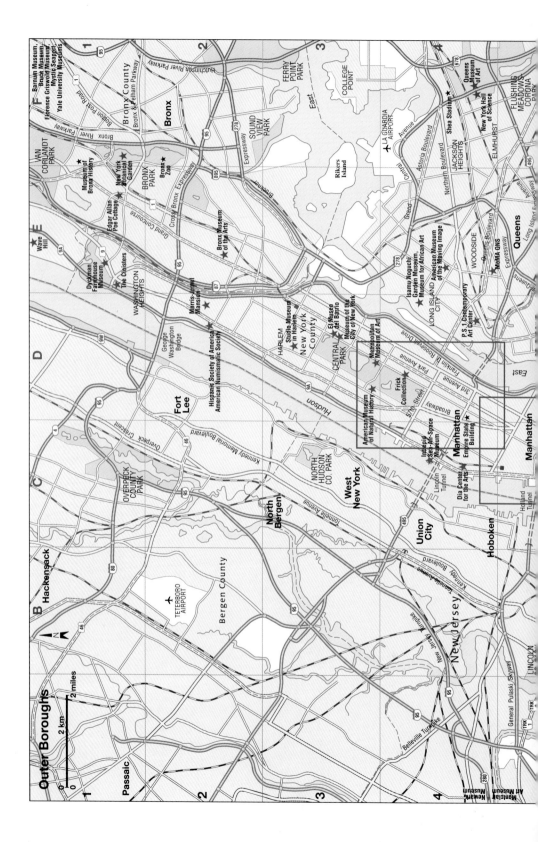

The Major Collections

The range is mind-boggling. Dinosaurs from when the world was young. Egyptian sphinxes. American classics. And the glories of the European masters. They're all here, in settings that are themselves wondrous.

Carleton Watkins

PHOTOGRAPHS

THE NEW GREEK GALLERIES

ANCIENT NEAR EASTERN ART

NEW INSTALLATION

Metropolitan Museum of Art

New York's premier cultural attraction is one of the world's great repositories of precious objects, from across the continents and the ages.

Map reference: pages 50–51, E2
1000 Fifth Ave at 82nd St, 10028.
Tel: 212-535-7710, www.metmuseum.org
Subway: 4, 5 or 6 (local or express) to 86th St.
Bus: M1, M2, M3 or M4 downtown on Fifth
Ave, uptown on Madison Ave; M79 crosstown
on 79th St; M86 crosstown on 86th St.
Fri–Sat 9.30am–9pm; Sun, Tues–Thurs
9.30am–5.30pm.
Admission fee, guided tours, lectures, films,
cafeteria, restaurant, wheelchair access.

She is the prima donna of Fifth Avenue, flaunting her attractions with colorful banners high overhead as art lovers and other strangers mount her steps and penetrate her labyrinth of corridors and galleries crammed with paintings and sculpture, glass and ceramics, furniture and textiles, knights' armor and rare violins, and all manner of precious objects.

Call her The Met, as New Yorkers do, a place that accommodates under one roof (not to mention her uptown sister, The Cloisters) an awful lot of cultural history. An errant step or two in this warehouse of art can take the unsuspecting visitor from a 5,000-year-old relic of Iranian pottery to a thoroughly modern manifesto of in-your-face expressionism – say, perhaps, Jackson Pollock's paint-splattered *Autumn Rhythm* of 1950.

It's an embarrassment of riches, a real success story. But if location is everything, what else would you expect from a place conveniently situated in this world-class seaport, this mecca that was coveted by New England colonials back when the Dutch still owned it? By the mid-19th century there was so much money around that Gotham's moguls and merchants had begun amassing their own private art collections. So when an American in Paris suggested in 1866, to his compatriots celebrating the Fourth of July at a restaurant there, that it was high time New York had a fine-arts institute of public scope, the stage was set.

Creative types such as poet-editor William

Cullen Bryant and architect Frederick Law Olmsted got involved, and the Metropolitan Museum of Art was founded in 1870, at the dawn of the Gilded Age. It shifted around for a while in temporary digs until the founders decided on a permanent home up in Central Park – Olmsted's great creation – far from the madding crowds of lower Manhattan. By 1880 the Met was in its new home on Fifth Avenue at 82nd Street.

The place was modest at first, before sprouting all those wings. On hand for the grand opening (March 30, 1880) was President Rutherford B. Hayes, up from Washington to declare the Met open and become the first visiting tourist. By 1894 north and south additions were tacked on and plans drawn up for the imposing central facade on Fifth Avenue, in neoclassical style, its Great Hall making for a truly grand entrance. The designer was Richard Morris Hunt, pet architect of the super-rich. The work was completed in 1902, a couple of years before the bulbous-nosed power broker J. P. Morgan took over as the Met's president and the Museum started amassing its rich collection thanks to some extremely generous gifts, fabulous bequests, its own excavations

Opposite: The Met's grand neoclassical entrance was designed by Richard Morris Hunt in 1902.

Below: *Don Manuel Osorio Manrique de Zuñiga, ca. 1790s, Francisco Goya.*

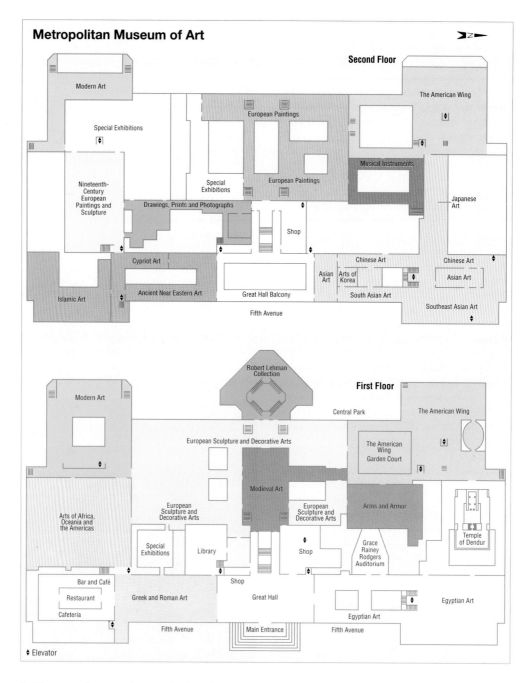

Metropolitan Museum of Art

Second Floor

Modern Art

Special Exhibitions

European Paintings

The American Wing

Nineteenth-Century European Paintings and Sculpture

Special Exhibitions

European Paintings

Musical Instruments

Japanese Art

Drawings, Prints and Photographs

Shop

Cypriot Art

Chinese Art

Chinese Art

Asian Art

Arts of Korea

Asian Art

Islamic Art

Ancient Near Eastern Art

Great Hall Balcony

South Asian Art

Southeast Asian Art

Fifth Avenue

Robert Lehman Collection

First Floor

Modern Art

Central Park

The American Wing

European Sculpture and Decorative Arts

The American Wing Garden Court

Medieval Art

Arts of Africa, Oceania and the Americas

European Sculpture and Decorative Arts

European Sculpture and Decorative Arts

Arms and Armor

Temple of Dendur

Special Exhibitions

Library

Shop

Grace Rainey Rodgers Auditorium

Bar and Café

Shop

Restaurant

Greek and Roman Art

Great Hall

Egyptian Art

Cafeteria

Egyptian Art

Fifth Avenue

Main Entrance

Fifth Avenue

‡ Elevator

in Egypt, and aggressive purchasing. Immense crowds were drawn to blockbuster exhibitions, perhaps most famously in 1963 when patrons lined up on Fifth Avenue for the chance to see the priceless Mona Lisa, nervously loaned by the Louvre. Today, attendance exceeds five million a year, and the Met has been declared officially untouchable as a National Historical Landmark.

Galleries have been reconfigured frequently in recent years. Visitors should consult floor plans, decide on their list of most-favored art, and be prepared to devote a full day for appreciation. There are three million objects, more or less, only a fraction of which can be shown at any one time.

Some genres are especially popular, like the relics of ancient Egypt, the Greek-Roman busts and sculpture, the famous European paintings, a mix of medieval objects, fine European furniture and decoration, high-class arms and armor, and 60,000 articles of garb and costumes that include everything from tribal headgear to glittering haute couture.

Ancient treasures

Egyptology has had mass appeal ever since Napoleon's invaders, including a small army of scavenger scientists, returned to France with everything but the pyramids. The Met's holdings in this field are as comprehensive as any museum outside Cairo, some 36,000 objects from dynastic and predynastic times. They're arranged chronologically in a series of rooms starting to the right of the Great Hall as you enter from Fifth Avenue. Among predynastic (before ca. 3200 B.C.) objects are an ivory comb, its teeth missing, that depicts elephants, birds and other creatures, and a painted jar with male and female figures who may be gods and goddesses. A painted limestone from ca. 2500 B.C. depicts archers in the earliest known rendering of an Egyptian battle scene. Funerary art was the dominant preoccupation. From about 1990 B.C. comes a wooden carving, vibrantly colored, of a female bearing a mortuary offering, as well as a graceful 22-inch-tall (56-cm) statuette in plaster and painted cedar of a *Ritual Figure* of royal attributes.

From the Middle Kingdom (2000–1786 B.C.) is a crouching sphinx honoring Senwosret III, carved from finely grained gneiss, while a sphinx in blue faience from a later era depicts another pharaoh, Amenhotep III (reigned 1417–1379 B.C.). Hatshepsut, who ruled as queen for 22 years during the fabled 18th Dynasty (1570–1342 B.C.), is depicted in pharaonic style, enthroned, in a life-sized limestone sculpture, one of many that filled her rich funerary temple at Deir el-Bahn in Thebes.

The famous Temple of Dendur, a gift from Egypt in 1965, occupies the Sackler Wing. It was erected in the Roman period, during the reign of Caesar Augustus, who is depicted in temple reliefs as making offerings to Egyptian and Nubian gods. The United States received it in recognition of efforts to save ancient monuments from flooding caused by construction of the Aswan Dam, and the Met was chosen (over the Smithsonian Institution) to house it.

From the Middle East

The "cradle of civilization" is part of the vast area represented in another large collection – art from the ancient Near East and the later Islamic period. Among ancient relics from the Iranian region: a terracotta jar from ca. 3500 B.C.; a figurine of a *Bull Holding a Vase* from ca. 2900 B.C.; a wonderfully expressive copper head thought to represent a ruler from ca. 2000 B.C. From the city of Babylon in the 6th century B.C. comes a section of a building wall, constructed of glazed bricks of various colors, depicting a ferocious lion, walking.

Iranian/Persian objects are predominant in the collection that represents the Islamic civilization that arose in the 7th century A.D., many of the artifacts being found in the Museum's own excavations at Nishapur in Iran just before and after World War II. There are outstanding examples of glass and metalwork, including many finely ornamental ewers and other vessels, in addition to ceramics, textiles, Egyptian and Persian carpets, and an exquisitely decorated prayer

LEFT: *Female figure*, early Cycladic period, ca. 2600-2400 B.C.

BELOW: The Temple of Dendur honored the goddess Isis and a pair of Nubian deities.

The Arms and Armor gallery exhibits weapons and armor from Europe, Japan and the ancient Near East.

rug from Ottoman Turkey in the late 16th century. Also from the Ottoman period is a sumptuous room of a house, with courtyard, built in 1707 in Damascus, Syria. The Nur ad-Din Room has marble floors, wood paneling with Arabic inscriptions in verse, and elaborate stained-glass windows.

Greek and Roman

Two marble sculptures illustrate the time span covered by the Greek-Roman collection: an exquisitely formed *Seated Harp Player* from the long-ago Cycladic civilization of the Aegean region, stretching back 5,000 years, and a *Colossal Head of Constantine* from the other end of the time spectrum, ca. 325 A.D. Some of the emperor's facial features were restored.

One of the earliest acquisitions was an Etruscan bronze *Chariot*, only 51 inches (130 cm) high, from the late 6th century B.C. It was found in a tomb in Monteleone, Italy, buried with its owner. A limestone *Sarcophagus with Lid* from Cyprus in the 5th century B.C. was one of the many objects acquired by Luigi Palma di Cesnola as American consul there years before he became the Met's first professional director. Also in the collection is the *Badminton Sarcophagus* of Roman times (260–65 A.D.), meticulously done in Greek marble.

The *Calyx Krater*, ca. 515 B.C., is a masterpiece of ceramic design and execution.

A bronze statue of a boyish prince may represent Lucius Caesar, grandson of Augustus. Another bronze from the same period depicts the Greek god Hermes, and the *Portrait Bust of a Child* portrays the head of a Roman boy in typical noble ringlet curls – was this the young Nero?

No Grecian urn is more highly prized than the *Calyx Krater*, a terracotta vessel that was the immortal fruit of a collaboration by potter (Euxitheos) and painter (Euphronios) about 515 B.C. Its blend of black and red is classic in design. And in a large

section devoted to Roman sculpture and wall paintings are the Boscoreale frescoes from a villa that was inundated in the Vesuvius eruption of 79 A.D. Boscoreale was a resort near Pompeii.

Art of the Byzantine Empire, from rise to fall (330–1453 A.D.), is displayed in newly expanded galleries by the Grand Staircase. Various cultures over a wide area stretching as far south as Egypt are represented.

Faith-based works

The centrality of religion in the Middle Ages is underscored by the collection of more than 4,000 works of medieval art in the main building on Fifth Avenue, in addition to the Met's collection at The Cloisters (see page 80). *Virgin and Child*, a French carving from the 12th century, shows Mary as exemplar of Divine Wisdom while the Holy Infant symbolizes the importance of the Word of God through whatever book or text he once held but which is now missing. Another French sculpture of the *Virgin and Child*, this one in limestone from the 14th century, shows a gentle Mary raising up her divine Son as apparent object of devotion.

A much larger though equally tender *Virgin and Child*, of apparent Netherlandish origin, depicts Jesus as a chubby infant interrupting the Blessed Mother as she reads while holding him in her lap. The sculpture is in limestone with polychromy and gilding and was probably created around the beginning of the 15th century. Also from that period comes a highly ornamental *Crib of the Infant Jesus* that is finely detailed. Such reliquary cribs were venerated in medieval Europe. In this Dutch creation a figure of the Christ Child that once lay beneath the silk coverlet is missing.

Of arms and warriors

The Museum also houses about 14,000 objects of armor and weapons from Europe and Japan, the Middle East, Asia and North America that date as far back as the 5th century. At the center of these popular Arms and Armor galleries is an Equestrian Court displaying European parade armor. A mounted knight wears German armor owned by the duke of Saxony in the mid-16th century. An 80-pound (36-kg) suit of English armor is believed to have been designed by Hans Holbein the Younger, portrayer of Henry VIII and his various wives. A parade helmet (1543) by legendary designer Filippo Negroli of Milan is a masterpiece – as much art as armor. A pair of pistols with ivory stocks were made in 1786 for Russia's Catherine the Great. A flintlock rifle was the work of the court gunsmith to Napoleon, and there are jewel-studded swords of various kinds.

Old favorites

Crowds thicken in the galleries that display European paintings, drawings and sculptures, genres that were favorites from the beginning. The works are hung in chronological fashion. Giotto helped point the way to Renaissance realism in paintings like *The Epiphany* (ca. 1320). Two centuries later another Florentine master, Fra Filippo Lippi, created a *Portrait of a Man and a Woman at a Casement*, showing a young well-to-do female, in scarlet wear and with prominent headdress, facing her beau at an open window.

Medici sophistication is vivid in *Portrait of a Young Man* (ca. 1540), showing a self-assured nobleman, apparently interrupted while reading, peering at us almost disdainfully as his finger marks the page. The artist was Agnolo Bronzino, court painter for Cosimo I. Raphael's famous altarpiece, *Madonna and Child Enthroned with Saints* (ca. 1505), displays his master-

ful gift of harmonic arrangement though he was barely out of his teens. Also in the collection are works by the Venetian masters, among them Tintoretto, Titian, Veronese and Tiepolo the elder. Some of El Greco's greatest work is here – *View of Toledo* (1597) and *Portrait of a Cardinal* (ca. 1600), depicting Seville's archbishop and Grand Inquisitor. Diego Velázquez, summoned to Rome in 1648 to paint the pope's portrait, practiced by using his own assistant and fellow traveler as model and in the process painted the incomparable *Juan de Pareja*. Another masterpiece of portraiture is that of the aristocratic boy in shining red holding a string tethered to a magpie – *Don Manuel Osorio Manrique de Zuñiga* (ca. 1786), by that other Spanish artistic visionary, Francisco de Goya.

Ancient Greek sculpture is featured in the Mary and Michael Jaharis Gallery.

In Rembrandt's renowned *Aristotle with a Bust of Homer* (1653), the Greek philosopher wears a gold chain that bears Alexander's likeness, and thus are three legendary figures united on canvas. In the last decade of his life (1660), Rembrandt recorded his identity for the ages in a *Self-portrait* in which he seems to regard us even as we peer at him. There are many more notable works: Vermeer's crystalline *Young Woman with a Water Jug*; Turner's shimmering *Grand Canal*; Poussin's classically dramatic *Rape of the Sabine Women*; Fragonard's luminous *Love Letter*; Elisabeth Vigée Le Brun's *Comtesse de la Châtre*, painted in 1789 as the old order was about to implode.

Different strokes

Rembrandt's Aristotle with a Bust of Homer was commissioned by a Sicilian nobleman in 1653.

Equally crowd-pleasing are European paintings and sculpture of the 19th century, grouped separately. Predominating are French works of the period's various styles. A neoclassical bent is evident in Ingres' crystal-clear portrait of Roman industrialist *Joseph-Antoine Moltedo* (ca. 1810), the Colosseum evident in the background.

Romanticism was in full swing by 1846, when Delacroix created his dramatic *Abduction of Rebecca*, inspired by Sir Walter Scott's *Ivanhoe*.

Realism undergirds Daumier's *The Third-Class Carriage*, a look at social juxtapositions in the industrial age at mid-century, and Courbet's provocatively nude *Woman with a Parrot*, harshly reviewed by Salon critics in 1866. Courbet, a realist rather than illusionist, was nonetheless influential with the Impressionist rebels by his daring choice of subject matter. An old favorite with Museum visitors is Rosa Bonheur's vividly realistic *Horse Fair*, shown at the Salon of 1853. To escape attention as she sketched, Bonheur dressed as a man for her regular trips to the Paris horse market.

There are many Impressionist treasures here. Monet's waters shimmer in *Garden at Sainte-Adresse* (1867) and *La Grenouillère* (1869). Renoir was well-paid for his charming rendering of well-to-do domesticity in *Madame Georges Charpentier and her Children* (1878), one of the Met's early Impressionist acquisitions, purchased in 1907. Among the Post-impressionists, Van Gogh painted his innovative *Cypresses* while confined to an asylum in 1889, and his erstwhile companion Paul Gauguin recorded his Edenic view of South Sea life in *La Orana Maria (Hail Mary)* of 1892.

Decorative gems

One of the Museum's largest collections falls within the purview of the Department of European Sculpture and Decorative Arts, established in 1907. Its 60,000 works include sculpture from Renaissance Italy and 18th-century France, plus richly decorated rooms from various periods and fine furniture, woodwork, glass, porcelain, jewelry, tapestries and many kinds of fixtures and goods.

Among the sculptures are Rodin's *The Thinker* (1880), a final study for his monumental tribute to Balzac (1897), and

others of his works; Antonio Canova's celebrated marble *Perseus with the Head of Medusa* – a second version, completed ca. 1808; Houdon's bust of the savant Diderot (1773); and Edgar Degas' arresting bronze of the *Little Fourteen-Year-Old Dancer*, first done in wax about 1880–81, with the addition of real shoes, a bodice, a muslin skirt and a horsehair wig.

The rich decoration includes a room from an English earl's residence near Worcester (*Tapestry Room from Croome Court*), whose design dates to ca. 1760. Its tapestries, beautifully woven in Paris, bear medallions illustrating classical myths. *Dining Room from Landsdowne House* in London was created ca. 1765–68. There are also a *Grand Salon from the Hôtel de Tessé*, a Paris mansion built in 1765–68; an actual Parisian storefront from the Quai Bourbon that was created ca. 1775 and is the oldest surviving structure of its kind; and an entire marble patio from a Spanish castle – *Patio from Vélez Blanco* – of the early 16th century that has Italian Renaissance design elements.

The paintings, sculpture and decorative arts housed in the Jack and Belle Linsky Galleries, a substantial private collection that was donated to the Museum in 1982, include a smoky-crystal ewer, made in Prague around 1680, that has a tangled and curious history. Fitted with gold mounts by a latter-day London craftsman, it was purchased by the eccentric William Beckford, the Gothic fantasist, who thought it to be a creation of the celebrated Renaissance goldsmith Benvenuto Cellini.

An even more famous private collection inherited by the Met is that bequeathed by the estate of Robert Lehman, the financier and aesthete. An entire pavilion was opened in 1975 to meet Lehman's stipulation that his gift of paintings, drawings, period rooms and other objects not be scattered. Among the works: Rembrandt's *Portrait of Gerard de Lairesse* (1665), Goya's *Countess of Altamira and Her Daughter* (1787–89); Ingres' luminous *Princesse de Broglie* (1853) – painted not long before her death at the age of 35.

The Museum has a rich collection of drawings and prints, supervised by a separate department created in 1993. Included are works by the major artists – Leonardo da Vinci, Michelangelo, Rembrandt, Albrecht Dürer, Rubens, Goya and others. The works are shown on a rotating basis in the Robert Wood Johnson, Jr. Gallery on the second floor. The space is shared with the Department of Photographs, created in 1992 and now possessing more than 20,000 images.

On native grounds

Paintings, sculpture and decorative arts by native sons are shown in the American Wing. The paintings cover a time span ranging from the late 18th century to the early 20th and include two famous renderings of George Washington – Emanuel Leutze's romantic *Washington Crossing the Delaware* (1851) and Gilbert Stuart's famous 1795 portrait. The president, during his second term, posed for Stuart in Philadelphia, then the capital.

ABOVE: *Garden at Sainte-Adresse*, 1867, Claude Monet.

BELOW: *Little Fourteen-Year-Old Dancer*, Edgar Degas.

Also in the collection are works by such notables as Winslow Homer (*Northeaster*, 1895), Thomas Eakins (*Max Schmitt in a Single Scull*, 1871), James McNeill Whistler's dark full-length *Portrait of Théodore Duret* (ca. 1883), and John Singer Sargent's provocative profile of *Madame X*, whose plunging neckline and off-the-shoulder strap (later repainted) was a Salon scandal in 1884. There are also works by Saint-Gaudens, Daniel Chester French, Frederic Remington and others; a fine Chippendale-style *High Chest of Drawers* crafted in colonial Philadelphia; and a Frank Lloyd Wright

John Singer Sargent's *Madame X (Madame Pierre Gautreau)* caused a stir at the 1884 Paris Salon.

achievement of 1912–14, his *Living Room from the Little House*, in a small Minnesota town. Wright insisted on total design for his interiors to assure a perfect integrity of the component parts.

Modern times

The Met did not take easily to modern art when it reared its bewildering head, as Calvin Tomkins (*Merchants and Masterpieces*, 1970) noted in writing of a trustee who gave reluctant approval for a purchase by covering his eyes and muttering, "I just can't look." The Museum now has a sizable number of paintings, sculpture, drawings, design and architecture in the modern manner. They have been housed since 1987 in the newly built Lila Acheson Wallace Wing, providing space on four levels for permanent and special exhibitions. Wallace, co-founder of the wildly successful *Reader's Digest*, was one of the Museum's major benefactors.

Gertrude Stein appears wise beyond her thirty-something years in Picasso's rendering, begun in Paris in 1905. Henri Matisse's simplified, luminous presentation of dancers, *Dance, I*, introduced him to American audiences at the Armory Show's great leap forward of 1913. André Derain, like Matisse one of the original Fauves (Wild Beasts) of extravagant color application, revealed his Cubist leanings in *The Table* (1911). Likewise Georges Braque in his rendering of a small round table, *Le Guéridon* (1921–22), done in oil with sand.

Many other notable works are in the collection: Georgia O'Keeffe's satirical use of a cow's skull in her 1930 statement on American nationalism, *Red, White, and Blue*; Willem de Kooning's sensuously abstract *Attic* (1949); the American Pop Art vision of James Rosenquist, *House of Fire* (1961), and Roy Lichtenstein, *Stepping Out* (1978); the arresting rearrangement of random marble pieces scavenged by the Japanese-American sculptor Isamu Noguchi in *Kouros* (1944–45). Large pieces of modern sculpture are exhibited in the outdoor Roof Garden (fifth floor) atop the Lila Acheson Wallace Wing overlooking Central Park.

Eastern delights

Precious objects from the Far East – India, China, Japan, Korea, South Asia, Southeast Asia – are exhibited in galleries on the second floor. The Museum has paid increased attention to them in recent years, creating new space in the 1980s and

1990s to spotlight the collection. It includes bowls and other pieces from the earliest Chinese civilization on record, the Shang Dynasty, going as far back as the 15th century B.C. There are many renderings of Buddha and the heavenly exemplars. A serene, composed *Standing Buddha*, carved from red sandstone, is from India's rich Gupta period around the 5th century A.D.

From Japan's Helan period around the 11th century is a bronze rendering of the cult figure Zao Gongen, a kind of local Buddha version. From 10th-century India come creations in bronze of a four-armed *Standing Vishnu* and a curvaceous *Standing Parvati*, consort of the Hindu god Shiva. There are also artistic creations of Pakistani, Afghani, Nepalese, Malaysian and Cambodian origin. One of the most elaborate of the Chinese objects in the collection is *The Astor Court*, a representation of a garden that was a gift to the United States from the People's Republic of China. It was opened in 1981.

Art from another vast region of the world is housed in the Michael C. Rockefeller Wing, opened in 1982. The region encompasses Africa, Oceania and the Americas – three continents and many islands – and a time span exceeding three millennia. Rockefeller, only 25 at the time, died accidentally while rafting in Papua, New Guinea, during a 1961 collecting expedition. His father, Nelson Rockefeller, presented the Museum with a

LEFT: A figure of *Diana*, after Augustus Saint-Gaudens, stands at the center of the Charles Engelhard Court in the American Wing.

commemorative gift of 3,300 works of art in 1969.

The collection, now numbering some 12,000 objects, includes many wood carvings and masks. *Mother and Child* from Mali, of uncertain age, is a dignified representation of a full-breasted, nurturing woman providing security to the baby she holds firmly in her lap. From the Benin Kingdom of 16th-century Nigeria is a *Pendant Mask*, fashioned from ivory with metal inlay, believed to

BELOW: Emanuel Leutze's idealized depiction of *Washington Crossing the Delaware*.

portray the queen mother. Around its periphery are diminutive representations of bearded Portuguese traders, who were attracted to Benin by such precious materials during their passage around Africa. There are many carved, stylized figures from recent times in Polynesia, New Guinea and other places, and artifacts in gold, ceramic and other substances representing Aztec, Mayan, Taino and various central and south American societies.

Music and garments

The Museum's encyclopedic dimension is illustrated by the presence of a Department of Musical Instruments that has more than 4,000 objects, including rare violins and the oldest surviving piano, and a Costume Institute that preserves garments dating as far back as Renaissance times.

OPPOSITE: The Great Hall.

BELOW: *Nasturtiums with "Dance, I"*, 1912, by Henri Matisse, is a view of the artist's studio with his painting *Dance, I* in the background.

The musical collection originated in 1889 with a donation of 270 instruments by Mrs. John Crosby Brown, the wife of an investment banker. She kept adding to it and by 1906 there were 3,500 instruments from around the world. They are displayed in second-floor galleries in a pattern that groups them by continent. Among them is the oldest extant piano, made in 1720 by Bartolommeo Cristofori, who invented the instrument about 20 years earlier at the Medici court in Florence.

Among other objects: a beautifully decorated *Double Virginal* made in 1581 by a Flemish harpsichord builder and discovered about 1915 in a Peruvian chapel; a Stradivarius, considered the finest of all Baroque violins – it was made by Antonio Stradivari in Cremona in 1691; a bowed sitar known as a mayuri ("peacock"), extending from a bird-like wooden carving and made in India in the 19th century. Another instrument of exquisite form and decoration is a *pi-pa*, or lute, from 17th-century China, when the Ming dynasty still held sway. Made chiefly of wood and ivory, it has 120 representations of animals, people, flowers and Buddhist symbols and must surely have been used at functions involving those in society's upper crust.

Besides displaying a wide range of garments – including the dress the unhappy Austrian empress Elizabeth ("Sissi") was wearing when she was fatally stabbed by an anarchist in 1898 – the Costume Institute serves as a research center for fashion designers, theater professionals and other specialists. It is situated on the Museum's ground floor and has study rooms and a library.

Food and drink: Food is available at the Met's own restaurant as well as at a cafeteria and bar/cafe, all on the first floor. Refreshments also are available in the Petrie Court Cafe on the second floor, and drinks are offered on Friday and Saturday, 4pm to 8.30pm, at the Great Hall Balcony Bar. Outside the Museum, the area is rich in dining opportunities. Directly across the street, in the Stanhope Park Hyatt Hotel, is the Melrose (995 Fifth Ave, 212-288-5800, moderate), featuring contemporary American dishes with a few Mediterranean touches. Also open on Sunday are Caffe Grazie (26 E. 84th St, 212-717-4407, moderate), serving reliable Italian favorites; Clove (24 E. 80th St, 212-249-6500, expensive), offering sophisticated New American cuisine in an upscale townhouse; and the coffeehouse Le Pain Quotidien (1131 Madison Ave, between 84th & 85th Sts, 212-327-4900, moderate). Uncommonly tasty pizza and more are served at Sofia Fabulous Pizza (1002 Madison Ave at 79th St, 212-734-2676, inexpensive).

American Museum of Natural History

New developments enliven this old favorite, which dazzles visitors with an encyclopedic tour of the natural world.

Map reference: pages 50–51, D1
Central Park West at 79th St, 10024-5192.
Tel: 212-769-5100, www.amnh.org
Subway: B or C to 81st St. Bus: M10, M7, M11 to 79th St or M79 to Central Park West.
Daily 10am–5.45pm, the Rose Center is open Fri to 8.45pm.
Suggested donation (separate fees for Space Show, IMAX films, and some special exhibitions), museum stores, cafeteria, music, films, guided tours, wheelchair access.

"**T**he best thing in that museum," says Holden Caulfield in *The Catcher in the Rye*, "was that everything always stayed right where it was … The only thing that would be different would be you."

Well, not exactly. Starting in the 1990s, this cavernous and rambling institution – the largest of its kind in the world – has renovated some of its most beloved exhibits and, in 2000, unveiled the glorious new Rose Center for Earth and Space. Holden would be happy to know that few of the old fixtures have been removed. The meteorites, totem poles, life-sized blue whale and dioramas of all creatures great and small are still in

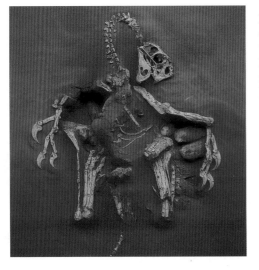

A brooding *Oviraptor* died with its legs draped around its eggs. This is one of the amazing specimens from the Museum's Mongolia expeditions.

place, though a few are showing their age. The dinosaurs remain too, completely revamped to reflect the latest thinking in paleontology.

Established in 1869 by natural-history professor Albert Smith Bickmore, the Museum launched some of the most significant scientific expeditions of the late 19th and early 20th centuries and continues to devote much of its resources to primary research, employing a staff of more than 200 scientists and technicians and sponsoring some 100 field projects every year. Laboratories and galleries were added in several stages over the decades, and the Museum now sprawls over 25 connected buildings on four square blocks.

Architecturally it's a bit of a hodgepodge, but the jumbled rooflines, conical towers and gothic arches suit an institution that functions as nothing less than a catalog of the natural world. It's been said that the Museum encompasses more than 32 million artifacts and specimens – probably a conservative estimate. At most, only two percent of the collection is on display at any given time, and still it's virtually impossible to see everything in a single visit, much less absorb what you've seen.

A better strategy is to limit yourself to two or three highlights, punctuated perhaps with an Imax movie or a tour of one of the smaller galleries. The Museum is also justly acclaimed for its temporary exhibits, which in recent years have included the delightful Butterfly Conservancy, a walk-through enclosure with nearly 500 free-flying butterflies, as well as an overview of genetics and a nostalgic look at baseball.

Skeletons in the closet

If you have time to see only one thing, head directly to the fourth floor, where you'll find the world's largest exhibition of dinosaur fossils. Return visitors will notice big changes here. A major overhaul of the dinosaur galleries in the late 1990s led to the repositioning of several skeletons, reflecting the view that the great beasts were agile, warm-blooded creatures instead of the ponderous, tail-dragging behemoths envisioned by early paleontologists.

Gone is the familiar chronological approach to the evolution of prehistoric life. In its place is "cladistics," a system developed in part by museum scientists that organizes living things into a sort of evolutionary family tree made up of groups, or clades, with shared anatomical features. The result, as science journalist Joan Gutin

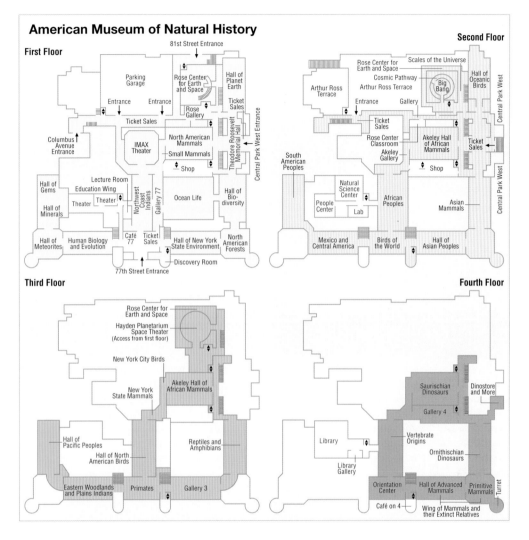

American Museum of Natural History

First Floor — 81st Street Entrance

Parking Garage · Rose Center for Earth and Space · Hall of Planet Earth · Ticket Sales · Entrance · Entrance · Rose Gallery · Ticket Sales · Columbus Avenue Entrance · IMAX Theater · North American Mammals · Small Mammals · Shop · Theodore Roosevelt Memorial Hall · Central Park West Entrance · Hall of Gems · Lecture Room · Education Wing · Theater · Theater · Northwest Coast Indians · Gallery 77 · Ocean Life · Hall of Biodiversity · Hall of Minerals · Hall of Meteorites · Human Biology and Evolution · Café 77 · Ticket Sales · Hall of New York State Environment · North American Forests · Discovery Room · 77th Street Entrance

Second Floor

Rose Center for Earth and Space · Scales of the Universe · Cosmic Pathway · Hall of Oceanic Birds · Arthur Ross Terrace · Arthur Ross Terrace · Big Bang · Entrance · Gallery · Ticket Sales · Rose Center Classroom · Akeley Hall of African Mammals · Ticket Sales · South American Peoples · Akeley Gallery · Shop · Central Park West · Natural Science Center · People Center · Lab · African Peoples · Asian Mammals · Mexico and Central America · Birds of the World · Hall of Asian Peoples

Third Floor

Rose Center for Earth and Space · Hayden Planetarium Space Theater (Access from first floor) · New York City Birds · New York State Mammals · Akeley Hall of African Mammals · Hall of Pacific Peoples · Hall of North American Birds · Reptiles and Amphibians · Eastern Woodlands and Plains Indians · Primates · Gallery 3

Fourth Floor

Saurischian Dinosaurs · Dinostore and More · Gallery 4 · Library · Vertebrate Origins · Ornithischian Dinosaurs · Library Gallery · Orientation Center · Hall of Advanced Mammals · Primitive Mammals · Café on 4 · Wing of Mammals and their Extinct Relatives · Turret

puts it: "Goodbye, Early Dinosaurs and Late Dinosaurs. Hello, Saurischian Dinosaurs and Ornithiscian Dinosaurs" – a distinction that has to do with the configuration of the hipbone. An introduction to cladistics is presented in a film narrated by Meryl Streep in the new Orientation Center. This is the logical place to start a tour and a worthwhile investment of time, although many visitors are too impatient to see actual dinosaur bones to sit through the entire program.

Adjacent to the Orientation Center is the Hall of Vertebrate Origins. Here the evolutionary tale starts about 500 million years ago when massive armored fish like *Dunk-*leosteus*, whose head was encased in bony (and beautifully preserved) armor, ruled the seas. Fossils of otherworldly creatures like *Diplocaulus* – sort of an oversized salamander with a boomerang-shaped head – chronicle the development of tetrapods (animals with limbs), amniotes (animals whose embryos develop in an amniotic sac), and synapsids (ancestors of mammals). Even more dramatic are flying reptiles like pterosaurs and real-life sea monsters such as ichthyosaurs, plesiosaurs and mosasaurs.

Follow the black stripe through a corridor exhibit on the 1994 discovery of an *Oviraptor* fossil in Mongolia. About the size of a large dog, this particular

Ancestors of the nautilus date back hundreds of millions of years.

Barosaurus rears up against an attacking Allosaurus in the grand rotunda.

and 1908. Broken ribs, damaged vertebra and a facial abscess were probably sustained in battles with other animals, though it remains unclear if *Tyrannosaurus* was a predator or scavenger. A second *Tyrannosaurus* skull, displayed at ground level, gives visitors a closer view of its powerful jaws and giant, razor-sharp teeth, designed to tear chunks of flesh from its prey.

A slightly smaller but no less lethal *Allosaurus* stands next to *T. rex*, munching on the tail of a sauropod. Other large theropods (two-legged, meat-eating dinosaurs), including a nearly complete *Albertosaurus*, are exhibited in a series of displays along the side wall.

Tucked into a corner, a pair of *Coelophysis* skeletons have the bones of immature *Coelophysis* in their abdominal cavities, evidence that this lightly built carnivore wasn't above an occasional bout of cannibalism. On the opposite end of the hall is the world's only display of a real fossil *Deinonychus*, an agile predator about the size of a human. It is shown in mid-leap, ready to rip into its prey with clawed hands and – deadliest of all – the sickle-like claw on the second toe of each foot. Just behind *Deinonychus*, several casts of *Archaeopteryx*, the earliest known bird (sometimes described as a "feathered dinosaur"), advance the theory that birds are descendants of dinosaurs, a notion that remains controversial among paleontologists.

Just across the aisle is *Apatosaurus*, one of the largest creatures to have ever walked the earth. Most people know it better by its old name, *Brontosaurus*, a misnomer propagated by 19th-century paleontologist O. C. Marsh in his haste to claim credit for a new species. Marsh was also

specimen is notable for having died while tending a nest full of eggs, the first direct evidence of dinosaur brooding behavior. Curiously, another *Oviraptor* nest was found at the site containing the skulls of two immature *Velociraptors*. Whether these fierce carnivores were present as prey or predators or, as some scientists suggest, as part of a parasitic child-rearing relationship (similar to that of the modern cuckoo), remains a mystery. Even more amazing is the discovery of an *Oviraptor* egg with an intact fossil embryo still inside. A model of the embryo is on display.

Better to eat you with

Just around the corner, the first of two dinosaur halls focuses on the saurischians, a group of "lizard-hipped" dinosaurs whose pubis (part of the hipbone) slopes forward, allowing some species to stand upright. In the center of the hall, representing the two major branches of the saurischian family, are the towering skeletons of *Tyrannosaurus rex* and *Apatosaurus*, both repositioned with tails held aloft for balance instead of dragging on the ground.

The *Tyrannosaurus* is actually composed of fossils from two individuals found in Montana by famed bone-hunter Barnum Brown in 1902

responsible for persuading the Museum to crown the specimen with the skull of a different species. The mistake was officially acknowledged in 1975, but *Apatosaurus* – née *Brontosaurus* – wore the wrong head until the skeleton was remounted in the 1990s.

Apatosaurus' long neck and peglike teeth were adapted to grazing treetops, and its long tapered tail was used as a powerful whiplash against predators. The animal may have also reared up on its hind legs (much like the *Barosaurus* in the rotunda at the main entrance) to bring its enormous forelimbs and clawed "thumbs" crashing down on an attacker.

The footprints below *Apatosaurus* are a section of the Glen Rose Trackway, a series of fossilized dinosaur tracks about 107 million years old found at the Paluxy River in central Texas. The smaller, three-toed prints are those of a theropod. The larger ones were left by a sauropod similar to *Apatosaurus*.

Armed and dangerous

The next hall covers the ornithiscians, dinosaurs with backward pointing hipbones. This group includes familiar armored and horned dinosaurs such as *Stegosaurus, Ankylosaurus, Triceratops* and *Styracosaurus* – all represented by impressive fossils, including a clutch of *Protoceratops* eggs. On the other side of the gallery are duckbill dinosaurs, whose rows of flat teeth were designed for grinding plant matter, unlike the sharp "beaks"of the horned dinosaurs – a difference clearly illustrated by a pair of motorized skulls that show the motion of the jaws.

The most significant specimen in the gallery is the so-called Dinosaur Mummy, a fossilized *Edmontosaurus* with rare samples of soft tissue, including a patch of skin clearly covered with little bumps, or tubercles, similar to those of an alligator. Skin impressions are also visible on a fossil *Corythosaurus*, a duckbill dinosaur with a bony crest honeycombed with nasal passages that may have been used to produce a trumpetlike call. More elaborate crests adorn the skulls of *Saurolophus, Lambeosaurus* and other duckbills, and several theories are proposed for their use – as a support for some kind of inflatable sac, a "resonating chamber to produce low-frequency calls," or a brightly colored visual signal.

Pachycephalosaurus also knew how to use its head. Its brain was protected inside a domed cranium about 10 inches (25 cm) thick; a small section is exposed for visitors to touch. Some scientists surmise that the helmetlike skulls were used in head-butting contests similar to those of present-day bighorn rams.

A nearby display case holds the remains of a *Psittacosaurus*, a two-legged herbivore with a parrotlike beak. Small polished stones found in its abdominal cavity are gastroliths, "stomach millstones" swallowed by the animal to aid digestion of fibrous plants.

Not warm and fuzzy

The next two halls – Primitive Mammals and Advanced Mammals – emphasize the diversity of the mammalian lineage. Many visitors are surprised to learn that mammals emerged at about

Primitive amphibians like this trematosaur were dominant before the emergence of dinosaurs.

A depiction of the Eocene period, about 50 million years ago, from the fourth-floor Orientation Center.

the same time as dinosaurs, although they rarely grew larger than well-fed rats until the dinosaurs died off about 65 million years ago.

The forebears of the mammalian line were anything but warm and fuzzy, a fact amply illustrated by the fossilized remains of *Edaphosaurus*, a large lizardlike creature with a spiny sail on its back. More familiar fossils include prehistoric anteaters, marsupials, monotremes (egg-laying mammals), giant armadillos, an 8-foot-tall (2.5-meter) ground sloth, and a *Gomphotherium*, an early ancestor of the elephant.

The last gallery is dominated by some of the creatures our Ice Age ancestors may have hunted (or been hunted by), including cave bears, saber-toothed cats, giant deer, a series of skeletons tracing the evolution of the horse, enormous rhino-like brontotheres with shovel-shaped prongs on their snouts, and wooly mammoths with enormous curled tusks.

Displays in the Hall of the Universe chronicle the evolution of stars.

A view of the universe

The other must-see at the Museum is the Rose Center for Earth and Space, a brand new facility that is both a state-of-the-art science center and an extraordinary architectural statement. Suspended in the center of the structure like a pearl in a glass box is the Hayden Planetarium, an aluminum sphere 87 feet (27 meters) in diameter split along the equator into two theaters. In the upper half is the 429-seat, dome-screened Space Theater, featuring *The Search for Life: Are We Alone?* – an investigation of the age-old question narrated by actor Harrison Ford. In the lower half is the much smaller Big Bang theater. Here viewers stand

around a rail and peer down into a basin-shaped screen while poet Maya Angelou narrates a laser-light interpretation of the universe's birth.

On a cantilevered walkway around the planetarium is a series of displays called the Scales of the Universe that demonstrates the relative size of objects in the cosmos, ranging from galaxies to subatomic particles, using the sphere as a point of reference. A second walkway, the 360-foot (110-meter) Cosmic Pathway, spirals down from the sphere. Illuminated panels along the edge chronicle the evolution of the universe from the Big Bang to the present. Each step represents about 75 million years. Remarkably, the past 30,000 years of human history occupies a space no wider than a single strand of hair.

The Cosmic Pathway leads to the Hall of the Universe, a large exhibition space with displays on star formation, asteroid collisions, black holes and other celestial phenomena. A 12-foot-wide (4-meter) high-definition screen called the Astro Bulletin flashes astronomy news along with images from the Hubble Telescope, and an interactive video features astrophysicists discussing their work. Near the center of the hall is the Willamette Meteorite, an eroded 15½-ton hunk of nickel-iron forged in the heart of a faraway star.

A stairway leads from the Hall of the Universe to the Hall of Planet Earth, which focuses on the geological forces that constantly reshape the planet. Displays utilize a variety of techniques and media to explore volcanism, plate tectonics, seismology, climatology and other aspects of earth science. Dramatic cross-sections of rock represent stages in the planet's evolution and illustrate the volcanic, sedimentary and metamorphic processes involved in rock formation. Models and videos are used to visualize the motion of the continental plates across the surface of the globe and show how their constant pushing and pulling engenders volcanoes, earthquakes, faulting and mountain building.

A display of model ice cores from Greenland demonstrates how glacial ice can be used to retrieve climatological data dating back more than 100,000 years. Also on display are several "black smokers," or sulfide chimneys, that once spewed scalding water about a mile beneath the surface of Juan de Fuca Sound. Some scientists speculate that the planet's earliest microbial life may have developed around such deep-sea vents, sustained by the flow of heat and minerals.

Visitors who want to learn more about earth- and space-borne rocks can trek over to the Halls of Minerals, Gems and Meteorites in the far corner of the Museum on the first floor. Highlights include the 563-carat Star of India, the world's largest star sapphire, and the 34-ton Cape York Meteorite, the world's largest meteorite on display. Also known as Ahnighito, the Cape York Meteorite is one of three retrieved from Greenland by Arctic explorer Robert E. Peary between 1895 and 1897. The so-called "iron mountain" had been used for centuries by the native Inuits as a source of iron for knives and other tools.

Representing wildlife

Permanent exhibitions elsewhere in the Museum fall into one of two categories – biological or anthropological. On the biological side are the famous wildlife dioramas situated in about a dozen halls devoted to birds, marine life, invertebrates, reptiles and mammals. The best of the lot is the Akeley Hall of African Mammals, the brainchild of its namesake Carl Akeley, a preparator and field researcher who revolutionized the art of taxidermy in the early 1900s. Akeley didn't merely stuff his specimens. He sculpted every muscle and tendon in painstaking detail, cast the figure in plastic, then applied the animal's skin.

It was Akeley's ambition to preserve the wild Africa he saw being ravaged by sport hunters and farmers. From a modern perspective, his tactics seem more than a little ironic. Killing and stuffing wildlife hardly seems like the work of a conservationist, especially when one learns that much of the hall was funded by wealthy patrons in exchange for accompanying Akeley and his colleagues on hunting (or "collecting") expeditions in Africa.

In fairness, it should be noted that Akeley was instrumental in establishing a gorilla sanctuary in the Congo, and there's no disputing that he elevated such dioramas to a new level of artistic mastery and scientific accuracy. Still, one can't help wondering how the animal skins were obtained. Perhaps Akeley himself gives us a clue in his two masterpieces – the gorilla diorama, which features a silverback beating his chest in defense of a nearby infant and, mounted on a pedestal in the center of the hall, a charging elephant herd protected by a single bull turned to face an unseen intruder.

Carl Akeley at work on *At Bay*, an elephant diorama for the Hall of African Mammals.

Alaska brown bear diorama in the Hall of North American Mammals.

Homo erectus on the African savanna about 500,000 years ago, a diorama in the Hall of Human Biology and Evolution.

Dioramas in other galleries sometimes fall short of those in the African hall. Fortunately, an ambitious renovation program is already in the works, starting with the Hall of Ocean Life, home of the beloved blue whale model, which is slated to reopen in 2003.

Far more dynamic than the old dioramas is the Hall of Biodiversity, a beautifully designed gallery unveiled in 1998 that is both a celebration of the planet's myriad life forms and a clarion call for their protection. The 100-foot-long (30-meter) Spectrum of Life is a spectacular array of more than 1,000 models and specimens, evoking the glorious variety of life on Earth from the humblest protozoa to the largest and most complex organisms. An adjacent display focuses on endangered species, suggesting that we are presently undergoing the planet's sixth great extinction – a loss of some 30,000 species every year. A bank of large, synchronized video screens illustrates the breadth and beauty of the world's ecosystems and surveys the damage that's being done to them. A walk-through diorama in the center of the hall recreates the Dzanga-Sangha Rain-

forest in the Central African Republic, one of the most diverse ecosystems on the planet. A series of video screens and computer stations along the far end of the hall addresses contemporary issues such as global warming, deforestation, and habitat fragmentation as well as the impact of day-to-day decision-making on biodiversity and what we can do to stem the tide of extinction.

The human family tree

The collection is no less impressive on the subject of human diversity. The Hall of Human Biology and Evolution tells the story of *Homo sapiens* beginning with a primer on genetics and anatomy, then tracing the course of human evolution from apelike australopithecines to the fully human people of Ice Age Europe. On display are casts of 3.2-million-year-old Lucy (*Australopithecus afarensis*) and 1.6 million-year-old Turkana Boy (*Homo ergaster*). Excellent dioramas depict scenes at various stages in human evolution. They include a *Homo erectus* couple shooing away a vulture from an antelope carcass, Neanderthals tanning a hide outside a cave entrance, and a Cro-

Magnon campsite with a hut made of mammoth bones. There are also replicas of Ice Age cave art from Lascaux and Altamira as well as fascinating animal and "Venus" figures crafted between 28,000 and 10,000 years ago. Melodies played on a replica of an Ice Age flute are piped into the gallery.

Indigenous cultures

Anthropology and archaeology have been mainstays of the Museum's research program since the landmark Jessup North Pacific Expedition of 1897–1903 led by Franz Boas – the "father of American anthropology" – who set out to document cultural connections between the tribes of Siberia and America's Northwest Coast. The bounty of art and artifacts collected by Boas and his colleagues can still be seen in the Hall of Northwest Coast Indians, which is lined with totem poles and display cases brimming with ceremonial masks, baskets and weavings made by the Bella Coola, Haida, Kwakiutl and other coastal tribes.

A 63-foot (19-meter) dugout canoe in the lobby was carved out of a single red cedar log by the Haida about 1878. The figures inside the canoe were sculpted with plaster face casts of actual Northwest Coast Indians made by Boas and his team during the expedition.

Boas eventually fell out with museum administrators and in 1905 took a seat at Columbia University. There he trained Margaret Mead, who later served as the Museum's curator of ethnology for more than 50 years and became one of the best-known social scientists of the 20th century. The Hall of Pacific Peoples – Mead's specialty – is named in her honor. Artifacts on display range from Indonesian batik textiles, Javanese shadow puppets and paintings by Australian aborigines to beautifully carved war clubs, swords lined with shark teeth, and body armor woven of coconut fiber from Micronesia. From the Philippines are a headhunting axe and a ceremonial gong with a handle fashioned from a human jawbone. From New Guinea's Sepik River is a rack of skulls modeled with clay, made as a war trophy or a memorial to honored ancestors.

Artifacts documenting the artistic traditions, religious beliefs and social lives of indigenous people from every corner of the globe fill halls devoted to Latin America, Africa, Asia, and North America, and almost all are among the finest collections in their respective fields. Among scores of Mesoamerican vessels, figurines and stone carvings are representations of musicians, acrobats and shamans as well as jade and gold ornaments, and ornate stone ax heads.

Among the most curious objects in this collection are the heavy stone yokes, or belts, some weighing more than 50 pounds (23 kg) that were apparently worn by players in a ceremonial ballgame. The largest artifacts are architectural fragments and replicas of statues and elaborately carved stela (stone columns) from Mayan temples at Uxmal in Mexico and Copan in Honduras.

From the Inca and other pre-Columbian cultures of South America come gold ornaments, copper and silver mummy masks, and ancient textiles. Also on view are elaborate feathered headdresses, blowguns up to 8 feet (2.5 meters) long, and other artifacts made by the traditional people of Amazonia. From the Plains Indians of North America are painted buffalo robes, ornate beadwork, cradleboards, ceremonial pipes, buckskin dresses and spectacular feathered headdresses.

Africa's diverse tribal cultures are represented by masks, musical instruments, ceremonial costumes, religious artifacts, and a variety of tools. Dioramas range from the Berbers of North Africa's Atlas Mountains to the Mbuti of the Congo rainforest. The vast Hall of Asian Peoples covers the development of paleolithic cultures, the rise of civilization in the Tigris valley, the invention of writing and the emergence of the world's great religions, as well as a dizzying array of traditional cultures stretching from Japan to Armenia.

Food and drink: The Museum Food Court (lower level, moderate) is several cuts above typical museum cafeterias, with fresh salads, sandwiches, grilled specialties, stone-oven pizza and an appealing choice of sweets. Otherwise, you'll find at least a dozen worthy eateries within a few blocks of the Museum. Choices range from red-hot Latino specialties at Calle Ocho (446 Columbus Ave between 81st and 82nd Sts, 212-873-5025, expensive), savory Vietnamese at Monsoon (435 Amsterdam Ave at 81st St, 212-580-8686, moderate), tapas at Sabor (462 Amsterdam Ave between 82nd and 83rd Sts, 212-579-2929, moderate), and Chinese at Silk Road Palace (447B Amsterdam Ave between 81st and 82nd Sts, 212-580-6294, moderate) to rib-sticking American fare at Good Enough to Eat (483 Amsterdam Ave between 83rd and 84th Sts, 212-496-0163, moderate).

A sacrificial dagger illustrates the skill of Aztec artists with wood and stone.

Brooklyn Museum of Art

Second in size only to the Metropolitan, New York's "other" great art museum contains more than a million objects, representing cultures and traditions reaching back to ancient Egypt.

Map reference: pages 52–53, D6
200 Eastern Parkway, Brooklyn, NY 11238.
Tel: 718-638-5000; www.brooklynart.org
Subway: 2 or 3 to Eastern Pkwy-Brooklyn
Museum. Bus: B71, B41, B69 or B48.
Wed–Fri 10am–5pm, Sat–Sun 11am–6pm (first Sat of each month to 11pm).
Admission fee, guided tours, lectures, films, concerts, museum store, café, wheelchair access.

Our Lady of Cocharcas under the Baldachin, 1765; created by an unknown artist in Peru, the painting records details of Spanish colonial life.

By the time of its assimilation into greater New York in 1898, Brooklyn was already a major city in its own right, boasting an expansive cultural and scientific museum called the Institute of Arts and Sciences. The Brooklyn Museum of Art (BMA) originated as a component of the Institute, which in 1897 dedicated the initial portion of the great McKim, Mead & White structure, an elegant Beaux-Arts design that today forms the core of the museum. Had this structure been completed as intended, it would have been the largest museum building in the world. Construction stalled in the 1920s, however, leaving only one-sixth of the project complete. Since then, the major capital improvements to the Museum have been a 1990s redesign and a new entrance pavilion in 2002, which unites both modern and neoclassical architectural elements in a 560,000-square-foot (52,000-sq-meters) space.

Until 1934, the Institute was dedicated to science as well as art, but in that year it divested itself of its natural-history holdings (many went to the American Museum of Natural History in Manhattan) and concentrated exclusively on fine art, including ethnographic objects from around the world. These latter holdings were among the first anywhere to be interpreted as works of art in their own right, rather than simply as anthropological artifacts.

Home and abroad

Several salvaged sculptures, once part of New York's "street furniture," are displayed in an outdoor space between the Museum's entrance and the parking lot. The finest of these, and surely the most melancholy for any student of the city's architectural past, is Adolph Weinman's *Night*, an allegorical representation of a drowsy, cloaked female figure sculpted of pink granite and rescued from the rubble of Pennsylvania Station after that grand terminal's much-lamented demolition in 1963. Along with its companion, *Day*, the 1910 work once flanked a clock at one of four main entrances to the station.

On the first floor, the Great Hall comprises exhibit areas for African, Pacific and indigenous American art. Among highlights of the African galleries – which were expanded and reinstalled in 2001 – are a large number of ceremonial pieces from the central portion of the continent. An 18th-century woodcarving of a *nyim*, or king, made by a member of Zaire's Kuba people displays the confident power and physical trappings of office, all in a 19-inch (48-cm) figure. The transcendent role of kingship is also suggested in the figure of a ruling *oba* carved in ivory on a rare 16th-century

bell from the court of Benin and a magnificently ornate beaded crown worn by a 19th-century Yoruba ruler. New to the installation is an extraordinary stone figure of a man holding a crocodile by an unknown Sapi artist of Sierra Leone in the 15th century, and a number of Ethiopian crosses created for ceremonial purposes between the 13th and 20th centuries.

Works from Polynesia, Micronesia, Melanesia and the islands of Southeast Asia make up exhibits drawn from more than 3,000 Pacific island artifacts. As with African art, the link between the visible world and the spirit realm is fundamental to creative expression in these far-flung archipelagoes. A 19th-century Kepong mask uses wood, fiber and shell fragments to represent a menacing bush spirit; from Vanuatu comes a mask of coconut fiber, hemp, bamboo and palm in which the wearer's ancestral ghosts reside. From Melanesia comes an early 20th-century splashboard for an oceangoing canoe, crafted to hold protective magic within its curved, polychrome design.

Native America

The BMA's Arts of the Americas collection constitutes one of the most important repositories of indigenous American art in New York. Comprising materials from both North and South America, the collection includes a treasury of important Andean textiles, among which is the famous *Paracas Textile*, dating back more than 2,000 years. South American ceramics, gold and stone carvings (a palm-sized Aztec jaguar smiles craftily through five centuries of time) also enrich the

ABOVE: *An Out-of-Doors Study (Paul Helleu Sketching with His Wife)*, 1889, John Singer Sargent.

LEFT: *Seated Buddha Sakyamuni*, China, Liao Dynasty, early 11th century.

collection, as do vivid Spanish colonial pieces, many with religious themes.

From North America come sleekly stylized mythic beasts and a monumental totemic house post from British Columbia's coastal tribes, and an early 19th-century Sioux chief's tunic ornamented with beads, feathers, porcupine quills, and human and horse hair. Other American Indian pieces range in age from a stone pipe bowl in the shape of a submissive prisoner, carved in the Southeast more than 500 years ago, to a lustrous black ceramic "melon" bowl, fired by a modern master in one of New Mexico's Indian pueblos.

Asian diversity

The BMA's Asian collection, housed on the Museum's second floor, is an ambitious attempt to encompass the continent's cultural diversity by displaying fine examples of divergent artistic traditions, from Turkey and Iran clear across to Japan. Korean and Persian art of the 19th and early 20th centuries are especially well represented. The Museum also possesses North America's largest collection relating to the little-known Ainu people of northern Japan.

A Medallion Ushak carpet from 16th-century Turkey is a brilliant example of how weavers created seemingly endless variations on a basic central design, using fine wool colored with brilliant vegetable dyes. A 10th-century Cambodian stone head of the Bodhisattva Avolokitesvara radiates wisdom and calm. On a folding paper screen from Japan's 17th-century Edo period, a party of kimono-clad picnickers strolls in fluid dignity against a bright gold background. And a plump little ewer, fired in Korea 900 years ago, wears its ethereal gray-green celadon glaze on a body of unfolding lotus leaves as perfectly as if it had just left the kiln.

Ancient worlds

The third-floor galleries contain Classical and Middle Eastern art and the Egyptian collection. Western antiquity is represented by pieces such as a 3,500-year-old Minoan slipware jug, decorated in stylized painted shellfish, and a splendidly realized Hellenistic black marble bust of a proud, pensive African. Middle Eastern pieces cover the region from Syria to Iraq. Especially striking are a seated *Syrian Sun God*, less than 6 inches (15 cm) tall and superbly cast in bronze about 1600–1700 B.C.; and an alabaster relief of a winged genie nearly 8 feet (2.4 m) in height, which adorned the palace of the Assyrian King Ashur-nasir-pal II some nine centuries before the Christian era.

The BMA possesses one of the world's great collections of ancient Egyptian art. The oldest pieces are predynastic, such as the foot-tall (30-cm) terra-cotta figure of a swooping, stylized female with a bizarrely beaked visage, crafted more than 5,000 years ago. From the Sixth Dynasty of the Old Kingdom comes a hauntingly translucent alabaster carving of the child king Pepy II, seated in his mother's lap. The faces of later kings and queens stare out from the Middle and New Kingdoms: Senwosret II, stern yet serene in black granite; Nefertiti looking sly in sandstone relief. The mummy case of the priest Nespanetjerenpere (ca. 945-653 B.C.) is a richly colored paean to the deceased's divine associations, while a much more recent mummy mask (ca. 100 B.C.–100 A.D.) reveals in gilt and pigment the Roman influence upon Egyptian depictions of the human face.

Decorative arts and American vision

The Museum's most engaging examples of decorative arts are a series of period rooms on the fourth floor. The oldest is from Brooklyn itself, a Dutch colonial interior from the 1675 Schenck House. This parlor/dining/sleeping room could have been the background for a Vermeer, with its blocky, foursquare furnishings softened by a "Turkey carpet," cheerful upholstery and Delft ceramics. Far more opulent is a room from a North Carolina mansion, the Cupola House, built nearly a century later, with Georgian paneling painted Prussian blue, Chinese ceramics, English-inspired American furniture and

Elaborate imagery on the *Cartonnage of Nespanetjeren-pere* identifies the deceased as a high-ranking priest.

faux-marble painted floorcloth. The 19th century is represented by a riotously ornate Victorian Moorish smoking room from John D. Rockefeller's New York town house – not a reflection of the oil titan's own simple tastes but that of the woman from whom he bought the ready-furnished mansion. Finally, simplicity of a particularly sumptuous mid-20th century sort is the hallmark of an Art Deco study from a late 1920s Manhattan apartment, complete with lalique crystal and geometric olive wood paneling.

American painting and sculpture galleries occupy much of the fifth floor of the museum's East Wing. Recently reorganized into an exhibition called *American Identities: A New Look* as part of the new Luce Center for American Art, the BMA's American holdings – which include decorative objects such as an Art Deco cocktail set and a Frank Lloyd Wright chair – span nearly three centuries. The colonial era is represented by several examples of the celebrated portraiture of John Singleton Copley and Gilbert Stuart, as well as lesser known artists such as William Williams, whose full-length 1766 portrait of Deborah Hall epitomizes 18th-century portrait painting as a signifier of social standing.

The 19th century in America was a great age of landscape painting, a trend that the BMA amply documents in its holdings of Hudson River School artists such as Thomas Cole (*The Pic-Nic*, 1846), and Albert Bierstadt (*A Storm in the Rocky Mountains, Mt. Rosalie*, 1866). As engaging in their way as Cole's romantic landscapes and Bierstadt's wildly majestic panoramas are the "genre" paintings of artists such as George Caleb Bingham, who took as his subjects farmers, boatmen and frontiersmen, as in *Shooting for the Beef* (1850), with its casual gathering of competing sharpshooters.

American landscape artists in the BMA include George Inness, whose naturalistic *A Day in June* (1882) represents a quiet departure from the grandiosity of the Hudson River painters, and the

George Washington, by Gilbert Stuart. The artist, one of the premier portraitists of the Federal period, felt his work was so distinctive that it was unnecessary to sign it.

luminist John Frederick Kensett (*Lake George*, 1870), for whom light working its changes across sky and water are as important as the composition's more tangible elements. Childe Hassam (*Poppies on the Isles of Shoals*, 1890) brought an Impressionist's eye to the American landscape, while Winslow Homer (*In the Mountains*, 1877, and *The Turtle Pound*, 1898) depicted human subjects and the natural environment with a stark and sentiment-free simplicity. As early as the 1880s, Homer's work, especially his watercolors, were gaining wide popularity for him among American art enthusiasts.

Twentieth-century and contemporary American painting and sculpture, much of which was formerly exhibited in galleries on the Schapiro Wing's fifth floor, are incorporated into *American Identities*. Works range from the dreamlike

of European paintings and sculpture, presently awaiting re-installation on the East Wing's fifth floor. The collection is especially strong in pre- and early Renaissance Italian and 19th-century French paintings. Nardo di Cione's *Madonna and Child Enthroned with Saints* (ca. 1360), tempera on a shimmering gold ground, harks back to a pre-Giotto formality in its grouping of figures while nevertheless employing a facial expressiveness that looks ahead to the next century. *Adoration of the Magi* (1480) by Bernardo Butinone is a warmly hued rendition of the kingly visit with charmingly contemporary Italian costumes and architectural background.

Jean-Francois Millet's *A Shepherd Tending His Flock* (1860s) and Gustave Courbet's *The Edge of the Pool* (ca. 1867) are French pastorals representing a gentle break from the academic tradition. A far more startling departure is Paul Cézanne's almost proto-cubist *The Village of Gardanne* (1886). Works by Degas, Lautrec, Gauguin and Matisse are also part of this worthy retrospective of the French 19th and early 20th centuries. Claude Monet's *The Ducal Palace at Venice* (1908) represents the shimmering summit of late Impressionism.

Camera works

The creative force inherent in the art of photography was recognized early by the Brooklyn Museum, first in the nation (1890) to establish a department focused on the world of the camera. The collection includes works by such leading practitioners as Edward Steichen, Margaret Bourke-White, Berenice Abbott, Paul Strand, Edward Weston and Lewis Hine. In one of Hine's best-known photos, satchel-toting immigrants climb the steps at America's gateway in 1908, symbolically moving on up in *Climbing into the Promised Land, Ellis Island*.

ABOVE: *Nude in a Wood*, 1906, Henri Matisse.

BELOW: *Angel*, William Edmondson, from *American Identity: A New Look*.

flower-and-bone desertscapes of Georgia O'Keeffe (*Ram's Head and White Hollyhock, New Mexico*, 1935) to Stuart Davis's riotous jazz-inspired *The Mellow Pad* (1945–51), and from one of Ad Reinhardt's celebrated "black" paintings (*Untitled Composition #104*, 1954–60) to the muted geometric color planes of Richard Diebenkorn's *Ocean Park No. 27* (1970).

Rodin and the Europeans

A central fifth-floor gallery contains the BMA's collection of sculptures by Auguste Rodin, the 1981 gift of Iris and B. Gerald Cantor. Highlights of the Rodin bequest include 12 figures and studies from *The Burghers of Calais* (1886–1888) as well as groups from *The Gates of Hell* (begun in 1880; incomplete at Rodin's death in 1917) and the *Monument to Balzac* (1898). There is also a reduction of *The Age of Bronze* (1876).

The Rodin exhibition anchors a small but important collection

Food and drink: For breakfast, lunch or dinner – and for what many Brooklynites consider the borough's best cheesecake – head for Junior's (386 Flatbush Ave, 718-852-5257, inexpensive), a deli-diner hybrid also offering plump cheese blintzes, corned beef and tongue sandwiches, and a wide variety of meat, fish and egg dishes. A neighborhood favorite with a Caribbean flavor is Mike's International (552 Flatbush Ave, 718-856-7034, inexpensive), where Jamaican jerk chicken and ribs are served with red beans and rice, and escoveitch fish is enlivened by vinegar and fiery scotch bonnet peppers. There's live music on summer weekends and occasionally in winter.

OPPOSITE: *Powerhouse Mechanic*, 1925, Lewis W. Hine.

The Cloisters

Perched high above the Hudson River in upper Manhattan, The Cloisters, in Fort Tryon Park, is America's only museum dedicated exclusively to the art of the Middle Ages.

Map reference: pages 52–53, E1
Fort Tryon Park, 10040.
Tel: 212-923-3700, www.metmuseum.org
Mar–Oct Tues–Sun 9.30am–5.15pm, Nov–Feb Tues–Sun. 9.30am–4.45pm.
Subway: A to 190th St (10 minute walk north on Margaret Corbin Dr). Bus: M4 to Fort Tryon Park-The Cloisters.
Admission fee, parking, museum store, seasonal café, limited wheelchair access (call 212-923-3700, ext. 7130, to make arrangements).

Right: *Descent of the Holy Spirit*, mid-12th century, Meuse Valley, France.

Below: *St. James the Greater*, ca. 1490, from the tomb of Juan II of Castile, Spain.

I f you'd like a Twilight Zone experience, come on up to The Cloisters. You'll find yourself transported back in time several hundred years to the Middle Ages. Here, in upper Manhattan overlooking the Hudson River, you get a sense of what medieval Europe was like and connect with its spiritual essence as expressed in a range of priceless art and precious objects.

Since its opening in 1938 as a public showcase, The Cloisters has been hailed as a gem, a museum par excellence, exhibiting incomparable art perfectly complemented by architectural splendor. The driving force behind this institution, as with so many others in New York, was John D. Rockefeller, Jr. But the man who really got it started was George Grey Barnard.

Born in 1863, Barnard was an American sculptor who studied in France – one important mentor was Auguste Rodin, the Michelangelo of his time. (Rodin, in fact, once compared the talented Barnard to a young Michelangelo.) Despite his association with the modern-day realist Rodin, however, Barnard remained essentially a neoclassicist who admired "the patient Gothic chisel."

While working in France, Barnard earned money by purchasing medieval church and monastery sculpture and architectural fragments from various landowners and then selling the pieces at a profit. He kept almost 700 objects for himself, shipped them to New York, and, upon his return in 1914, opened a church-like brick museum on Fort Washington Avenue, next to his residence in Washington Heights. He called the place "the Cloisters," intending it as a benefit for the widows and orphans of French sculptors. The works weren't displayed in any kind of historically accurate context, but Barnard's museum was the first of its kind to display medieval art in the United States.

When Barnard's Cloisters was put up for sale in 1924, Rockefeller couldn't pass it up. An avid collector himself, the multimillionaire donated funds to the Metropolitan Museum of Art to purchase it, and threw in more than 40 of his own medieval works. Some years later, when the Met decided that a larger space was needed to display the collection in a more appropriate manner, Rockefeller provided the money to convert some 66 acres (27 hectares) of land just north of the original museum into a public park – Fort Tryon Park – with the new museum as its centerpiece. (Rockefeller had purchased the property in 1909 for $1.7 million and spent more than $3.5 million on its improvement.) At the same time, Rockefeller guaranteed that the view across the Hudson would remain pristine by donating additional land to New Jersey, on the other side of the river, to be incorporated into its Palisades Park.

Peace and quiet

Elements of five medieval cloisters are incorporated into the framework of the museum, whose overall design is evocative of buildings of the Middle Ages. What are cloisters? They are covered walkways, or quadrangles, enclosed by a vaulted passageway or arcade, surrounding open courtyards. Today these monastic hand-medowns provide a peaceful spot for visitors to relax and contemplate troves of medieval art. There are roughly 1,200 works of art on exhibit. They date from as early as 800 A.D., but they're centered on the High and Late Middle Ages. Supplementing them are some 6,000 more treasures downtown, at the Met's main Fifth Avenue showcase.

As installed here, the cloisters lead to galleries whose exhibits focus upon the treasures of the collection, especially the Romanesque and Gothic periods – paintings, sculptures, stained glass, metalwork and textiles, including the renowned *Unicorn Tapestries*. There are medieval manuscripts exquisitely illuminated, ivories, enamels and much more. And the adjacent medieval gardens are recognized as the finest of their kind in the world.

The architect for the Rockefeller-financed Cloisters was Charles Collens, who had designed Manhattan's grandly ornamental Riverside Church (yet another Rockefeller project). Rather than recreate an actual medieval building for this new project, Collens chose to incorporate medieval proportions, styles and actual portions of the arcades of five medieval cloisters into a decidedly 20th-century structure.

As for the exhibits themselves, that job went to Joseph Breck, a curator of decorative arts and assistant director at the Met. He laid out the exhibits in roughly chronological order, from about 1000 A.D. to 1520 A.D. When he died, in 1933, James Rorimer worked with Rockefeller to complete the installation.

Tapestry treasures

The museum is on two levels. On the first floor are the famous *Unicorn Tapestries*, woven in Brussels about 1500 and long regarded as the crown jewel of The Cloisters collection. All of the brilliant colors in the seven tapestries were derived from only three dye plants (yielding red, yellow and blue) and depict the hunt of the mythological unicorn, whose capture, death and restoration may represent the incarnation, death and resurrection of Jesus Christ.

Tapestry weaving was a tradition from ancient times in Egypt, Greece and China, and it developed in Europe starting in the 10th century. The first important French tapestries date from the 14th century. Hunting the unicorn was a familiar subject of tapestry weaving in the late Middle Ages and the Renaissance. The Cloisters' *Unicorn Tapestries* were once owned by the family descended from François VI, duc de la Rochefou-

The Unicorn Tapestries: The Unicorn in Captivity, 1495–1505, northern France.

cauld, at the time of the French Revolution in 1793, when they were taken by peasants from his family estate at Verteuil. The peasants used them, it is thought, to protect their produce from frost until they were recovered, with some damage, in 1850. These renowned tapestries were purchased by Rockefeller in 1922. He donated them to the Metropolitan in 1937.

A place for monks

Three of the five cloisters are also on this floor. Directly in front of the Tapestries room is the Saint-Michel-de-Cuxa Cloister, from a Benedictine monastery founded in southern France in 878. The cloister's covered arcades surround a garth, or enclosed yard with no ceiling. Traditionally, it was in this space – generally on the south side of the church – that monks sat in contemplation, read and bathed. The Romanesque marble capitals on the cloister's columns are characterized by intricately carved scrolling leaves, acanthus blossoms, and

animals with two bodies and a common head. Today, a fountain in the center of the crossed paths divides the garden into four grassy quadrants, each with a fruit tree and bordered by herbs and flowers. In winter, the cloister's arcades are glassed in and the interior walkway is filled with pots of brightly colored flowering plants, including lily of the valley, jasmine, narcissus and fritillaria.

Artists who created the capitals (all pre-1206) in the cloister from the Benedictine abbey of St.-Guilhem-le-Désert, founded in 804 in southern France, carved intricate acanthus plants and palm trees in cream-colored limestone, then drilled holes in intricate honeycomb patterns to contrast with the foliage and give it a crisp laciness. Demons on the Mouth of Hell capital drive sinners down into the pit.

Visitors to the Romanesque Hall separating the two cloisters enter through a massive rounded arch supported by huge limestone blocks. Crafted around 1150, the arch's capitals are carved in low

TOP AND RIGHT: Visitors tour gardens designed according to horticultural information from medieval art and literature.

OPPOSITE: Stained-glass panels adorn The Cloisters' galleries and reconstructed chapels.

relief with animated floral and animal carvings. Across from this entrance is a mid-13th-century pointed Gothic archway from the Burgundian monastery of Moutiers-Saint-Jean. A third doorway, the late 12th century Reugny Door from the Loire Valley, has a pointed and deeply recessed arch. Statuary on display include sculptures of Clovis, the first Christian king of France, and his son Clothar.

There are two chapels off the Hall. Under the altar canopy in Langon Chapel is a wooden sculpture of the *Virgin and Child*. Originally painted, the entire work (except the head of the Christ Child, attached with a dowel and now missing) was carved from a single block of birch. The Fuentidueña Chapel, with its imposing rounded apse, was originally a part of the church of San Martín in the Spanish village of Fuentidueña north of Madrid. Although the rest of the church was in ruins, the chapel was salvageable and was painstakingly dismantled and reconstructed here. Up in the half dome is a fresco of the *Virgin and Child* from the Catalonian church of San Juan de Tredós.

In the Gothic mode

Adjacent to the Cuxa Cloister is an architectural reconstruction of the Chapter House from Notre-Dame-de-Pontaut, a 12th-century abbey in southwestern France. Used by the monks as a gathering place, the rectangular room has the signature thick walls and small windows of the Romanesque period. The rib-vaulted ceiling, however, is Gothic. Gothic architects had learned how to transfer the ceiling load from the walls to supporting columns, making possible the graceful interiors and ample windows that typified the architecture of the period.

The stained-glass windows in the Early Gothic Hall next to the Chapter House are superb examples of the new style that was succeeding the Romanesque in churches throughout Europe in the 12th century. Statuary displayed here includes the sandstone *Virgin* (ca. 1250) from Strasbourg Cathedral and the limestone *Virgin and Child* from the île de France of the mid-14th century.

A stairway descends to the Gothic Chapel (also accessible from the lower level), where the effigy of crusader knight Jean d'Alluye, armed in chain mail with sword and shield, lies upon his tomb – a popular mode of burial for prominent individuals in the late 11th century. Acquired by Barnard, the

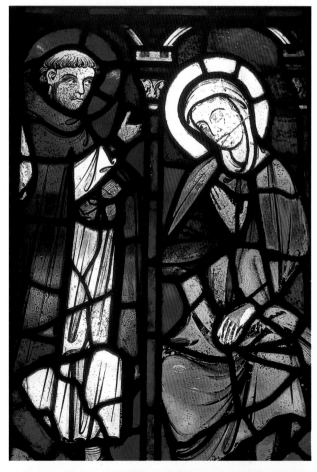

tomb – now empty – was originally in the cloister of an abbey near Le Mans.

There are several stained-glass windows in the chapel, as well as funerary monuments, including the tombs of the Spanish counts of Urgel. Upstairs are fragments of the *Nine Heroes Tapestries*, part of a 15th-century series of French pictorial textiles thought to have been commissioned by a nobleman of the House of Valois. The subjects of the tapestries are heroes from pagan, Hebrew and Christian history and mythology: Hector, Alexander, Julius Caesar, David, Joshua and Arthur. The tapestries were cut up and disbursed over the years; it took two years to reassemble the fragments, and it is believed that the works are now two-thirds complete.

In the Boppard Room, ornate canopies with intricate twisting arches and leafy ornaments frame six late-Gothic stained-glass panels originally installed in the church of the Carmelite convent at Boppard am Rhine. An elaborate alabaster altarpiece was created in Spain in the 15th century.

Adjacent, in the Campin Room, secular and religious themes are intricately blended by 15th-century painter Robert Campin in his three-paneled *Altarpiece of the Annunciation*, which portrays the Archangel Gabriel's announcement to the Virgin Mary that she has been chosen by God to be the mother of Christ. A wealthy Flemish couple commissioned the work, and Campin chose to place the scene in a setting that his patrons would find familiar and comfortable. The gallery, with a Spanish painted ceiling, is furnished with objects similar to those depicted in the Virgin's room.

The Dormition of the Virgin, a 15th-century oak carving from Cologne, Germany.

In the Late Gothic Hall are sculptures dating from the latter part of the 15th century representing the Magi, or Wise Men, who visited Jesus after his birth. They were originally integrated into a large altarpiece at a convent in Baden-Baden. A carved oak relief *Death of the Virgin*, also German, is a work of the same era.

Three cloisters

Outside the Late Gothic Hall, Froville Arcade, built around nine pointed arches from the Benedictine priory of Froville, is the third of the five cloisters. On the lower floor are the Bonnefont Cloister, the Trie Cloister, the Gothic Chapel, and the Glass Gallery.

The late-13th or early 14th-century Bonnefont Cloister has capitals and columns from the Cistercian abbey at Bonnefont-en-Comminges and other religious foundations in southern France. The simplicity of the capitals here is indicative of the strict asceticism of the Cistercian order, whose monks considered ornamentation a distraction from the contemplation of God. The raised beds in the Bonnefont Cloister's herb garden hold one of the world's most specialized plant collections, based on more than 300 species used in the Middle Ages for cooking, medicine, art, industry, housekeeping and magic.

The Trie Cloister displays richly carved capitals, bases and shafts from the Carmelite convent and other religious orders in the Bigorre region of southwestern France, as well as from monasteries near Toulouse. Under the tiled roof, the arcade, with its central fountain, frames a garden filled with plants typical of the European countryside: bluebells and irises from the meadows, cattails that grow along streams, and woodland primroses and violets. Many of the plants here are depicted among the flora of the *Hunt of the Unicorn* tapestries.

Stained glass, sculpture and tapestries in the Glass Gallery are representative of late medieval works created for the burgeoning class of wealthy merchants and tradesmen as well as for churches, the traditional patrons. As such, they reveal the growing secularization of European life at the close of the Middle Ages.

The aptly-named Treasury is a repository for pieces created, according to the 12th-century monk Theophilus, to embellish the House of God "with such great beauty and variety of workmanship ... without which the divine mysteries and the administering of the offices cannot continue."

The collection includes a walrus ivory altar cross from the 12th century – *The Cloisters Cross* – carved with more than 100 figures and 60 Greek and Latin inscriptions, and yet another prized possession – the *Book of Hours* of Jeanne d'Evreux, a miniature illuminated prayer book created around 1325–29 for the queen of France. Among the other objects in the collection: an elephant-ivory *Plaque of St. John the Evangelist* from the 9th century and a pot-metal glass *Martydom of Saint Lawrence*, made ca. 1175 in Canterbury, England.

Lightweight audio guides are available, providing information on the history of The Cloisters, its architecture, its gardens and some 70 works of art. The guide includes 75 stops (about two hours of programming) and allows visitors to customize a tour to suit their interests.

The Gothic Chapel, with the tomb of Jean d'Alluye and Austrian stained glass from the 14th century.

Food and drink: Visitors can enjoy sweets, sandwiches and coffee at a café in the walkway of the Trie Cloister, open May–Oct. Nearby, at the southern entrance to Fort Tryon Park, is the airy, oak-paneled New Leaf Café (212-568-5323, moderate), which turns out creative salads, sandwiches, and beef and chicken dishes. The restaurant, in a restored 1930s limestone building, is run by the New York Restoration Project, founded by entertainer Bette Midler, and all profits go to improvements in the park. A snack bar on the lower level prepares food to go. Open for lunch Tues–Sat and Sun brunch.

The Frick Collection

Steel magnate Henry Clay Frick built his New York mansion around a spectacular collection of art dating from the Renaissance through the late 19th century. Intended from the beginning as a legacy to future generations, it remains one of the world's finest testaments to an individual connoisseur's vision.

Map reference: pages 50–51, E3
1 E. 70th St, 10021.
Tel: 212-288-0700; www.frick.org
Tues–Sat 10am–6pm, Sun 1pm–6pm.
Subway: 6 to 68th St. Bus: M1, M2, M3, M4 southbound on Fifth Ave to 72nd St or northbound on Madison Ave to 70th St.
Admission fee, museum store, concert series, free audio tour, wheelchair access.

Sir Thomas More, 1527, Hans Holbein the Younger.

Largely self-educated, but a millionaire by the time he was 30, Henry Clay Frick (1849–1919) had a lifelong interest in art, although he confined his collecting to the modest acquisition of prints and sketches during his early years in the business of providing coke to the burgeoning steel industry in his native Pennsylvania. His appreciation of painting grew more sophisticated following an 1879 trip to Europe with another young collector, Andrew Mellon, eventual benefactor of the National Gallery of Art in Washington, D.C. By 1895 Frick had achieved great wealth as an executive in the Carnegie Steel Company and was ready to indulge his passion in earnest. He purchased 30 paintings in that year and acquired 92 more by 1900.

Frick's tastes ran at first to the French Barbizon school along with works by contemporary American and European artists, but soon deepened to include Flemish, Dutch, Italian and Spanish masters. Portraits and landscapes were his favorite subjects. Among them was the earliest Frick acquisition remaining on exhibit, Corot's *Ville-d'Avray*.

As he entered his fifties, Frick's tastes turned more towards 17th-century Dutch masters and 18th-century English portraits. He bought his first Vermeer shortly after 1900 as well as works by Gainsborough and Lawrence. He added a Titian – his first Italian Renaissance painting – to his collection in 1905, and in the same year bought a Van Dyke and an El Greco. Renaissance, Baroque and 17th-century Dutch works figured significantly among Frick's acquisitions of the decade that followed and included paintings by Veronese, Velázquez, Holbein and Vermeer, although more recent painters such as Constable and Turner also commanded his attention.

Many of the finest paintings in the collection were purchased during the last five years of Frick's life. In 1914 and 1915, he acquired major works by Goya, Whistler, Manet, Degas, Millais and Gainsborough, as well as Renaissance canvases by Titian and Bellini and the series by Fragonard called *The Progress of Love*. A final Vermeer was added to the collection in 1919, the year of Frick's death.

Be it ever so humble

In 1906, Frick had spent $2.4 million to acquire the block on Fifth Avenue between 70th and 71st streets, where the Lenox Library stood. By 1907 the old library building was demolished (the collection was transferred to the successor New York Public Library, at Fifth Avenue and 42nd Street), and Frick was free to begin building.

(Ironically, one of the reasons Frick left his turreted Pittsburgh mansion and moved to New York, where for several years he rented the old William H. Vanderbilt mansion on Fifth Avenue, was that he felt the steel city's sooty air was bad for his paintings. A small portion of his collection, however, remains at his restored Pittsburgh home, Clayton.) He commissioned Carrère & Hastings, architects of the New York Public Library, to build a residence on the site. The style of the limestone mansion was to be 18th-century English, as inspired by Italian neoclassicism. In furnishing his new home, Frick leaned heavily towards 17th- and 18th-century French antiques, English dining room and library pieces, and Italian bronzes. His sculpture collection, largely Italian Renaissance with some French and northern European work, was well integrated with the furnishings.

Frick's residence, as completed in 1914, is essentially the home of the Frick Collection that we see today, with a 1930s modification – conversion of an outside courtyard into an interior Garden Court – by architect John Russell Pope, and the addition of the Oval Room, East Gallery and a lecture hall/music room. Following Frick's death, his widow Adelaide Childs Frick lived in the building for the 12 remaining years of her life, after which, under the terms of Frick's will and $15 million endowment, the home was converted into a museum. Under the endowment's terms, funds available after maintenance requirements were met could be used to purchase additional artworks. Since Frick's death, the collection has been increased in size by roughly one third.

The collection opened to the public in 1935, without any drastic alteration of the premises from their original residential appearance. Although strict maintenance of the status quo in interior decoration and arrangement of artworks was not required as part of the Frick legacy, the paintings in one room, the Living Hall, are displayed as they were in Frick's lifetime.

First Impressions

From the entrance hall on East 70th Street, visitors proceed to the left, where the East Vestibule is dominated by Tiepolo's mythological narrative

Perseus and Andromeda, a study (ca. 1730) by the Venetian for a now-destroyed ceiling fresco in Milan. In the adjacent Anteroom is Memling's *Portrait of a Man* (ca. 1470); van Eyck's early 15th-century *Virgin and Child, with Saints and Donor*; El Greco's *Purification of the Temple* (ca. 1600); and *The Three Soldiers* (1658) by Pieter Brueghel the Elder. The Anteroom opens onto the Boucher Room, where François Boucher's eight-panel series *The Arts and Sciences* (ca. 1750) depicts juvenile parodies of adult pursuits. Boucher also painted the *Four Seasons* in the West Vestibule.

The Dining Room, off the West Vestibule at

The Garden Court, originally an outdoor courtyard, was converted into an interior space in the 1930s.

The Fragonard Room features 18th-century French furniture and *Progress of Love*, a four-canvas series by Jean Honoré Fragonard.

the building's southwest corner, showcases several fine examples of 18th-century English portraiture. Hogarth, Romney, Reynolds and Gainsborough are all represented, the latter by his 1783 *The Mall in St. James's Park*, a charming portrayal of leisurely urban life.

The West Vestibule opens onto the South Hall and the Fragonard Room. In the former are two of the Frick's three Vermeers (out of some mere three dozen accepted as the artist's work): *Officer and Laughing Girl* (ca. 1655–60) and *Girl Interrupted at Her Music* (ca. 1660). Both demonstrate the Dutch artist's mastery of lighting and perspective. Renoir's *Mother and Children*, dating to the middle 1870s, also hangs in the South Hall.

The four-panel Fragonard series *The Progress of Love*, which dominates the eponymous room between the West Vestibule and Living Hall, were

THE MAN BEHIND THE MANSION

Although Henry Clay Frick's maternal grandfather, distiller Abraham Overholt, was the richest man in western Pennsylvania, Frick made his own way in the world. He began work at 16, clerking in his uncle's store, and invested his savings in a coal vein that proved spectacularly productive. He was the "Coke King" of Pennsylvania in the days when iron had yet to give way to steel, and his Frick Coke Company was, in the 1870s, positioned to profit enormously from the rising new steel industry.

During the 1880s, steel titan Andrew Carnegie became the largest stockholder in Frick's company. This gave Carnegie a reliable source of high-quality coke for his furnaces, and also brought Frick into the management of the Carnegie firm. Frick served as chairman of Carnegie Steel from 1889 to 1900 but was ousted in a dispute with Carnegie over the price of coke purchased from Frick's original firm. "I'll see him in hell, where we both are going," was Frick's reply to a proposed reconciliation with his old associate shortly before his death.

Frick was an ardent foe of organized labor and earned notoriety for his ruthless suppression of the Homestead, Pennsylvania, steel strike of 1892. Shortly after, Frick was shot and seriously wounded by a young anarchist named Alexander Berkman. The wounded man's insistence upon finishing his paperwork before being taken away for medical attention only added to the Frick legend.

painted in the early 1770s for Madame du Barry, mistress of Louis XV. They represent the final flowering of French Rococo painting and are complemented by seven smaller paintings by the same artist completed some 20 years later, in what was by then an antique style. A Houdon sculpture, *Comtesse du Cayla*, rests on the Fragonard Room's mantel.

The Living Hall, as was noted above, is the one room in which the arrangement of artworks has not been altered since Frick's lifetime. Two portraits by Hans Holbein the Younger are reminders of tumultuous English politics under Henry VIII: *Sir Thomas More* (1527) reveals the adamant character of the canonized author and administrator executed by the king for refusal to recognize his self-appointed position as head of the English Church; *Thomas Cromwell* (1532) depicts one of More's chief persecutors, who himself fell out with Henry and was likewise executed. The Venetian School is represented by two Titians, *Man in a Red Cap* (ca. 1516) and *Pietro Aretino* (ca. 1550), a portrait of a popular satirical poet of the day; and by Bellini's *St. Francis in the Desert* (ca. 1480).

A room with personality

The Living Hall leads into the Library and North Hall. Of all the mansion's rooms, the Library, overlooking the Lawn on Fifth Avenue and dominated by Henry Frick's massive table-desk custom made in England by White, Allom and Company, best conveys the steel magnate's commanding personality. Its walls are hung with 18th- and early-19th-century English canvases, including portraits by Gainsborough and Reynolds, and one by Romney of Lady Hamilton – famed as the mistress of Admiral Horatio Nelson – in allegorical guise as "Nature."

The Library also contains three fine English view paintings: Constable's *Salisbury Cathedral from the Bishop's Garden (*1826) and Turner's *Fishing Boats Entering Calais Harbor* (1803) and *Mortlake Terrace: Early Sunday Morning* (1826). Several 18th-century French bronzes also adorn the room.

Over in the North Hall, Theodore Rousseau's *The Village of Becquigny* (ca. 1857) recalls Frick's early enthusiasm for the Barbizon painters, the coterie of French landscapists influenced by Constable and named after a village near Fontainebleau. Watteau's *The Portal of Valenciennes* (ca. 1710), a departure from his usual romantic subject matter, and Monet's 1879 *Vétheuil in Winter* underscore the North Hall's eclectic character, as does Ingres' captivating *Comtesse d'Haussonville (*1845), an exquisitely skilled study in pensiveness and coquetry combined.

Ingres' rendering of the beautiful, beguiling countess displays his uncanny mix of cool neoclassic form with sensuous romantic expression, and the master portraitist was in his 65th year when he painted this picture. The Hall also contains a pair of Italian Renaissance bronzes and a marble bust by Houdon.

The tiny Enamel Room, at the Fifth Avenue and 71st Street corner of the mansion, houses the collection of painted Limoges Renaissance enamels purchased by Frick from the J. P. Morgan estate. The room also houses several small paintings attributed to Piero della Francesca or his workshop; a Veneziano *Coronation of the Virgin* (1358); and a late Gothic *Temptation of Christ on the Mountain* (ca. 1310) by di Buoninsegna.

Eclectic taste

The West Gallery, accessible from the North Hall, is the largest of the mansion's rooms and the one that best exemplifies the breadth and quality of the Frick Collection. Here is the third of the collection's Vermeers, *Mistress and Maid*, painted during the final decade of the artist's life (1665–79). The gallery displays three Rembrandts: a 1658 *Self-Portrait*, showing the artist at age 52; *Nicolaes Ruts* (1631), a portrait of a prominent Dutch businessman; and *The Polish Rider* (1655), an unusual subject for the artist

Mother and Children, ca. 1876–78, Pierre-Auguste Renoir, is exhibited in the South Hall.

and perhaps an allegorical one, suggesting the progress of life as a journey. Seventeenth-century Dutch painting is also represented in the West Gallery by the four Hals canvases: *Portrait of an Elderly Man* (ca. 1628); *Portrait of a Woman* (1635); *Portrait of a Painter* (early 1650s); and *Portrait of a Man* (1660); and by two Van Dycks, both painted about 1620: *Frans Snyders* and *Margareta Snyders*.

El Greco's military portrait *Vincenzo Anastagi* (ca. 1575) and Velázquez's *King Philip IV of Spain* (1644) further illustrate the eclecticism of Frick's taste, especially as represented in the West Gallery, as does Goya's *The Forge* (ca. 1817), a powerful portrayal of men at work. Veronese's busy allegories of *Virtue and Vice* and of *Wisdom and Strength*, both painted about 1580, contrast markedly with the gallery's pair of Turners – *Cologne: The Arrival of a Packet Boat* and *Harbor of Dieppe*, both dating to 1826. Constable's

RIGHT: *The Forge*, ca. 1817, Francisco Goya.

BELOW: *Self-Portrait*, 1658, Rembrandt.

The White Horse (1819) and Corot's *The Lake* (1861) help round out the collection's evidence of Frick's attention to painters who lived in times closer to his own.

Late additions

Leaving the West Gallery, visitors enter the series of rooms added to the mansion in the 1930s. The elegantly proportioned Oval Room contains a pair of Van Dyck portraits – the Cavalier poet *Sir John Suckling* (ca.1630s) and the *Countess of Clanbrassil* (ca. 1636). These are balanced by two Gainsborough portraits of Georgian society women of the 1770s and 80s, and by a life-size terra-cotta *Diana the Huntress,* sculpted by Houdon in the same era.

The small East Gallery contains a remarkable collection of portraiture, including a David, two Van Dycks, three Goyas and four Whistlers, as well as works by Turner (*Antwerp: Van Goyen Looking Out for a Subject*, 1833), Millet (*Woman Sewing by Lamplight*, ca. 1870), and Corot (*Ville-d'Avray*, ca. 1860). Claude Lorrain's 1656 *The Sermon on the Mount* strikes an odd note in what is – Van Dyck aside – essentially a 19th-century room, until we recall the French painter's influence on Turner.

The Frick's Garden Court was never intended as a gallery but was a carriage court enclosed according to architect John Russell Pope's plans during the 1930s remodeling of mansion into museum. Accessible from the Oval Room, East Gallery or circular Music Room (used for free concerts and orientation lectures), the court is a serene and relaxing place, with a central pool and fountain around which are arranged portrait busts dating from the 16th through 19th centuries. Jean Barbet's bronze *Angel* (1475) presides over the court's restful atmosphere.

Food and drink: *The Japanese tea salon Toraya (17 E. 71st St, 212-861-1700) serves light lunches along with a choice of five kinds of tea. Dishes might include sansai okawa (rice with Japanese vegetables), served with steamed egg custard, salad and soup. For the less intrepid, Bella Blue Restaurant (967 Lexington Ave, 212-988-4624) serves pizza and a broad selection of Italian entrees.*

The Comtesse d'Haussonville, 1845, Jean-Auguste-Dominique Ingres. The Comtesse was a noted author and, for a woman of her status, an independent and liberal thinker.

Museum of Modern Art

Moving onward and upward, New York's premier showcase for what's new in the visual arts keeps looking to the future.

Map reference: pages 50–51, C5
11 W. 53d St (between Fifth and Sixth Aves), 10019.
Tel: 212-708-9400; www.moma.org
Thurs–Tues 10.30am–5.45pm, Fri to 8.15pm.
Subway: E or F to Fifth Ave and 53rd St; B, D, F or S to 47-50 Sts/Rockefeller Center. Bus: M1, M2, M3, M4 or M5 to 53rd St.
Admission fee, restaurant, café, museum stores, guided tours, lectures, films, wheelchair access.

Note: *MoMA is occupying a temporary exhibition space in Queens until 2005, while the main building is closed for renovations.*
Map reference: pages 52–53, E4
45-20 33rd St, Long Island City, NY, 11101.
Tel: 212-708-9400.
Subway: 7 local to 33rd St. Bus: Q32, Q60 to Queens Blvd/33rd St.

Call her MoMA. Yes, it's true, her heart belongs to Dada, as to everything else that was new in the modernist imagination betwixt and between Post-Impressionism and Pop Art and whatever else is brewing – as you can see by the 100,000 or so objects in her collection. And now she herself is poised to take a great leap forward in cultural history.

Girl Before a Mirror, 1932, Pablo Picasso.

She is the Museum of Modern Art, now undergoing a major face-lift. She'll be quite a different place by the time the year 2005 rolls around and she reopens her doors on West 53rd Street to let the public back in. Capacity will be doubled, affording 630,000 square feet (58,500 sq m) of new and reconfigured space for all the exhibitions and special programs she puts on in her mid-Manhattan roost.

The architect, Yoshio Taniguchi, has arranged it so that the main galleries will be housed in a brand-new building while another structure accommodates MoMA's activities in education and research. There'll be much more space for those activities than previously. And the prominent sculpture garden will be greatly enlarged.

While all this is going on, a new facility in Long Island City has been arranged to handle the Museum's operations. It's known as MoMA QNS – as in Queens County. Once a factory, it's been reconfigured and will have, in addition to gallery space for the permanent collection and special exhibitions, a combination café/bookstore, offices and other facilities. Shows lined up for MoMA QNS during this interim period include works by Matisse, Picasso, Pollock and Ansel Adams.

Cubes, cups and saucers

MoMA's bounty is replete with offerings of Cubism, Futurism, Fauvism, Surrealism, Abstract Expressionism and all the labeled and unlabeled trophies of modernist design. And besides all the paintings and sculpture are loads of drawings and prints, books and photos, films and videos and a wide range of distinctive objects ranging from chairs and sewing machines to cups and saucers and examples of Machine Art like highly functional – and in their own way beautiful – ball bearings.

In the beginning, there were only eight prints and a drawing. That was in 1929, when the Museum was founded as the first of its kind devoted to modern art. The founders were three ladies of means – Abby Aldrich Rockefeller, Mary Quinn Sullivan and Lillie P. Bliss – who were mad *about* mod when a lot of people were mad *at* mod. It was not so many years earlier, at the groundbreaking Armory Show of 1913, that a largely disbelieving New York press and public got their first look at the modern stuff and in effect asked: Is this serious?

The ladies, serious indeed, enlisted the help of an astute young art fancier named Alfred H. Barr,

Jr., who became MoMA's first director, and the initial show was held in November 1929 (right after the stock market crash). That opening show was devoted to works by Cézanne, van Gogh, Gauguin and Seurat, those exemplars of the second wave that followed in the wake of the original modernist breakthrough of the 1860s: Impressionism.

The exhibition was held on the 12th floor of a building at Fifth Avenue and 57th Street. A few years later, in 1932, Abby's well-heeled husband, John D. Rockefeller, Jr., provided space for the new Museum at 11 W. 53rd Street (personally, he much favored the Old Masters). Then, in 1939, came a new building at that address. Like the art it housed, it was nontraditional in design – functional, rectilinear, free of fussy ornament – the so-called International Style as executed by architects Edward Durell Stone and Philip Goodwin. There were major additions in 1951 and 1964.

One embellishment of note was the Abby Aldrich Rockefeller Sculpture Garden created by Philip Johnson in 1953 and expanded in 1964. With its stone creations, pools, fountains and plantings, it offered a pleasant ambience, at once sophisticated and relaxing, amid the sights and sounds of helter-skelter midtown Manhattan. The Museum's last big expansion came in 1984, when gallery space was doubled.

In with the new

At the heart of the Museum's collection are some 3,500 paintings and sculpture dating to the 1880s when rebellious artists began a process that favored abstraction over old-fashioned objective representation, setting new aesthetic standards even as their product was (and often still is) criticized by holdouts as somehow dehumanizing, perverse, arbitrary and just plain ugly.

The twists and turns in modern art's development are evident in the chronological arrangement of the works. Edgar Degas eluded easy classification as a stylist, though his later works influenced such groundbreakers as Gauguin and Picasso. Here, in his pastel *At the Milliner's* (ca. 1882), the woman trying on the hat is Degas' inti-

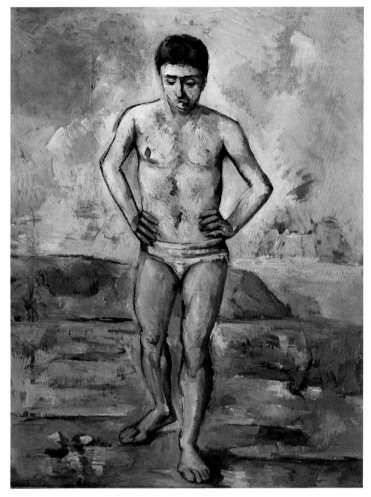

The Bather, ca. 1885, by Paul Cézanne, the painter whom Henri Matisse described as "the father of us all."

mate friend Mary Cassatt. Another work from the early period is Vincent van Gogh's tempestuous *The Starry Night* (1889). It is popular with Museum patrons but must have come as quite a shock when first shown.

George Seurat's analytic, rationalist detachment is evident in seascapes like *Port-en-Bessin, Entrance to the Harbor* (1888). Henri de Toulouse-Lautrec bestowed an immortality of sorts on the Moulin Rouge dancer of gluttonous appetite tagged *La Goulue* in his 1891–92 cardboard painting, as he did for the cabaret dancer known as "Cha-U-Kao" in his color lithograph *The Seated Clowness* (1896).

Paul Cézanne's *Still Life with Apples* (1895–98) showed the new compositional approach that profoundly affected how artists would perceive the shape of things to come. Paul

Above: *La Clowness assise (The Seated Clowness)*, 1896, Henri de Toulouse-Lautrec.

Right: Detail from *Sleeping Gypsy*, 1897, Henri Rousseau.

a Surrealist attitude. One of the Museum's long-time fixtures was Picasso's large mural *Guernica*, evoking the horror of the Spanish Civil War, until it was returned to post-fascist Spain in 1981. In its place, as it were, is *The Charnel House* (1944–45), Picasso's mixture of oil and charcoal suggesting the first grim black-and-white newspaper accounts of the Nazi death camps.

Matisse's primitivist design in his lyrical *Dance* (1909 version) echoes Cézanne's abstract reductiveness. A similar quality is evident in Matisse's quartet of large bronze sculptures of a human figure seen from the rear – *The Back* – which he worked on for over 20 years starting in 1909. Earlier (1905–06), Matisse showed his Fauvist colors in *Girl Reading*, the subject of the painting being his daughter Marguerite. In the anomalous arrangement of colors and shapes entitled *Piano Lesson* (1916), the pupil is his son, Pierre.

Georges Braque, after painting *Landscape at La Ciotat* (1907), collaborated with Picasso in launching Cubism. The name of this major new creative force arose when a critic observed that Braque reduced everything to cubes. *Bathers* (1907) demonstrates André Derain's early modernist sensibility, years before he rejected the new approach and embraced classical conception. Henri Rousseau's peculiar mix of fantasy and primitivism is famously reflected in *The Sleeping Gypsy* (1897) and *The Dream* (1910), the latter painted in the last year of his life.

Umberto Boccioni's *States of Mind: The Farewells*, depicting the busy scene at a railroad station (1911), reflects the Italian Futurists' affinity for materialism and the machine age. *Reclining Nude* (ca. 1919) is Amedeo Modigliani's affirmation of the centrality of the human figure. Paul Klee's *Cat and Bird* (1928), oil and ink mounted

Gauguin rejected Western convention in favor of primitive wonder in works like *The Moon and the Earth* (1893). Separate space is set aside for Claude Monet's luminous *Water Lilies*, rendered late in life at his shimmering garden in Giverny, where the Impressionist master died in 1926.

Picasso and Matisse

The collection is strong in works by those two giants of 20th century creation, Pablo Picasso and Henri Matisse. Picasso's *Boy Leading a Horse* (1906), with its bold brush strokes and flat composition, is Cézannist in design. *Les Demoiselles d'Avignon* (1907) is Picasso's great breakthrough, his solicitous Barcelona women with distended mask-like faces and piercing eyes portending Cubism and ushering in a new aesthetic world order. The Museum acquired the famous work in 1939. Picasso fused sheet metal and wire to create *Guitar* (1912), which he later presented as a gift to MoMA. *Three Musicians* (1921), including a Harlequin figure, is one of his famous Cubist renderings. *Seated Bather* (1930) and *Girl before a Mirror* (1932) have

on wood, exemplifies his fantastic-satirical symbolism. *Zapatistas* by José Clemente Orozco (1931) is one of the social-protest works typical of him and fellow Mexicans Diego Rivera and David Alfaro Siqueiros, both also in the collection.

Beyond reality

MoMA's standing was enhanced in the 1940s as New York emerged as the world capital of art. A retrospective exhibition in 1945 memorialized the Dutch-born painter Piet Mondrian, who himself had paid homage to the fascinating rhythm of both jazz and the city in his last completed painting, *Broadway Boogie Woogie* (1942–43). Mondrian had been absorbed by Cubism before embracing nonobjective abstraction in works like *Colour Planes in Oval* (1914), *Composition, V* (1914) and *Composition with Color Planes, V* (1917).

The collection illustrates the shift to non-figurative abstraction by others, such as Fernand Léger. *The Divers, II* (1941–42), captures young male swimmers in action off Marseilles and was painted while Léger was a refugee in New York. Surrealism, with its unnatural and fantastic images, developed in the mid-1920s. *The Birth of the World* (1925) exemplifies the lyricism in Surrealist Jóan Miró's work. Among the most famous of Surrealist works in the Museum's collection are Salvador Dali's *The Persistence of Memory* (1931), with its weirdly shaped limp timepieces, and René Magritte's *The False Mirror* (1928).

Marcel Duchamp, meanwhile, rattled convention with his Dada-ist approach in works like *The Passage from Virgin to Bride* (1912) and his metal *Bicycle Wheel* – as he excited Armory Show patrons with his *Nude Descending a Staircase, No. 2*. Realism was not abandoned by everyone, however, as evidenced by the work of Edward Hopper, who had also exhibited at the Armory Show. His *House by the Railroad* (1930) was the Museum's first painted acquisition. Hopper, "painter of loneliness," conveyed the sense of a brooding modern urban anomie. Realism was similarly the approach taken by the idiosyncratic

The Starry Night, 1889, Vincent van Gogh. "Looking at the stars," he said, "always makes me dream."

Andrew Wyeth, whose *Christina's World* (1948) is one of the Museum's popular possessions.

Pollock's progress

Jackson Pollock studied under Thomas Hart Benton before abandoning realism for Picasso-like design in *Stenographic Figure* (1942). By the time of his death in 1956, Pollock had become legendary for his Abstract Expressionism and leading status in the so-called New York School. The Museum has many of his works, including *The She-Wolf* (1943), *Gothic* (1944), *Full Fathom Five* (1947) and his wall-sized O*ne (Number 31, 1950)*.

Pollock's paper drawings, too, were important for their layered patterns, as in one of two untitled works of 1950–51 owned by the Museum in which line and color are fused, the lines crossing and recrossing in a kind of energetic outburst – "action painting." MoMA was the site of the first retro-spectives of Pollock's work, in 1956 and 1967.

Woman, 1 (1950–52) is one of a series of six oils on the female subject by Willem de Kooning, who was co-leader with Pollock in the so-called New American Painting. *Agony* (1947) is the beautiful but anguished work of Armenian national Arshile Gorky, who was another influential Abstract Expressionist; he committed suicide in 1948. Color fields were a preoccupation with Mark Rothko, as in *Red, Brown and Black* (1958). Jasper Johns put the national banner to famously unconventional use in his collage *Flag* (1954–55).

Claes Oldenburg displayed his plaster sculp-tures of dessert-as-art, *Pastry Case, 1* (1961–62), in his storefront studio on the Lower East Side, at the same time as Roy Lichtenstein (*Girl with Ball* and *Drowning Girl*), Andy Warhol and others were making waves with campy, comic Pop Art.

Sculpture and more

One of the most celebrated works of sculpture in MoMA's collection is Auguste Rodin's bronze, *Monument to Balzac* (1897–98). Among some other notable works are Aristide Maillol's massive

The She-Wolf, 1943, Jackson Pollock. "The modern artist is expressing an inner world … expressing his feelings rather than illustrating."

LEFT: *The False Mirror*, 1928, René Magritte.

BELOW: *Side 2*, 1970, Shiro Kuramata, from MoMA's architecture and design collection.

What the Museum calls architecture and design is what might traditionally be called decorative arts. MoMA's focus is on mass-produced objects that were made to serve a useful purpose and at the same time have aesthetic interest. There are more than 3,000 decorative objects in the collection that meet this standard.

Especially prominent are chairs of superior quality by top-flight designers. Charles Eames, working with Eero Saarinen, designed a revolutionary side chair made of molded plywood secured to a frame of aluminum tubing. It attracted attention after winning a MoMA design competition in 1940, before "Eames chairs" became an American original.

Similarly famous is the Barcelona side chair (1927) designed by architect Ludwig Mies van der Rohe. It is made of chrome-plated tubular steel and leather. The Finnish designer Alvar Aalto was acclaimed for modernist creations like his *Paimio Armchair* (1931), in birch plywood. Also notable is a table by Isamu Noguchi (1944), of ebonized birch with glass top; strikingly original chairs designed by architect Le Corbusier and Marcel Breuer, of Bauhaus standing, in the 1920s; and an *Office Armchair on Swivel Base* (1904) by Frank Lloyd Wright.

Industrial design is also included. Exhibits range from vacuum cleaners, teakettles and ball bearings to a Cistalia "202" GT sports car and a Bell & Howell helicopter. You'll never look at an ordinary object the same way again.

female nude, *The River* (ca. 1939–43), cast in lead; Constantin Brancusi's bronze *Bird in Space* (ca. 1928); Henry Moore's bronze abstract *Large Torso: Arch* (1962–63); Alberto Giacometti's characteristically elongated *Man Pointing* (1947) and his forbidding *Woman with Her Throat Cut* (1932); and David Smith's stainless-steel *Cubi X* (1963).

The Museum had a meager collection of drawings until the 1960s, when it began amassing a sizable number that now exceeds 6,000. Established in 1971, the Department of Drawings oversees a treasure trove that includes van Gogh's gouache-watercolor *Hospital Corridor at Saint Rémy* (1889), created during his confinement there; Picasso's reconstructed Cubist conception in *Man With a Hat* (1912), in which he used cut and pasted paper in a most unconventional way; and Joan Miró's attractive arrangement of symbols in *The Beautiful Bird Revealing the Unknown to a Pair of Lovers* (1941).

The four remaining categories of visual arts represented in the Museum's six holdings are architecture and design; prints and illustrated books; photography; and film and video. The photos date as far back as the 1840s. The Museum has more than 140,000 books and periodicals. And the collection of about 14,000 films includes the work of distinguished moviemakers in cinematic history, including D. W. Griffith, Eisenstein, Murnau, Pabst, Fritz Lang, von Sternberg, Lubitsch, Jean Renoir, King Vidor, Capra, Bunuel, Ford, Welles, Hitchcock and many more.

Food and drink: *A new café and restaurant are on the drawing board for MoMA's renovated midtown building, due to open in 2005. Nearby eateries of note in this high-rent neighborhood include the high-profile China Grill (52 W. 53rd St, 212-333-7788, expensive); the Scandinavian-flavored Aquavit (13 W. 54th St, 212-582-8993, expensive); and prix-fixe Italian at Ciao Europa (63 W. 54th St in the Warwick Hotel, 212-247-1200, moderate to expensive). A café/bookstore at MoMA QNS offers a modest selection of sandwiches, sweets, salads and beverages.*

Solomon R. Guggenheim Museum

A daringly original structure by America's master architect provides the framework for creations of soaring imagination in the modern vein.

Map reference: pages 50–51, F1
1071 Fifth Ave (between E. 88th and 89th Sts), 10128.
Tel: 212-423-3500; www.guggenheim.org
Sun–Wed 9am–6pm, Fri–Sat 9am–8pm.
Subway: 4, 5 or 6 (local or express) to 86th St.
Bus: M1, M2, M3 or M4 downtown on Fifth Ave or uptown on Madison Ave.
Admission fee, museum store, café, guided tours, lectures, films, live music, wheelchair access.

Woman with Yellow Hair, 1931, by Pablo Picasso, was inspired by the artist's young lover.

Founded in 1937, the Guggenheim was relatively new among the city's leading art repositories, but this was no disadvantage. Newcomer though it was, the Guggenheim shared top billing on the city's cultural marquee thanks largely to Frank Lloyd Wright, America's most renowned architect. He was asked in 1943 by mining magnate Solomon R. Guggenheim to design a place where Guggenheim could show off his collection of paintings. It was Wright's first and only New York commission, and what he came up with could only be called unique.

Wright favored "organic" creations, at one with nature, not the kind of unreal landscape he saw in Gotham's artificial skyscraper jungle. His final blueprint called for a concrete structure on Fifth Avenue, across from Central Park, that reminded people of everything from a giant inverted snail to a corkscrew, a washing machine, a marshmallow and a seashell. Perched on a rectangular base, it would curl around itself in an unbroken conical sweep from top to bottom for six levels and a quarter of a mile, natural light streaming in from outside. The interior was to be honeycombed with bay areas for display of art works, its central circular space grandly capped by a dome letting in more light from the sky above, while the building's curvilinear design was meant to be at one with the twists and turns of its Central Park backdrop.

Building officials raised various objections and artists, too, were less than thrilled by this biomorphic museum-in-the-round which they thought offered a dizzy field of vision for art appreciation. Wright dismissed the complaints and holed up at the plush Plaza Hotel while overseeing his work in progress, no doubt enjoying the fuss. The Museum opened in October 1959 to mixed reviews and much buzz, but Wright missed out on the fuss, having died a few months earlier.

Today his building is officially classified as a landmark, the youngest in New York ever to be so designated. There was more controversy in 1990 when an addition to the Museum was proposed. Designed to conform to the look of Wright's structure, it came across as a giant toilet bowl and was rejected. The architect went back to the drawing board and came up with a 10-story tower annex, facing East 89th Street, that provided ample gallery space for exhibitions of large objects as well as a sculpture terrace. In the process, new attention was drawn to the Wright stuff in architectural design.

From old to new

At the core of the collection housed in (if not overshadowed by) Wright's standout building are the works of some of the leading artistic names since modernism reared its head in the latter part of the 19th century. Many were associated with the various movements such as Expressionism,

Cubism and the general trend toward abstraction – such painters as Klee and Kandinsky, Mondrian and Modigliani, Léger and Moholy-Nagy, Picasso and Pollock, such sculptors as Archipenko, Brancusi, Calder, Giacometti, Moore and all the rest.

They were a revelation for Solomon R. Guggenheim, the fourth of seven sons of a Swiss emigrant who came to America in 1847 and made a fortune in merchandising and mining. Solomon enlarged the fortune and took up art collection in more or less standard millionaire fashion, acquiring traditional works generally by 19th-century French and American painters. But that changed when he met Hilla Rebay von Ehrenwiesen, a German baroness with a passion for abstraction, which she regarded as the endgame of modernism, its logical culmination. She was an artist herself, close to the Expressionists and others on the cutting edge in European art circles.

Arriving in America in 1927, she met the 66-year-old Guggenheim and turned him on to painters such as Max Ernst, Jean Arp, Hans Richter, Rudolf Bauer and, most notably, Vasily Kandinsky. On a European tour with Guggenheim in 1929 she introduced him to Kandinsky, chief theoretician for the new wave in artistic expression. Kandinsky, author of the 1912 manifesto *On the Spiritual in Art*, focused on the interplay between color and abstract forms and downplayed the traditional mimetic approach – reproducing nature's surface features rather than distilling the true, inner essence of things.

Rebay advised and Guggenheim purchased, starting with Kandinsky's *Composition 8* (1923), the first of many over the years to come from that artist – the Museum became the chief repository of his work. Many paintings by Bauer, who was Rebay's amour, were purchased as well – there were some 200 of his in the collection by 1939. Guggenheim bought works by Robert Delaunay, Marc Chagall, Albert Gleizes, Moholy-Nagy and

The Football Players, 1908, by Henri Rousseau; the artist, a toll clerk, only began painting seriously in his forties.

many others of the European modernists, storing them in his Plaza Hotel apartment at first, then at a Carnegie Hall office.

He planned originally to leave his collection to one of the major institutions, but then decided to establish a museum of his own. In 1937 the Solomon R. Guggenheim Foundation was established, and two years later it opened the Museum of Non-Objective Painting in a former auto showroom at 24 E. 54th Street. The Museum was shifted in 1947 to the Fifth Avenue site on which Wright's building would be erected. A new era began in 1952. The sole obsession with abstract, nonrepresentational paintings was abandoned and the name changed to The Solomon R. Guggenheim Museum to honor its founder (he had died in 1949). Rebay, who had clashed with Frank Lloyd Wright, was replaced as director by James

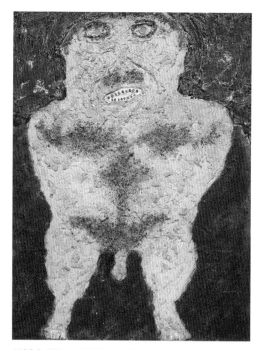

Johnson Sweeney, and the institution began broadening its mission. Sweeney pushed for acquisition of works of art from other periods and genres, including sculpture, and the Guggenheim came into possession of several collections of exceptional scale and quality.

Back to Pissarro

The estate of New York art dealer Karl Nierendorf was purchased in 1948, gaining for the Museum works by Chagall, Oskar Kokoschka, Lyonel Feininger and others. Especially imposing was the group of paintings presented by Justin K. Thannhauser, a dealer whose holdings included Impressionist and Post-Impressionist masterpieces; they would be installed in a separate Thannhauser Wing in 1965. Earliest among them was Camille Pissarro's *The Hermitage at Pontoise*, a landscape painted about 1867 in traditional style. Pissarro was hailed as a master by both Cézanne and Gauguin.

Pre-Impressionist, too, is Renoir's *Woman with Parrot* (1871), while the shimmering Impressionist look is reflected in Manet's *Before the Mirror* (1876). Both paintings were Thannhauser gifts. The great post-Impressionists are represented, too. Vincent van Gogh painted *Mountains at Saint-Rémy* just a year before his suicide in July 1890. Paul Gauguin's *In the Vanilla Grove, Man and Horse*, painted on burlap, is from his Tahiti sojourn in 1891. Also, Paul Cézanne's *Plate of Peaches* (1879–80); *Mme. Cézanne*

Top: *Will to Power (Volonté de puissance)*, 1946, by Jean Dubuffet, who described his style as Art Brut, or "raw art."

Below: *Sketch for Composition II*, 1909–10, Vasily Kandinsky.

(1885–87); and *Man with Crossed Arms*, painted about 1899 when the master innovator was entering his seventh decade.

Modernist times

The collection offers a glimpse at modernist influences and development. Among the works acquired in the Thannhauser bequest is Toulouse-Lautrec's frank evocation of ennui in a Paris brothel, *Au Salon* (1893). That artist's influence is shown in an early (1900) Picasso work, *Le Moulin de la Galette*, the first painting Picasso did in Paris after arriving from Barcelona. One of his Cubist renderings is *Accordionist*, done in 1911, while his colorful still life *Mandolin and Guitar* is from 1924. Picasso's distortions and plastic approach to human features are evident in the pastel *Three Bathers* (1920) and *Woman with Yellow Hair* (1931). Thannhauser acquired the latter work from the artist himself in 1937.

The *Football Players* (1908) is by the idiosyncratic Henri Rousseau, whose singular work has been labeled "naive art." Like van Gogh, Edvard Munch, *Sketch of the Model Posing* (1893), was a vital influence in the development of German Expressionism. Georges Braque's early association with Fauvism's "wild" colors is represented by the

brilliant *Landscape near Antwerp* (1906), suggesting van Gogh's emotionalism. Braque moved on to Cubism soon after, as attested to by such works as *Piano and Mandola* and *Violin and Palette*. The subject of Henri Matisse's *L'Italienne* (1916) is an Italian model named Laurette who posed for him between 1915 and 1918.

Paris Through the Window (1913) is Chagall's fantastic rendering of his newly adopted city as seen with the mind's eye, complete with parachutist, upside-down train, two-faced man and other bizarre figments of his imagination. Musical references were a constant in Chagall's work, as in his *Green Violinist* (1923–24).

Flowers were constant early on for Piet Mondrian, as in his charcoal *Chrysanthemum* (1908–09), before his work turned increasingly abstract. *Composition 8* and *Composition 1916*, both from the World War I period, are Cubist-like. In the grid *Composition 2* (1922), he uses only vertical and horizontal lines framing blocks of color.

Houses in Paris (1911) is one of the Cubist works of Juan Gris; he, Picasso and Braque are considered the foremost exponents of that style. *Nude* (1917) is one of Amedeo Modigliani's typically sensuous creations. He restricted virtually all his work to the human figure, painting 26 reclining female nudes in one period (1916–19)

of his brief, bohemian life (he died at 35). Some were banned from public display. Modigliani's mistress, Jeanne, is his subject in *Jeanne Hébuterne with Yellow Sweater*.

Kandinsky's *Blue Mountain* (1908–09), with its stylized, flattened masses of forms and colors, prefigures his move away from representation. His compositional approach is radically different in later works like *Painting with White Border and Black Lines*, both from 1913, or *Several Circles* (1926). Kandinsky plumbed the implications of shapes, lines and colors in a kind of aesthetic strip-mining in his pursuit of spirit matter.

Homegrown talent

New York succeeded Paris as the vital center of the art world by the 1940s, as reflected in the Museum's holdings of works by American artists, including the leading figure in Abstract Expressionism: Jackson Pollock. Among his vigorous

Nude, 1917, Amedeo Modigliani, one of many nudes produced by the artist before his untimely death in 1920.

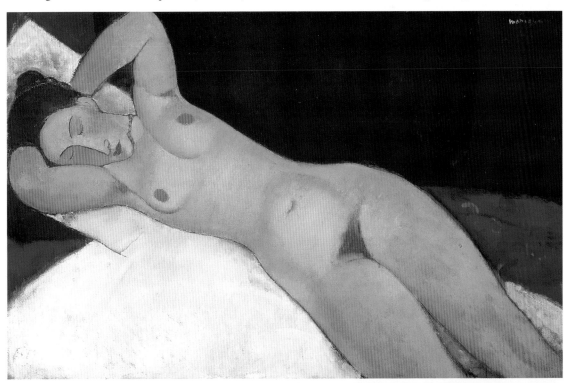

oilcloth, thereby rendering a figure in motion. Archipenko's works have been described as "sculpto paintings."

One of the best-known works by the Romanian sculptor Constantin Brancusi is *The Seal*, which he crafted from marble over a dozen years starting in 1924. Also familiar are the works of the Swiss sculptor Alberto Giacometti, among them his bronze *Spoon Woman* (1926) and *Nose* (1947). The latter, in Giacometti's characteristically elongated style, combines bronze with wire, rope and steel. The collection has mobiles by Alexander Calder going back to the 1930s. Aristide Maillol's *Woman with Crab* dates to 1902. Among relatively recent acquisitions are David Smith's *Cubi XXVII* (1965) and Richard Serra's *Right Angle* (1969).

Branching out

Among other notable bequests to the Museum have been works from the estates of Hilla Rebay, who died in 1967, and Guggenheim's niece, Peggy. Since the late 1930s, Peggy Guggenheim had amassed her own collection of avant-garde art, works by Europeans at first and then by Americans; she relied on Dada founder Marcel Duchamp for artistic advice as her Uncle Solomon had been guided by Rebay. Peggy Guggenheim installed her collection in a palazzo on the Grand Canal in Venice. She died in 1979 and the Solomon R. Guggenheim Museum absorbed her collection. In addition to the Venetian presence, the Guggenheim has been expanding its franchise into other territories as well. In Spain there is Guggenheim Museum Bilbao, designed by Frank Gehry (and acclaimed as the last great building of the 20th century). And the newest presence is the Guggenheim Hermitage Museum in Las Vegas. It is a collaborative effort involving the Guggenheim and the famous St. Petersburg institution in Russia.

Food and drink: Starting with breakfast, and including afternoon tea, light meals and desserts are served in the Guggenheim Café, restored in recent years to Wright's original design. Nearby, right off Fifth Avenue, is Joanna's (30 E. 92nd St, 212-360-1103, expensive), offering quality Northern Italian fare, and Ciao Bella Cafe (27 E. 92nd St, 212-831-5555, moderate), specializing in soups and sandwiches. Pizza fanciers can satisfy their craving at Pintaile's, (26 E. 91st St), much favored for its thin-crusted pies.

ABOVE: *Grrrrrrrrrr!!,* 1965, by Roy Lichtenstein, who mimicked comic-book lettering, lines and Benday dots.

RIGHT: Constantin Brancusi's *King of Kings* may have been inspired by African art and Romanian folk carving.

OPPOSITE: The central atrium is surmounted by a skylit dome.

drip-splash "action paintings" is *Ocean Greyness* (1953). Willem de Kooning's large and equally vigorous *Composition* is a clash of charcoal and thickly painted colors. The title of Mark Rothko's 1949 painting shows his own attraction to luminous colors: *Violet, Black, Orange, Yellow on White and Red*. Ellsworth Kelly used five panels for his own large horizontal exploration in color: *Blue, Green, Yellow, Orange, Red* (1966). Roy Lichtenstein used his comic-strip technique to convey an impression of mechanism and militarism in *Preparedness* (1968), and Andy Warhol's *Orange Disaster* (1963) replicates the electric chair in a garish hue.

Works of sculpture

An early work of sculpture is Edgar Degas's *Dancer Moving Forward*, which he started crafting in 1882. One of the modernist innovators in the field was the Kiev-born sculptor Alexander Archipenko, who used polychrome construction in welding together *Médrano II* (1913–14) of painted tin, wood, glass and painted

Whitney Museum of American Art

Strong in both historical and contemporary trends, the Whitney is generally regarded as possessing the world's finest collection of 20th-century American art.

Map reference: pages 50–51, E3
945 Madison Ave at E. 75th St, 10021.
Tel: 212-570-3676; www.whitney.org
Subway: 6 to 77th St. Bus: M1, M2, M3, M4, M30, M72, M79 to Madison Ave and 75th St.
Tues–Thurs 11am–6pm, Fri 1pm–9pm, Sat–Sun 11am–6pm.
Admission fee, museum store, café, lectures, films, wheelchair access.

My Egypt, 1927, by Charles Demuth, reflects a fascination with industrialism during the "Machine Age" of the 1920s.

Gertrude Vanderbilt Whitney was rich as well as arty, so when she was rebuffed by the Metropolitan Museum of Art in 1929, she said, in effect: The heck with them, I'll start my own museum. And so she did. Ever since then, the Whitney Museum of American Art – with the accent on "American" – has long ranked

as one of the so-called Big Five of New York City museums, sharing top billing with the Met itself, the Museum of Modern Art, the Guggenheim, and the Brooklyn Museum.

When it came to art, Mrs. Whitney was more interested in live Americans than dead Europeans. This heiress to part of the immense fortune left by the railroad baron Cornelius Vanderbilt was an accomplished sculptor in her own right. Back in 1907 she opened a studio in Greenwich Village, and quicker than you can say "salon," it became a gathering place for young artists. It was called the Whitney Studio Club, and it was located in what would later be the heart of New York bohemianism at 10 West 8th Street. Seven years later, Mrs. Whitney purchased the adjoining town house and established the Whitney Studio, catering to younger painters and sculptors whose avant-garde work was all too often overlooked by the art establishment.

No less than Auguste Rodin wrote of both her sculpture and her efforts on behalf of fellow creators: "Aristocratic and very rich, she works with the sincerity and fervor of a poor artist whose ideals are the only luxury." Which probably explains her reaction when the Met's director, Edward Robinson, turned down her offer of an entire collection, numbering 500 mostly home-grown paintings and pieces of sculpture. Robinson told her, in so many words: Sorry, but your collection is not really our cup of tea.

Greatly annoyed, Mrs. Whitney stormed away. Two years later, in 1931, her own new museum got off the ground in a row of West Village brownstones. Years later, in 1954, it moved up to West 54th Street. Since 1966 the Whitney has been on Madison Avenue, its home a striking work of architecture by Marcel Breuer. Cloaked in gray granite, its sleek bulk arranged in progressively overhanging masses, the building shows the influence of a youthful Breuer's apprenticeship to Walter Gropius of Bauhaus fame.

The collection

Today the Whitney has about 12,000 works of art – paintings, sculptures, prints, drawings, photographs – representing the creative energy and imagination of more than 1,900 artists. At its core is the legacy of Gertrude Whitney herself, about 600 works that reflect her own well-informed and highly individualistic tastes. Although she

enjoyed a close relationship with many of the artists who put the stamp of abstraction on the vibrant New York art scene, Mrs. Whitney personally was inclined toward the traditional mode of representation, both in her own work and in her acquisitions. Her founding collection, for example, includes paintings by Thomas Hart Benton, George Bellows, Edward Hopper, John Sloan, Robert Henri and Maurice Prendergast.

Inevitably, over seven decades of expansion, the Whitney's directors have broadened the scope of the Museum's holdings. Abstraction is well represented, particularly works by the so-called Abstract Expressionists, or New York School, who rose to dominance right after World War II. Nonetheless, visitors to the Whitney will still encounter a higher profile for realism than will be found at, say, the Museum of Modern Art.

Sculpture has also become a larger component of the Whitney collection over the years (Mrs. Whitney, curiously, collected few pieces by artists working in her own chosen medium).

And since 1991 the Museum has maintained a photography department.

In addition to the acquisitions by Gertrude Whitney and her successors, the Whitney collection has been augmented by a number of generous gifts. Outstanding among these were some 2,500 oil paintings, watercolors, drawings and prints by Edward Hopper, donated in 1970 by his widow, Josephine. Also notable were Felicia Meyer Marsh's 1979 gift of more than 850 paintings, drawings and sketches by her late husband Reginald Marsh, and the 1976 Lawrence H. Bloedel bequest of works by Milton Avery, Charles Demuth, Georgia O'Keeffe, Larry Rivers and Charles Sheeler.

The Whitney has long prided itself on its policy of purchasing works within a year of their creation, often prior to wide recognition of the artists. This predilection for being "ahead of the curve" extends to retrospectives of newly recognized artists. Jasper Johns, Cy Twombly, Nam June Paik and Cindy Sherman were all given their

Gertrude Vanderbilt Whitney, a portrait of the Museum's founder, painted by Ashcan School artist Robert Henri in 1916.

Lily and the Sparrows, 1939, Philip Evergood.

the Lauder Galleries are rooms devoted to three of the century's giants: Edward Hopper, Georgia O'Keefe and Alexander Calder.

Hopper was the painter of melancholy who found isolation and dejection on big-city nighttime streets no less than in lonesome houses by the seashore. O'Keefe captured the austere light of the Southwestern desert and peered into the substance of dry bone and voluptuous iris alike. Calder was the inventor of the mobile and master of sculptural whimsy. His *Circus* (1926–31), a Whitney fixture since 1976, is installed in the Lauder Galleries, and several other of his works are exhibited elsewhere in the Museum.

The Whitney's permanent collection, rotating among the other galleries, encompasses the panoply of major 20th-century American art movements. The Ashcan School, that loose affiliation of urban realists who flourished in New York in the early 1900s, is represented by one of George Bellows' explosive prizefight scenes, *Dempsey and Firpo* (1924), and John Sloan's *Backyards, Greenwich Village* (1914), a telling vignette of city kids building a back-alley snowman. Robert Henri, the Aschan School's founder, is represented by *Gertrude Vanderbilt Whitney* (1916), a full-length portrait of the Museum's founder, stretched out regally on a divan in her salad days in Greenwich Village.

Henri was an early influence on Edward Hopper, whose *Early Sunday Morning* (1930), *Railroad Sunset* (1929) and *Second Story Sunlight* (1960) explore the interior architecture of loneliness and alienation as well as the outward reality of bricks and mortar. Stuart Davis was also a student of Henri, although he converted to modernism after being bowled over by the landmark Armory Show of 1913. Davis' renderings of consumer products and packaging in the 1920s presaged Pop Art by some 40 years. *The Paris Bit* (1959), an extension of his work in geometric abstraction, reflects the dynamism of urban life in large, flat shapes of blue and black and the prominent use

first museum retrospectives at the Whitney. And the Museum has made a name for itself by recognizing a wide array of creative expression in such media as film, video, architecture, decorative arts, jazz and various other modes not traditionally associated with museum exhibitions.

Art on a roll

The Whitney rotates works from its permanent collection throughout its galleries at intervals of three to four months. For this reason, it is not possible to identify precisely where and when visitors might encounter particular pieces. An exception is a recently designed fifth-floor space, the Leonard and Evelyn Lauder Galleries, which permanently showcase more than 200 works – paintings, drawings, sculptures and photographs – from the first half of the 20th century. Central to

of words and lettering.

Among notable early modernists in the collection are Marsden Hartley, whose *Painting, Number 5* (1914–15), an assembly of abstracted shapes, symbols and insignia, is a "portrait" of his lover, a German officer who was killed in World War I. Georgia O'Keefe, in *Summer Days* (1936), integrates images that recur throughout her New Mexico work – bones, flowers and the eroded hills outside Taos. Abstraction is more pronounced in her *Music— Pink and Blue II* (1919), whose soft shapes and colors are clearly inspired by natural forms.

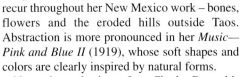

Nature is nearly absent from Charles Demuth's *My Egypt* (1927) and Charles Sheeler's *Rouge River Plant* (1932), which transcribe the man-made shapes of grain silos and smokestacks with almost photographic exactness. Precisionism, as the style came to be known, found its inspiration in industrial architecture, equating the massive structures of steel and concrete with the monuments of the ancient world.

The grandeur and dynamism of the Industrial Age is expressed with dizzying exuberance in Joseph Stella's *The Brooklyn Bridge: Variation on an Old Theme* (1939). The bridge was one of the great engineering feats of the 19th century and one of the artist's favorite haunts, evoking in him intense feelings of awe. "It impressed me," he wrote of the bridge, "as the shrine containing all the efforts of the new civilization of America – the eloquent meeting of all forces arising in a superb assertion of their powers, in apotheosis."

The Social Realists of the 1930s took a dim view of industrial society and chronicled the human toll of the Great Depression. Brothers Raphael and Isaac Soyer recorded the boredom and hopelessness of the unemployed in works like *The Mission* (ca. 1935) and *Employment Agency* (1937). Reginald Marsh captured the tawdry side of city life in *Twenty Cent Movie* (1936), in which a theater offers celluloid fantasies such as "Sins of the Flesh" and "Bare Naked" while street characters modeled after Hollywood "types" loiter outside. Paul Cadmus caused a stir with his depiction of drunken servicemen in *Sailors and Floozies* (1938), and Ben Shahn lashed out at the legal system in *The Passion of Sacco and Vanzetti* (1932–32). Shahn's celebrated work, part of a series of 25 gouaches and temperas on the subject, shows the Italian-American anarchists in coffins ostensibly being mourned by the three members of a blue-chip commission that upheld their death sentences.

In our times

Since the 1950s the Museum has devoted itself exclusively to 20th-century (and now 21st-century) art. It breaks down the most recent art periods

LEFT: In *Little Big Painting*, 1965, Roy Lichtenstein parodies the impetuous drips and brush strokes of the Abstract Expressionists.

BELOW: Typical of Edward Hopper, the two figures in *Second Story Sunlight*, 1960, are oddly disconnected.

into two categories: postwar and contemporary. The moral uncertainties of the postwar era prompted a return to abstraction. For Jackson Pollock and other members of the New York School, art was not merely a depiction of an object or idea but an "enactment" of the unconscious mind – hence the improvisational drips and splashes of "action" paintings like Pollock's *Number 27* (1950) and the impulsive brush strokes of Willem de Kooning's *Door to the River* (1960) and *Woman and Bicycle* (1953). It was de Kooning

The Brooklyn Bridge: Variation on an Old Theme, 1939, a subject Joseph Stella painted many times during his career.

who credited Pollock with having "broken the ice" by unleashing line from its traditional role in paintings.

At the same time, Mark Rothko (*Four Darks in Red*, 1958, and *Untitled*, 1953) and Barnett Newman (*Day One*, 1951–52) created expansive "color fields" devoid of figures, intending to induce transcendental states of mind by enveloping the viewer in resonant hues. William Baziotes' paintings have a whiff of violence about them, as in *Green Form* (1945–46). Piet Mondrian's abstract celebration of New York hipness (as in *Broadway Boogie-Woogie*) is called to mind by Burgoyne Diller's *Third Theme* (1946–48) and Fritz Glarner's *Relational Painting* (1949–51).

The Pop Artists of the 1950s and 60s turned away from the heroic themes and intentions of the Abstract Expressionists and embraced the burgeoning consumer culture of the postwar era. They not only took pop culture as subject matter – as did Jasper Johns in *Three Flags* (1958), widely considered his masterpiece, and Andy Warhol in *Green Coca-Cola Bottles* (1962) – but integrated ordinary objects into their work, as Robert Rauschenberg did in *Satellite* (1955), which, among other things, incorporates a pair of socks and a stuffed pheasant.

Highlights in sculpture include Elie Nadelman's *Tango* (1919), inspired by American folk art; Alexander Calder's wire "drawing" *The Brass Family* (1927); Theodore Roszak's streamlined, machine-like *Bi-Polar in Red* (1940); Louise Bourgeois' totemic *Quarantania* (1941); Isamu Noguchi's interlocking *Humpty Dumpty* (1946); Louise Nevelson's *Black Majesty* (1955) and *Rain Forest Column IV* (1967); Claes Oldenburg's droopy vinyl *Soft Toilet* (1966); and the plaster body casts of George Segal's *Walk, Don't Walk* (1976).

The Whitney has staged many notable special exhibitions, a recent standout being *The American Century: Art and Culture 2000*. Among

others of the past several years: *Over the Line: The Art and Life of Jacob Lawrence*, a showing of works by the renowned African-American artist; *Hopper to Mid-Century: Highlights from the Permanent Collection*; Irving Penn's works, *Dancer: 1999 Nudes*; and *Louise Nevelson: Structures Evolving*. The Museum owns 97 works by Nevelson, the Russian-born sculptor whose favorite medium for her abstract creations was wood.

The Biennial

Since 1932, the Whitney has mounted an important series of exhibitions held every other year and called, appropriately, the Whitney Biennial. An invitational show, each Biennial is dedicated to work produced in America during the preceding two years – "a mirror of our culture and of who we are now," as its curators attest. Approximately 15 smaller exhibitions are held each year, along with six film and video programs. The Whitney was in the vanguard of promoting the efforts of non-commercial independent filmmakers and has presented the New American Film and Video Series (originally the New American Film-makers Series) since 1970.

The Whitney also maintains a midtown branch gallery at the Philip Morris Building on 42nd Street (see page 139) across from Grand Central Terminal. The Whitney at Philip Morris features a sculpture court, with a 42-foot-high (13-meter) space that permits the showing of pieces too large for the main location on Madison Avenue, and a gallery devoted to a series of changing exhibitions of contemporary paintings and smaller sculptures.

Food and drink: A branch of Sarabeth's Kitchen (212-570-3670, moderate) in the Museum serves up American café fare at New York City prices. But along with the $15 hamburgers, club sandwiches and chicken pot pies are some great breakfast bargains, which are served all day. Weekend brunch is a popular event. For something a bit more substantial, renowned French-born chef Daniel Boulud combines family and regional specialties with haute cuisine to create classic French dishes with a country flair at the elegant Café Boulud (20 East 76th St, 212-772-2600, expensive). The menu features treats such as braised lamb shanks and peekytoe crab salad, along with fabulous desserts.

Above: Thomas Hart Benton painted *Poker Night (from A Streetcar Named Desire)* in 1948 as a gift for the producer of the stage play.

Left: *Bi-Polar in Red*, 1940, reflects sculptor Theodore Roszak's enthusiasm for technology and science-fiction imagery.

Fine Art

Paintings, drawings, sculpture and other precious works of creative expression, across a spectrum of artistic design and media, are on display at four lesser-known but imposing institutions

Dahesh Museum of Art

One of the city's newer repositories for the visual arts focuses anew on creative representation in the "old" style.

Map reference: pages 50–51, C6
601 Fifth Ave, between 48th and 49th Sts, 10017.
Tel: 212-759-0606, www.daheshmuseum.org
Subway: 6 to 51st St or E, F to Fifth Ave. Bus:
M1, M2, M3, M4, M5 to 49th St or M27, M50
to Fifth Ave.
Tues–Sat 11am–6pm.
Free admission, guided tours, museum store,
wheelchair access.

Who knew that the old-fashioned kind of art pushed aside by the likes of Picasso and all the modernists would make a comeback some day? That seems to be the case at the Dahesh Museum of Art, opened in 1995 and built around a collection of paintings, sculpture, prints and drawings – all in the great European tradition of neoclassical realism – amassed by the Palestinian-born art lover Saleem Moussa Achi.

Moussa Achi came to be known as Dr. Dahesh in Beirut, Lebanon. His collection, moved to America after civil war erupted in that country in 1975, has examples of the "academic art" and "historical painting" that was the prevailing approach before Impressionism and scenes from everyday life relegated such work to oblivion in museum basements and downplayed once important Salon names like Bouguereau and Gérôme. Dahesh was particularly interested in Orientalism, a 19th-century movement among European artists that focused on exotic subjects from the Middle East such as Arab horsemen, snake charmers and harem slaves.

Among the highlights is *The Water Girl* (1885) by Adolphe-William Bouguereau, in which the comely peasant subject bears an earthenware vessel over her shoulder as she gazes frankly at the artist. *Working in Marble* (1890) is a bronze sculpture by Jean-Leon Gérôme. *Cattle by a Lake* is the work of Auguste Bonheur, brother of the accomplished painter Rosa Bonheur. Another notable work is Gustav Bauernfeind's *Jaffa, Recruiting of Turkish Soldiers in Palestine*, a celebrated 1888 oil depicting conscripts being rowed to an Ottoman vessel off the coast of present-day Tel Aviv. The tableau includes some 100 colorfully dressed Arabs in different attitudes and captures the scene's potent emotions and chaotic movement.

The Museum features rotating exhibitions from its permanent collection, and sponsors lectures and symposia on classical art.

Food and drink: Try Avra (141 E. 48th St, between Third and Lexington Aves, 212-759-8550, moderate) for grilled fish and a selection of Greek specialties prepared with minimal fuss. Or stroll down a few blocks to Café Centro (200 Park Ave at 45th St, 212-818-1222, moderate), a large brasserie with cassoulet, a tasty bouillabaisse and other Mediterranean delights served in a chatty, spirited atmosphere.

OPPOSITE: The late Isamu Noguchi, with one of his sculptures.

LEFT: *The Water Girl*, 1885, Adolphe-William Bouguereau, from the Dahesh Museum of Art.

Isamu Noguchi Garden Museum

The studio of sculptor Isamu Noguchi provides an ideal viewing space for shapes that are alternately serene and unsettling, stolid and lyrical.

Map reference: pages 52–53, D4
32–37 Vernon Blvd, Long Island City, NY 11106.
Tel: 718-721-1932, www.noguchi.org
Subway: N to Broadway, walk west on Broadway, left on Vernon.
Wed–Fri 10am–5pm, Sat–Sun 11am–6pm.
Admission fee, museum shop, café, guided tours, wheelchair access.

Note: *The Museum is occupying a temporary exhibition space at 36-01 43rd Ave, Long Island City, until spring 2003, while the main building is closed for renovations. The temporary space will house changing exhibitions from the permanent collection.*

Noguchi with his sculpture *Undine (Nadja)* in 1925, before studying with Constantin Brancusi in Paris.

For Isamu Noguchi (1904–88), sculpture was about contrasts – the play between light and shadow, and the stark distinction between the randomness of the raw stone shapes he selected and the precise, polished incisions he made in them. When the Japanese-American sculptor purchased an old photoengraving plant in Queens to use as a studio and later a museum, he engineered one of his boldest studies in contrast. In this gritty neighborhood that looks across the East River to the skyscrapers of Manhattan, Noguchi created both a practical work space and a superbly appropriate environment for viewing some of his most intriguing works.

The old plant and a modern addition house pieces from the sculptor's early career – several small bronzes reflect the influence of his mentor, Constantin Brancusi – as well as small sculptures of clay and wood, and models and photographs of large installations located all over the world. But the Museum's most dramatic works are the great stone sculptures of Noguchi's later career, tranquil on the surface but with a curious, unsettling edge. Some look as if Noguchi had managed to discover and expose secret channels within the stone; others seem to have responded to his touch with a decidedly un-stonelike display of plasticity, as if they were made of a pliant metal to which a gentle torque had been applied. Others appear to be portions of gigantic knots tied in stone, as if the material was taking on yet another mysterious characteristic. Often, the pieces exude the sculptor's fascination with shapes that suggest rather than reveal, with themes that are implied but not actually present.

Another aspect of Noguchi's genius with shape and space are his Akari lights, paper sculptures illuminated from within. Their abstract geometric designs are intriguing, often whimsical versions of the traditional paper lanterns of Japan. (Scaled-down versions of the lights are sold in the museum shop).

In the Museum's ivy-walled Japanese-inspired garden, stone sculptures play counterpoint to plantings that resemble giant bonsai. Magnolia, juniper and white birch provide texture, scent, shade and rustling leaves. Near the center of the garden, an irregular, 4-foot-high (1.2-meter) block of basalt is constantly bathed in a shimmering skin of flowing water that gurgles from within. Its surfaces are at once softened and animated by the water, and radiate calm into the surrounding garden.

Food and drink: *The Museum's café offers pastries, coffee and other light fare.*

National Academy of Design

A venerable 19th-century taste-maker continues to train and exhibit contemporary artists while celebrating the work of its illustrious members.

Map reference: pages 50–51, F1
1083 Fifth Ave at 89th St, 10128.
Tel: 212-369-4880; www.nationalacademy.org
Subway: 4, 5 or 6 to 86th St. Bus: M1, M2, M3, or M4 on Fifth and Madison Aves to 89th St.
Wed–Thur noon–5pm, Fri 10am–6pm, Sat–Sun 10am–5pm.
Admission fee, museum store, lectures, guided tours, wheelchair access.

The National Academy of Design has a golden history, a majestic setting, and a quiet devotion to resurrecting the work of important artists. The Academy was established in 1825 and has been described by art critic Robert Hughes as "the most powerful taste-forming body of the American Renaissance." Its founders included Hudson River School masters Thomas Cole and Asher B. Durand, as well as artist and inventor Samuel F. B. Morse, who wished to pattern the institution after London's Royal Academy, where his own work had been displayed to much acclaim. Students still receive traditional instruction at the Academy's School of Fine Arts.

The country's oldest artist-run organization upholds a quaint custom: Members – including, over the decades, such notable figures as Frederic E. Church, Winslow Homer, John Singer Sargent, Robert Henri, Louise Bourgeois, Robert Rausch-enberg and Jasper Johns – are required to submit both a self-portrait and a representative example of their work, a tradition that fortifies the Academy's collection of 2,200 paintings, 240 sculptures, and 5,000 works on paper.

Situated next to the Solomon R. Guggenheim Museum, directly across from Central Park's lovely Jacqueline Kennedy Onassis Reservoir, the Academy occupies an elegant Beaux-Arts townhouse on Fifth Avenue's Museum Mile. The

The Noguchi Garden is an oasis of tranquility in an industrial neighborhood.

lobby entrance gives onto a luxe rotunda room with a dramatic spiral staircase. Rising from the center of the room is the sculpture *Diana of the Chase*, a 1922 bronze by Anna Hyatt. Diana's arm, her loose covering and the dog at her feet fuse into an entrancing coil, culminating in the huntress's upraised bow and beguiling viewers with a chance reference to the spiral staircase.

Upstairs, the Academy's spacious galleries offer a sanctuary of parquet floors, French doors and ornamental plaster ceilings. In a small walnut-paneled room with a marble fireplace and a lavish wood cornice hang a selection of works from the Academy's permanent collection. Curators regularly change the lineup here in order to concur with temporary exhibitions.

Recent shows have ranged from cheeky and vibrant Pop artists to the masters of the Hudson River School. The Academy also conducts the nation's oldest juried show during its Annual Exhibition, which presents new work by contemporary artists.

Food and drink: Hungry patrons line up for freshly baked muffins, pastries and other breakfast goodies at Sarabeth's Kitchen (1295 Madison Ave between 92nd and 93rd Sts, 212-410-7335, moderate), although some customers find the cutesy décor a bit hard to stomach. Lunch and dinner are equally tasty. Pintaile's Pizza (26 E. 91st St between Fifth and Madison Aves, 212-722-1967, inexpensive) specializes in pizza with paper-thin crust and dusted with herbs, although the tiny restaurant has precious little elbow room.

Queens Museum of Art

Housed in a building constructed for the 1939 World's Fair, the Museum exhibits contemporary art as well as an assortment of unexpected treasures, like Tiffany lamps and the world's largest architectural model.

Map reference: pages 52–53, F4
New York City Building, Flushing Meadows Corona Park, Queens, NY 11368.
Tel: 718-592-9700, www.queensmuse.org
Tues–Fri 10am–5pm, Sat–Sun noon–5pm.
Subway: 7 to 111th St (walk south on 111th St to park entrance at 49th Ave). Bus: Q48 to Roosevelt Ave and 111 St, Q23 or Q58 to Corona Ave and 51st Ave.
Donation suggested, museum store, guided tours, workshops, wheelchair access.

The Queens Museum of Art comes off as something of a hodgepodge. The largest galleries are devoted to changing exhibitions of contemporary art, with an emphasis on international artists intended to reflect, perhaps, the ethnic diversity of Queens itself. Shows in recent years have focused on the work of Asian performance artists, contemporary Indian artists and those of Indian descent, Greek-American artists, and one-person shows devoted to noted Japanese and Chinese artists. Numerous shows launched at the QMA tour other major museums in the United States and abroad, including a recent survey of conceptual art representing the work of more than 130 artists from around the world.

The QMA is also dedicated to preserving the legacy of New York's two 20th-century World's Fairs. Housed in the only major structure remaining from the 1939 and 1964 World's Fairs (look for the enormous steel globe *Unisphere* in the front plaza), the Museum exhibits artifacts, memorabilia and photographs from the fairs that

speak volumes about American culture in each period. Particularly instructive are notions about the future – some remarkably prescient, others laughably off-key.

As a special attraction for the 1964 World's Fair, Robert Moses – the "master builder" and political dynamo whose public works transformed the city in the 1930s, 40s and 50s – commissioned a scale model of New York City. The result is the *Panorama of the City of New York*, the world's largest architectural model, containing 895,000 individual structures and occupying 9,335 square feet (867 sq meters). The public could take a simulated helicopter ride over the model, accompanied by an audio narration by Lowell Thomas, who praised New York as "the world's best run city."

Moses intended to update the *Panorama* after the World's Fair and use it as a tool for urban planners, but funds for the project ran dry during the fiscally rocky 1970s, and the model was slated to be dismantled and shipped off to the respective boroughs. A cash infusion in the 1980s rescued the *Panorama* from the chopping block, and a thoroughly refurbished version was unveiled in 1994.

Another highlight of the Museum's permanent collection are works in glass by Louis Comfort Tiffany, manufactured at the nearby Tiffany studio in Corona, Queens. The exhibit traces the evolution of Tiffany glass from simple favrile, or handmade, designs to highly complex floral lamps, which were painstakingly constructed over wooden armatures.

The QMA is also a community museum and seeks to engage the public in a variety of programs, including free screenings of international films, gallery tours, family workshops, and live performances. Art Zone, a hands-on educational experience for children, gives kids the opportunity to make art that is immediately displayed on the Museum walls.

Food and drink: Dining in the immediate area is limited to hot dogs and ice cream sold by vendors in Flushing Meadows Corona Park. Otherwise, your best bet for a convenient bite is to pack a lunch, although those willing to take a 15-minute walk or a short bus ride will find authentic southern Italian dishes at Park Side (107-01 Corona Ave, 718-271-9276, expensive), a lively neighborhood trattoria.

Folk Art

Native genius is showcased at a couple of repositories for traditional arts and crafts in midtown Manhattan. The works stretch back in time to colonial America and forward to the contemporary scene

American Folk Art Museum

Traditional work and that of contemporary self-taught artists are the mainstays of this museum, now in new and much expanded surroundings.

Map reference: pages 50–51, C5
45 W. 53rd St, 10019.
Tel: 212-265-1040; www.folkartmuseum.org
Subway: E or V train to 53rd St and Fifth Ave.
Bus: M1, M2, M3, M4, M5, M7 to 53rd St.
Tues–Sun 10am–6pm, Fri to 8pm.
Admission fee, museum store, café, research facilities, wheelchair access.

Welcome to the city's newest full-fledged art museum, the first since the Whitney opened on Madison Avenue in 1966. The new kid on the block is the American Folk Art Museum, which late in 2001 moved into a $22 million, eight-story home on 53rd Street. The new digs give it four times as much space as previously to show off the 4,000 articles in its extraordinary collection. Now it can display 500 such pieces at any given time while also mounting several special exhibitions each year.

The institution has shifted around since its founding by private collectors in 1961 as the Museum of Early American Folk Arts. It quickly developed into a major repository of 18th- and 19th-century works. And in recent years, curators have broadened the collection to include not just the good-old-days objects but also 20th-century and contemporary works by self-taught artists, domestic and foreign. The holdings were expanded considerably in 2001 when Ralph Esmerian, chairman of the Board of Trustees, donated his personal collection of more than 400 paintings and objects. It was the largest gift in the Museum's history.

Seven of the floors in the new American Folk Art Museum have exhibit space ranging from intimate rooms suitable for displaying small objects to expansive areas where large pieces are showcased. A coffee bar on the mezzanine level overlooks a two-story atrium. Offices, a reference library and educational facilities are situated on two levels below ground, including the Contemporary Center, dedicated to the study of works by 20th-century, self-taught artists.

The timing is right, it would appear. There seems to be heightened interest of late in so-called primitive work by vernacular artists. Known also as outsider art (a term the Museum avoids), its distinctive quality was recognized in the 1940s by Jean Dubuffet, who used a "rough" approach in some of his own paintings. He saw artistic vision in works by psychiatric patients and others in abnormal states and used the term "art brut," or raw art, to refer to such expression.

Unschooled genius

Esmerian's generous gift augments other donations made by him over the years. They include a great variety of objects, ranging from distinctive Pennsylvania German fraktur – illuminated manuscripts and documents – and rare Shaker gift drawings to illustrated books created by an imprisoned Union soldier during the Civil War. Among the most important pieces is *Girl in Red Dress with Cat and Dog* by Connecticut-born portrait artist Ammi Phillips (1788–1865), one of the era's best itinerant painters or "limners," who traveled the countryside painting likenesses on commission.

Among other notable pieces in the permanent collection are the painted wooden *Flag Gate*, a garden gate in the form of a 38-star American flag created by an unknown artist in Jefferson County, New York, around the time of the U.S. Centennial celebration of 1876; the molded copper *St. Tammany Weathervane* (mid-1900s), consisting of an Indian figure standing on an arrow; and *Animal Carnival*, a series of wooden carvings of a catfish, tiger and other beasts by Felipe Benito Archuleta (1910–91), a New Mexican artist known also for his religious shrines, or *bultos*.

Opposite: *Girl in Red Dress with Cat and Dog*, created by Ammi Phillips between 1830 and 1835; the artist is credited with more than 500 portraits.

Below: The Museum exhibits about 500 works by self-taught artists.

Also represented is the Reverend Howard Finster (b. 1916), self-proclaimed "Father of Folk Art," who gave up preaching one Sunday – no one could remember what his sermon was about, he says – and turned to "sermons in paint" to "preach to the congregation of the world."

The Shakers, a utopian religious community that settled in New York and New England in the late 18th century, are represented at the Museum by an assortment of chairs, rugs, boxes, work tables and gift drawings. Needlework is celebrated in an extensive collection of quilts, hooked and braided rugs, samplers and other household textiles from the 18th to the 20th centuries.

The museum's collection also includes a comprehensive body of work by Chicago recluse and self-taught artist Henry Darger (1892–1973), including 26 mural-size watercolors, drawings, archival material and the complete manuscripts of three books. *Realms of the Unreal* has a 15,000-page epic fantasy that Darger worked on for 60 years. He augmented the book with hundreds of watercolors – some up to 9 feet (3 meters) long

– and smaller drawings. The American Folk Art Museum was the first institution in New York City to exhibit the work of Darger, now recognized as one of the great self-taught American artists of the 20th century.

The Museum holds a year-round series of special exhibitions, lectures, symposia and performances by folk musicians, dancers and storytellers. Its former home, the Eva and Morris Feld Gallery at 2 Lincoln Square (Columbus Avenue at 66th Street) continues to function as a branch gallery for smaller exhibits. Visiting hours there are 11am–7.30pm daily except Monday, when closing time is 6pm.

Food and drink: La Bonne Soupe (48 W. 55th St between Fifth and Sixth Aves, 212-586-7650, moderate) has been satisfying customers for decades with authentic bistro fare at reasonable prices. Fixed-price meals are a bargain. An indoor waterfall gurgles pleasantly in the background at Aquavit (13 W. 54th St between Fifth and Sixth Aves, 212-307-7311, expensive), a sleek and spacious Scandinavian restaurant with artfully prepared salmon, arctic char, smoked herring and other regional specialties. Don't miss the opportunity to sample one of several aquavits, a vodka-like spirit flavored with fruit and spices and served ice cold. The upstairs café is a good value.

American Craft Museum

Fine artisanship – from handmade jewelry to Appalachian basketwork – is the focus of the nation's premier resource for contemporary craft.

Map reference: pages 50–51, C5
40 W. 53rd St (between Fifth and Sixth
Aves), 10019.
Tel: 212-956-3535; www.americancraftmuseum.org
Subway: E or F to Fifth Ave; B or D to Seventh
Ave; N or R to 49th St; Q to Rockefeller Center.
Bus: M1, M2, M3, M4, M5 southbound on Fifth
Ave or M5, M6, M7 northbound on Sixth Ave.
Daily 10am–6pm, Thurs to 8pm.
Admission fee, museum shop, lectures, adult
and children's workshops, wheelchair access.

Housed since 1987 in an airy, four-level space, the Museum's permanent collection encompasses more than 1,175 craft objects that embody an exemplary union of function and beauty. The emphasis here is on 20th-century work; most pieces were made by American artists after World War II.

The museum follows a carefully planned three-part acquisition program, with an eye towards academic rigor as well as public education and enjoyment. The first component is what the curators call "contextual collections," documenting the history of craft in the United States from the late 19th-century Arts and Crafts movement to the present. The second is an archive of material such as drawings, diaries, sketches, models, prototypes and video recordings that chronicle the creative process and provide background information on the objects in the primary collection. Finally, the museum is committed to creating "thematic collections," focusing on a wide range of issues addressed by craftspeople and interpreting various styles and techniques. Recent acquisitions represent an array of media and styles, including jewelry, handmade paper, textiles, sculpted wood, hand-blown glass and ceramics.

In addition to its permanent collection, the museum mounts an ambitious roster of special exhibitions. One recent show, *Objects for Use*, surveys some of the finest work of 200 American craftsmen, including unconventional items such as kayaks, snowshoes and musical instruments. Other shows focus on particular artists – Frank Lloyd Wright's leaded-glass windows, for example – or a specific form, like a recent show of diminutive stickpins created by some of the world's leading jewelry artists.

Visitors who want to try their hand at crafting should inquire about upcoming workshops, many suitable for both children and adults. One recent class introduced participants to the art of making "poem kites" and was followed by a kite-flying session in Central Park. Other workshops offer basic instruction in handmade books, basketry, jewelry, origami and other crafts; many are taught by artists whose work is shown at the Museum. Lectures by artists and curators are presented on Thursday nights, and various "Meet the Artist" functions are held throughout the year. The museum store, filled with beautiful handmade objects, is a shopper's bonanza, perfect for stocking up on unusual gifts.

Food and drink: *Power lunchers and minor celebs (and those who wish they were) gather at the China Grill (52 W. 53rd St, between Fifth and Sixth Aves, 212-333-7788, expensive) for Asian and international specialties served in a stunning architectural setting. For something sweet and filling, try Ferrara's (1700 Broadway, between 53rd and 54th Sts, 212-581-3335, moderate), a midtown outpost for cappuccino and cannoli, though some locals say this location falls short of the original in Little Italy.*

Kites "float" above visitors in a dramatic three-story atrium.

Cultural adornments from a kaleidoscope of nationalities and ethnic groups — Tibetan, Iberian, Slavic, Kurdish, African, Latino — are spotlighted at several locations in the Big Apple. Common to all is the creative imperative

Americas Society

In an elegant old house is a showcase for the creative achievements of the nations of the Western Hemisphere.

Map reference: pages 50–51, E4
680 Park Ave at E. 68th St, 10021.
Tel: 212-249-8950; www.americas-society.org
Subway: 6 to 68th St. Bus: M1, M2, M3 or M4
(uptown on Madison Ave, downtown on Fifth Ave); M101 or M102 (uptown on Third Ave, downtown on Lexington Ave).
Tues–Sun noon-6pm.
Admission fee, readings, lectures, concerts, wheelchair access.

First it was a capitalist's town house. Then it became the residence of the Soviet delegation to the United Nations. Finally it wound up as the base of operations for the Center for Inter-American Relations, out of which came the Americas Society.

The Society, a kind of economic and social clearinghouse for the Western Hemisphere, is a not-for-profit institution that aims to foster awareness in the United States of neighbors north and south of the border. This includes a cultural consciousness, and to that end changing exhibitions of visual arts are mounted in a public art gallery on the ground floor of the building.

Shows in recent years have included paintings, sculpture, photos, ceramics and works in other media by Brazilian, Argentinian, Uruguayan, Guatemalan and other artisans. Among the exhibits: *Abstract Art From the Rio de la Plata: Buenos Aires and Montevideo, 1933–1953* and *Picturing Guatemala: Images From the Cerma Photography Archive, 1870–1997*. There are also occasional musical programs, lectures, literary events and film screenings, as well as panel discussions on matters of socioeconomic development pertinent to the Americas.

The building has had its own interesting development. It was constructed as an elegant town house of neo-Federal design for the financier Percy Rivington Pyne in 1911; the architect was the prestigious firm of McKim, Mead & White. Russian diplomats occupied it from 1948 to 1963, it was the scene of frequent anti-Soviet demonstrations as the Cold War raged, and Premier Nikita Khrushchev attracted wide notoriety when he stayed here with his flamboyant public appearances from a second-story window. The building was saved from a developer's wrecking ball by a Spanish marquesa of Rockefeller descent who purchased it and three adjoining Park Avenue properties in 1965 and made a gift of them to the Center for Inter-American Relations.

Food and drink: Expect lively people and luscious food at Circus (808 Lexington Ave between 62nd and 63rd Sts, 212-223-2965, expensive), a spirited Brazilian place a few blocks from the museum. Other notable picks in this strictly upscale neighborhood are Le Charlot (19 E. 69th St between Madison and Park Aves, 212-794-1628, expensive) and Ferrier (29 E. 65th St between Madison and Park Aves, 212-772-9000, expensive), both with a fine French flavor.

Asia Society and Museum

From the East, artifacts covering a broad range of time and space are showcased on Park Avenue in an extensive collection and special exhibitions.

Map reference: pages 50–51, E4
725 Park Ave at 70th St, 10021.
Tel 212-288-6400; www.asiasociety.org
Subway: 6 to 68th St. Bus: M1, M2, M3 or M4
(uptown on Madison Ave, downtown on Fifth Ave); M101 or M102 (uptown on Third Ave, downtown on Lexington Ave).
Tues–Sun 11am–6pm, to 9pm Fri.
Admission fee, guided tours, store, café, lectures, films, wheelchair access.

Out of Asia have come very fine specimens of art and precious objects, forming the basis of great museum collections in the New York area. You'll find much at the Metropolitan, of course, and also at the Japan Society, the Brooklyn and Newark museums, the Jacques Marchais center on Staten Island and, not least of all, the Asia Society and Museum.

The Society came into being in 1956 thanks to John D. Rockefeller III. He had become enamored with life in the Far East after traveling there, and he wanted a center to facilitate good relations and cultural

OPPOSITE:
Self-Portrait with Horn,
1938, Max Beckmann, from the Neue Galerie New York.

BELOW: *Figure of a Man,*
Japan, 7th century, from the Asia Society and Museum.

Mrs. John D. Rockefeller III Gallery, where selections from the Society's permanent collection are exhibited. Among the holdings: a sensitive Japanese portrait of a Boddhisattva; Chinese scroll paintings; Buddhist statuary from Southeast Asia; a copper statue of a kneeling woman from 11th-century Cambodia; a many-armed copper sculpture of a 9th-century Indonesian goddess.

Through exhibitions, curators seek to enhance understanding of the broad sweep of Asian creativity, in terms of both time and space. The inaugural exhibition marking the reopening of the renovated galleries, for example, was entitled *Monks and Merchants: Silk Road Treasures from Northwest China, Gansu, and Ningxia*. Although centered on Chinese art, the exhibition underscored the regional diversity of art-making along the famous Silk Road, enterprises that ranged from jade and gold burial masks to ceramics and Buddhist statuary in stone.

Food and drink: The café serves light Asian-inspired cuisine. Off the premises, China Fun (1221 Second Ave at 64th St, 212-752- 0810, inexpensive) offers dim sum, Cantonese barbecue dishes and first-rate noodles at reasonable prices. Expect a noisy crowd and little in the way of atmosphere.

El Museo del Barrio

The arts and culture of Puerto Rico, Latin America and the Caribbean are preserved and brought to life with a series of vivid exhibitions and special events.

Map reference: pages 52–53, D3
1230 Fifth Ave at 104th St, 10029.
Tel: 212-831-7272; www.elmuseo.org
Subway: 6 to 103rd St. Bus: M1, M3 or M4
to 104th St.
Wed–Sun 11am–5pm.
Admission fee, performances, concerts,
workshops, wheelchair access.

Celestial Entertainer, 10th century, from the Asia Society's collection of Indian art and sculpture.

exchange between the U.S. and Asia. Art exhibitions have been held ever since. In 1979 the Society received from Rockefeller a gift of 300 works of the paintings, sculpture and other objects he and his people had spent years collecting from across the Asian world, some dating to 2000 B.C.

Newly renovated gallery space at the Society's home on Park Avenue (once known as Asia House) features a glass-enclosed garden court that floods the lobby with natural light. The building's three floors are united by a dramatic spiral staircase fashioned of white steel and laminated glass. Combined with blue marble floors, the staircase is intended to evoke colors of traditional Chinese porcelain.

Digital signage and touch screens allow visitors to interactively explore Asian art and culture. On the third floor of the building is the Mr. and

Born in a schoolroom in East Harlem in 1969, El Museo del Barrio has evolved into the country's only organization devoted to the preservation of Puerto Rican, Caribbean and Latin American art and culture.

The museum traces the roots of Latino culture to the indigenous peoples of the Caribbean. Its holdings of pre-Columbian artifacts include an extensive collection of ceramic, stone, bone and shell figures made by the Taino Indians, who inhabited Puerto Rico before the arrival of Europeans.

Exploring the fusion of cultures that took place following the Spanish conquest, selections from the permanent collection focus on folkloric and religious artifacts from throughout Latin America, including a large number of Santos de Palo, naive wooden sculptures depicting saints traditionally used as votive objects in the home. Most of the santos are a century or more old. Secular artwork and craft objects trace the movement of Puerto Ricans and other Latinos to the urban centers of North America. These include musical instruments; toys and dolls; and the masks, costumes, and piñatas associated with festivals.

Paintings, prints, sculptures and photographs round out the museum's holdings. Some 3,000 works on paper chronicle the development of printmaking in Puerto Rico and Latin America since the mid-20th century. The collection of paintings and sculpture are particularly strong on works from the 1960s and '70s. Photographs, films and videos are mostly devoted to docu-

menting life in Puerto Rico and the Latino immigration to New York.

El Museo mounts at least four special exhibitions each year, frequently highlighting individual artists and artistic movements arising within the Latino communities of the metropolitan area, and examining their influence on the art world. Festivals and workshops held throughout the year are designed to involve the immediate community as well as visitors in art projects often related to current exhibitions.

Images of Spain: *Portrait of a Little Girl* (left), ca. 1642–43, by Diego Velázquez, and *Galician Milkmaid* (below), 1925, by Ruth Anderson, from the Hispanic Society of America.

Food and drink: *Tangy Puerto Rican dishes await hungry museum-goers at La Fonda Boricua (169 E. 106th St between Third and Lexington Aves, 212-410-7292, inexpensive), an arty, upbeat spot for pork chicharrones, beef in citrus sauce, octopus salad, plantains, mounds of rice and beans, and other specialties.*

Hispanic Society of America

Iberian culture of Old World and New, from ancient times to the 20th century, is savored in a rich assemblage of visual arts, books and archaeological items.

Map reference: pages 52–53, D2
Audubon Terrace, 613 W. 155th St (at Broadway), 10032.
Tel 212-926-2234; www.hispanicsociety.org
Subway: 1 to 157th St. Bus: M4 or M5 to Broadway and 155th St.
Tues–Sat 10am–4.30pm, Sun 1pm–4pm, closed August.
Admission free (donations accepted), museum shop, no wheelchair access.

When he was still young, Archer M. Huntington, the multimillionaire son of a railroad baron, became interested in Iberian culture. He wrote books on Spain, translated the classic *El Cid* poem, and received a degree from the University of Madrid. Before he died in 1955 he gave away a good part of the fortune he had inherited from his father, Collis P. Huntington, founding and supporting museums, including the Hispanic Museum.

It opened its doors in 1908, four years after Huntington established The Hispanic Society of

America. The museum is part of Audubon Terrace, a cultural complex Huntington conceived and largely funded (the land in upper Manhattan was once owned by the ornithologist John James Audubon). A master plan for the complex was conceived by Archer's architect cousin, Charles Pratt Huntington, who designed the Beaux-Arts-style buildings along with notables Stanford White and Cass Gilbert.

Though its blue-collar setting lacks the glitz of Museum Mile or trendy Lower Manhattan, the Hispanic Museum is a worthwhile venture. Centered on a typical Spanish courtyard, it includes paintings and drawings, sculpture, decorative arts, antique furniture, ceramics, tiles and mosaics, textiles dating from the time of Arab rule in the Iberian Peninsula, and a library containing more than 200,000 books and manuscripts on Spanish and Portuguese history, literature and art.

Heraldo de Madrid, ca. 1910, Joaquín Sorolla y Bastida.

Some of the objects were brought over by Huntington, who first visited the peninsula in 1892. They included gravestone fragments, jewelry and other items from an archaeological camp near Seville known as Italica, which was the first Roman colony in Spain.

The collection includes works by some of the immortal names of Spanish painting – notably El Greco (*Pietá, St. Jerome, The Holy Family, St. Luke*), Velázquez (*Portrait of a Little Girl*) and Goya. The latter's famous *The Duchess of Alba* (1797), prominently displayed in the main exhibition room, depicts the alluring beauty with whom he is said to have conducted a stormy affair while both were married to other partners. The collection also has Goya's *Manuel Lapena, Marquis of Bondad Royal*, as well as the portraits *Alberto Foraster* and *Pedro Mocarte*.

The art represents the various schools – Catalan, Aragonese, Valencian and Castilian – of earlier times as well as Spain's Golden Age of the 16th to 18th centuries. Among other notable names in the collection are Ribera (*The Ecstasy of Mary Magdalene*), Zurburán (*Saint Lucy*), Miranda (*The Immaculate Conception*), Barnuevo (*Saint Joseph*), Cano, Murillo and the prolific Joaquin Sorolla y Bastida (1863–1923). The Hispanic Society owns more than 100 of Sorolla's 350 paintings, including 14 large canvases in his *Provinces of Spain* series commissioned by Huntington in the early 1900s.

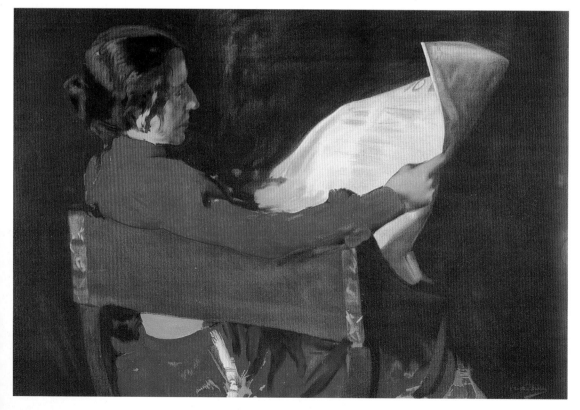

The museum's main gallery is two stories high, decorated in red terracotta. On the terrace between the main and north buildings are a bronze equestrian statue by Huntington's second wife, the sculptor Anna Hyatt Huntington, of the triumphant *El Cid Campeador*, brandishing a lance while mounted on his stallion. Especially rare pieces of sculpture are ivories from the 7th century B.C., engraved in Phoenician style, as well as Greek and Roman bronzes, and works of Roman marble.

Among the fine works of furniture is a 16th-century Moorish-Spanish *vargueño*, an ivory box that is an example of the Moslem-European Renaissance encounter. There is a wide range of other objects, including a singular wood carving *Mater Dolorosa* from the 13th century; pottery from Mexico; glass from the Barcelona area in Renaissance times; brilliantly colorful Hispano-Moresque bowls and platters from the 15th century; Gothic crucifixes, locks and ironwork; silks woven in the 13th and 14th centuries and gold-brocaded embroideries from later times. In addition to the books and manuscripts are prints, maps and globes contained in the Museum's Iconography Collection.

Food and drink: Options are limited in this area, so consider packing a lunch. ALCA Pizzeria (Broadway at 157th St, 212-491-4300, inexpensive) serves pizza and other Italian specialties. Sandwiches, meatloaf, burgers and other diner standbys are on the menu at Coral's Diner (Broadway at 159th St, 212-927-7545, inexpensive).

Jacques Marchais Museum of Tibetan Art

Situated amid gardens on a Staten Island hillside is the country's only museum to display Tibetan art in an authentic setting.

Map reference: pages 52–53, A9
338 Lighthouse Ave, Staten Island 10306.
Tel: 718-987-3500, www.tibetanmuseum.com
Bus: Staten Island Ferry from Battery Park; from ferry terminal, bus S74 to Lighthouse Ave and walk 15 minutes up hill.
Apr–Nov Wed–Sun 1pm–5pm, Dec–Mar Wed–Fri 1pm–5pm.
Admission fee, museum shop, performance series, workshops, no wheelchair access.

The Jacques Marchais Museum is built in the style of a Tibetan *gompa*, or temple, and reflects its founder's lifelong enthusiasm for the art and culture of Tibet. Jacques Marchais was the pseudonym of Jacqueline Klauber, a Manhattan art dealer who as a child was fascinated by a collection of 13 metal figurines brought from Sikkim by her great-grandfather.

The figurines, most likely made in northern Nepal to represent Buddhist deities, are still on display in the museum founded by Klauber in 1947 to house her collection. Galleries in the architecturally correct Tibetan buildings also house representations of deities such as Chenrezig, 11-headed god of mercy and compassion; ritual masks; images in metal and clay of lamas, Tibetan Buddhist priests; and statuettes of early Dalai Lamas, political and spiritual leaders of Tibet in the days before the mountain nation's absorption into neighboring China and the exile of the current holder of the title.

TOP: *The Duchess of Alba*, 1797, Francisco Goya, from the Hispanic Society and Museum.

BELOW: A Tibetan-style building on the wooded grounds of the Jacques Marchais Museum.

Most Tibetan art is created for ritual or devotional purposes. Appropriately, one interior wall of the museum is arranged as a three-tiered altar. On the first tier are vessels for offerings; on the second are figures of Buddhas and lamas; and on the top tier are representations of bodhisattvas, individuals who attain partial enlightenment but remain on the physical plane to help others.

Behind the museum structures, secluded from the surrounding residential streets (visitors should note that parking is limited), there is a sculpture garden with a fish and lotus pond.

Food and drink: Although the museum has no dining facilities, visitors are welcome to bring lunch and eat in the gardens.

Japan Society

The mood is gentle here, a laid-back ambience that exudes art and tranquility in equal measure.

Map reference: pages 50–51, E7
333 E. 47th St, 10017.
Tel: 212-832-1155, www.japansociety.org
Subway: 6 to 51st St, E or F to Lexington Ave and 53rd St. Bus: M15, M101 or M102 to 47th St.
Tues–Fri 11am–6pm, Sat–Sun 11am–5pm.
Admission fee, lectures, performances, films, wheelchair access.

A 16th-century vessel from *Five Tastes,* an exhibition of traditional Japanese design at the Japan Society.

Actually, you don't feel like you're in midtown Manhattan when you come here. You feel like you're in a teahouse, close to a garden. The building that houses this place known as the Japan Society was designed by architect Junzo Yoshimura. What he liked was the sense of indoor gardens, a waterfall, a reflecting pool complete with tall bamboo (which thrives indoors). So what you get here, more than at any other New York museum, is a break from crowds, traffic, noise.

The Society was founded in 1907 to promote U.S.–Japan cultural and economic ties, which it does with great style. The building's interiors are crafted from Japanese cypress, Virginia slate and rice paper. Yoshimura, the architect, managed to illuminate much of the building with natural light (through clerestory windows). The chairs, tables and benches you find here were designed by the eminent Japanese-American woodworker and designer George Nakashima, who incorporates traditional Japanese joinery and massive slabs of hardwood in his furniture.

You can learn the Japanese language here. The Society offers classes taught in the ultra-modern Toyota Language Center. Visitors who already speak the language can enjoy the library, which has books covering many aspects of Japanese history, politics and culture. There are also films with Japanese subtitles, all part of a program supported by top-flight critics and directors, among them Martin Scorsese.

And there's contemporary Japanese plays, theater pieces, dance. These events are held in the Lila Acheson Wallace Auditorium, an elegant 278-seat hall with hand-rubbed Scandinavian ash paneling and Japanese flat curtains. Recent productions have included Tadashi Suzuki's adaptations of *Oedipus Rex*, which explore the relationship between Greek tragedy and traditional Noh drama.

But the jewel in the crown for the Japan Society is its gallery exhibitions. In 2001 they included a long overdue retrospective of Yoko Ono's pioneering work as a conceptual artist. This included her early instruction paintings and documentation of her performance work with John Cage, David Tudor and Mayuzumi Toshiro at the Sogetsu Art Center in Tokyo. *Frank Lloyd Wright and the Art of Japan: the Architect's Other Passion* was one of the most extraordinary exhibitions of the season. As a young man, Wright traveled to Japan and later spent years in Tokyo realizing the Imperial Hotel, one of his grand creations. Throughout his life he collected Japanese woodblock prints, and all these many years later we can appreciate their influence on the pure lines

An indoor "garden" at the Japan Society is a welcome respite from hectic midtown Manhattan.

and simplicity of his architecture. The sale of Japanese prints, as it turns out, helped him to support his work as an architect.

Food and drink: There are excellent Japanese restaurants in the neighborhood, including Seo, a new sushi bar with an outdoor garden (249 E. 49th St, 212-355-7722, expensive). Bellini (208 E. 52nd St, 212-308-0830, expensive) offers fashionable Italian fare for beautiful people and all the rest of us.

Kurdish Library and Museum

The only institution in North America devoted to Kurdish history and culture provides a unique insight into a nation without political borders.

Map reference: pages 52–53, D6
144 Underhill Ave at Park Place, Brooklyn 11238
Tel: 718-783-7930.
Subway: Q to 7th Ave, 1 or 2 to Grand Army Plaza
Mon–Fri 1pm–5pm.
Free admission, no wheelchair access.

Kurdistan is an ancient land sprawling across some 170,000 square miles (440,000 sq. km) of mountainous territory in Turkey, Iraq and Iran, and parts of Syria and Armenia. Its people, the once-nomadic Kurds, were subjects of the Ottoman Empire before its disintegration in the aftermath of World War I. Although the 1920 Treaty of Sèvres proposed the establishment of a political entity called Kurdistan, hostility to the concept among neighboring states ultimately prevented its ratification. The Kurds have consequently remained stateless, despite periodic nationalist uprisings.

Established in 1988 under the auspices of the State University of New York, the Kurdish Library and Museum promotes awareness of the precarious political situation of the Kurds and their struggle for human rights. It also maintains a collection of Kurdish art and cultural artifacts, among which are fine examples of textile arts developed over centuries of nomadic and village life. Traditional Kurdish carpets, costumes and ornamental weavings have long been celebrated for their color and complexity.

Special collections include the early art of Mahdat Ali; photographs taken by Dana Adams Schmidt during the Kurdish revolution in Iraq; and women's costumes donated by Hero Talabani. The museum also maintains an extensive library of slides, musical cassettes and videos.

Two special exhibits are mounted annually.

Recent subjects have included the Jews of Kurdistan; Kurdish poster art; Kurdish crafts; the legacy of emperor Saladin; and collections of Kurdish village jewelry.

Food and drink: Junior's (386 Flatbush Ave, 718-852-5257, inexpensive) is a favorite for cheesecake, thick sandwiches, blintzes and other deli specialties.

Museum for African Art

The nation's only independent institution of its kind takes a mixed-media approach to African art.

RIGHT: A silver brooch by Josef Hoffman from the Neue Galerie's inaugural exhibition.

Map reference: pages 52–53, D4
36-01 43rd Ave, Long Island City, Queens
Tel: 212-966-1313; www.africanart.org
Subway: 7 to 33rd St. Bus: weekend Queens Artlink shuttle from the Museum of Modern Art (call 212-708-9750 for schedule)
Tues–Fri 10.30am–5.30pm, Sat–Sun noon–6pm
Admission fee, concerts, lectures, workshops, museum store, wheelchair access.

BELOW: The Museum for African Art offers hands-on workshops, children's programs and concerts as well as seasonal exhibitions.

Note: *The museum will occupy this interim site until moving to a permanent location at 110th St and Fifth Ave in 2005.*

I n a review of an exhibit at this museum, the *New York Times* critic Holland Cotter reported that African art "is often physically kinetic. It moves, dances, kicks up dust, makes noises, changes shape, seeks you out, seduces you, tickles you, tells you to get serious but also lighten up. It is mood-altering: by alternately soothing and provoking its audience, it stimulates people's complex feelings about themselves and about the world."

Cotter might just as well have been describing the mission of the Museum for African Art. Each year, drawing on resources ranging from private collections to institutions overseas, the museum mounts several exhibits designed to increase understanding and appreciation of African art and culture by involving audiences directly, often combining a range of media including music, dance, puppetry and native crafts.

Whatever the theme, the exhibitions have earned a reputation for originality. In the past, they've included subjects such as *Secrecy: African Art That Conceals and Reveals*, displaying 100 works from sub-Saharan Africa; and *ART/artifact*, which exhibited works in a variety of imaginative settings.

In addition to its regular exhibits, the museum presents works by contemporary African artists. It also hosts family workshops, such as puppet and basket making, which are linked to current exhibitions. Concerts, including a series known as *Satonge!*, on Saturday evenings, features African music of various styles. All programs are free with museum admission.

Food and drink: It's not much to look at, but family-run Manducati's (13-27 Jackson Ave at 47th Ave,718-729-4602, moderate) serves first-rate Italian dishes, complemented with a fine wine cellar.

Neue Galerie New York

Modern works of a German and Austrian stamp are highlighted against the backdrop of an elegant New York townhouse with a continental savor.

Map reference: pages 50–51, F1
1048 Fifth Ave (at 86th St), 10028.
Tel: 212-628-6200, www.neuegalerie.org
Subway: 4, 5, 6 to 86th St. Bus: M1, M2, M3,
M4 to 86th St, M86 to Fifth Ave.
Sat–Mon 11am–6pm, Fri 11am–9pm.
Admission fee, museum shop, café, lectures,
chamber music, cabaret, wheelchair access.

There was a Neue Galerie in Vienna in the 1920s devoted to German and Austrian art, and now there's one in New York. This latter-day version on Fifth Avenue's Museum Mile opened in November 2001. It's one of the city's very newest museums, and the press notices were generally glowing.

The credit goes to Ron Lauder. He's the son of Estée Lauder and heir to her cosmetics fortune.

He's also a former U.S. ambassador to Austria and a collector long interested in German-Austrian art, and he has deep pockets to indulge his whim for fine art and precious decorative objects. The fine things in his Neue Galerie collection are quite at home at its swanky address; the mansion, erected 1912–14, was the work of the firm (Carrére & Hastings) that gave us the grandly elegant New York Public Library and bears its same Paris-based Beaux-Arts influence.

For something like $20 million, Mr. Lauder bought the six-story house (Vanderbilts, no less, once lived here) and had its interior redecorated. The first show, a survey of art and design from the Viennese Secession to the Bauhaus, was called *New Worlds: German and Austrian Art, 1890–1940*. There were paintings, sculpture and drawings by Egon Schiele, Oskar Kokoschka and Gustav Klimt, just to name some of the major Austrians; German artistic luminaries such as Max Beckmann, George Grosz, Kurt Schwitters and Oskar Schlemmer; and still others of major artistic pedigree – Kandinsky, Moholy-Nagy, Klee, Feininger. Future shows will focus on the work of Kokoschka and designer Dagobert Peche.

Portrait of Hans Tietze and Erica Tietze-Conrat, 1909, Oskar Kokoschka, from the Neue Galerie New York.

At the Neue Galerie, too, are prints, photos and the decorative arts, all decidedly modernist in design. That opening show devoted separate galleries to German Expressionism, to Bauhaus design and to social realism of a kind known in the 1920s as New Objectivity. More than a few of the works by the artists represented here were later blacklisted by Hitler's Nazi regime as exponents of "degenerate art."

The building houses a relatively small amount of exhibition space – 4,300 square feet (400 sq. meters) on two floors. The opening exhibition included furniture by Marcel Breuer, a famous Barcelona Pavilion-style table and chair by Ludwig Mies van der Rohe and, on the second floor, paintings by Schiele, Kokoschka and Klimt as well as decorative objects designed by Josef Hoffmann and other prominent members of the Austrian circle.

Mr. Lauder built his collection with the assistance of a Vienna-born dealer, the late Serge

Self-Portrait in Brown Coat, 1910, Egon Schiele. The young Austrian, regarded by many as Klimt's successor, died prematurely in 1918.

Sabarsky, who came to be his mentor of sorts. Starting in 1968, Sabarsky's gallery on Madison Avenue was the leading place in America for German and Austrian Expressionist art.

Food and drink: In the paneled Café Sabarsky on the ground floor, visitors can savor the dark coffee and excellent desserts of an old Viennese-style restaurant. Replicas of period banquettes and bentwood furniture, plus a Josef Hoffmann chandelier, provide a setting that is luxurious and distinctive. A cabaret performance and prix-fixe dinner are presented at the café on selected Friday evenings.

Studio Museum in Harlem

The art of African Americans and the African diaspora is the focus of a dynamic museum in the heart of Harlem.

Map reference: pages 52–53, D3
144 W. 125th St (between Lenox and Seventh Aves), 10027.
Tel: 212-864-4500, www.studiomuseum inharlem.org
Subway: 2 or 3 to 125th St. Bus: M7, M102 or M2 to 125th St.
Wed–Fri noon–6pm, Sat 10am–6pm, Sun noon–6pm.
Admission fee, educational programs, wheelchair access.

Although the Studio Museum presents a wide range of African-American and African art, its strongest exhibitions are devoted to 20th-century and contemporary work. A permanent collection of some 1,500 objects encompasses both traditional and modern expression from North America, the Caribbean and Africa, but what lures most visitors to this airy, attractive space are the compelling temporary shows.

Topics cover a wide swath of thematic territory, ranging from explorations of cultural identity, racism and gender roles to the re-evaluation of black artists whose work has been overlooked by mainstream galleries and critics. Previous exhibitions, for example, have examined the long-ignored contribution of Norman Lewis to the Abstract Expressionist movement of the 1940s and '50s. A show with similar intentions is scheduled for 2003, surveying the role of African American and Caribbean artists in the development of American modernism. Much better known is the work of Jacob Lewis, who did some of his most significant paintings – including the landmark *Migration Series* – in the early 1940s in the waning days of the Harlem Renaissance. A selection of his pieces, including a few from the Museum's permanent collection, were installed in the lobby in late 2001.

Cutting edge work by contemporary artists, solo or in groups, is prominently featured, and at least one show a year is reserved for the Museum's artists-in-residency program, dedicated to cultivating emerging talent. Extensive renovations, including the addition of 2,500 square feet (230 sq. meters) of gallery space, are slated for 2002.

Food and drink: A new café is on the Museum's to-do list. Until it opens, try Sylvia's (328 Lenox Ave, between 126th and 127th Sts, 212-996-0660, moderate), a Harlem landmark famous for soul food – fried chicken, barbecued ribs, collard greens, sweet potato pie and such. Some locals say the food isn't always what it used to be, but the Sunday gospel brunch is truly uplifting.

Traditional costumes at the Ukrainian Museum.

Ukrainian Museum

Exhibits ranging from painted Easter eggs to photographs of life on the steppes make up one of America's best collections of Ukrainian folk art and culture.

Map reference: pages 48–49, E3
203 Second Ave, 10003.
Tel: 212-228-0110; www.ukrainianmuseum.org
Subway: N, R, 4, 5 or 6 to 14th St-Union Square.
Bus: M1, M2, M3, M6 or M7 to Union Square
Wed–Sun 1pm–5pm.
Admission fee, museum store, workshops, wheelchair access.

The genesis of the Museum was the display of 400 pieces of Ukrainian folk art at the 1933 Chicago World's Fair. By the time the Museum was founded in 1976 by the Ukrainian National Women's League of America, the collection had nearly doubled in size. Today, with more than 40,000 objects dating from the 19th to the mid-20th century, this rapidly growing museum houses a broad representation of Ukrainian folk art.

The collection includes colorful festival apparel, ritual weavings and richly embroidered textiles from throughout Ukraine. Decorative ceramics, metalwork, brass and silver jewelry, and an outstanding assemblage of 900 brilliantly colored Easter eggs (*pysanky*) round out the display.

Among recent acquisitions are paintings, drawings, sculpture and graphics by such prominent artists as Nikifor (1896–1960) and Vasyl Krychevsky (1873–1952) and sculptor Chreshnovsky (1911–94). Other well-known artists represented here include Alexander Archipenko (1887–1964) and Petro Cholodny the Younger (1902–90).

The latter years of Ukraine's rich and tumultuous history, which began in the 7th century B.C. when Scythians rode across the steppes north of the Black Sea and culminated in the nation's independence following the collapse of the Soviet Union, are chronicled in the Museum's archives. Photographs and documents trace political, social and cultural life in Ukraine, as well as a century of immigration to the United States.

Plans to build a new museum to house the growing collection were given a major boost when the project received a $3.5 million grant in 2000. A new, three-floor facility at 222 E. Sixth Street is slated to open in 2003.

Food and drink: Service and decor take a back seat at Ukrainian East Village (140 Second Ave, between 9th St and St Marks Place, 212-529-5024, moderate) and Veselka (144 Second Ave at 9th St, 212-228-9682, moderate), which dish out rib-sticking portions of blintzes, pierogi, borscht and other East European specialties.

Contemporary Art

What's new in painting, sculpture and other media is put front and center at several showcases for emerging artists, including a converted schoolhouse in Queens and a garden overlooking the Hudson River

Artists Space

**A museum where experimentation is the
rule features the work of emerging artists.**

Map reference: pages 48–49, C5
38 Greene St (at Grand St), 10013.
Tel: 212-226-3970, www.artistsspace.org
Subway: A, C or E to Canal St. Bus: M1 or M6
to Grand St.
Tues–Sat 11am–6pm.
Free admission, wheelchair access.

ABOVE: Detail from Willie Cole's installation *The Elegba Principle* from the Bronx Museum of the Arts.

OPPOSITE: *Underpass*, by Lee Boroson, at the Whitney Museum at Philip Morris.

Artists Space was founded in 1972 at a
time when trying to hang the work of
unknown artists in a public forum was
more difficult than nailing jelly to a tree. Since
then, this citadel of the alternative space movement has exhibited the work of more than 5,000
emerging artists, offering a place in the sun for
subterranean talents who take risks in the fields of
visual art, film, architecture, design and performance. Expect the provocative – a naked woman
sweeping flour off a floor, perhaps, a 9-by-5 inch
display of rice bags and boxes, a video created
by affixing a camera to a dog.

This sassy nonprofit, which curates many temporary exhibits each year, isn't afraid to muddy its
ivory tower with politics. One of its controversial
exhibits, *Witness: Against Our Vanishing*, tackled
the AIDS crisis in 1989 and not only scared up
headlines across the nation but incited the temporary withdrawal of funding from the National
Endowment for the Arts.

A recent exhibit, *Purloined*, featured the work
of Sophie Calle. The French artist posed as a
chambermaid and took a series of photographs
inside hotel rooms, training her lens on such
warmly suggestive items as a hot-water bottle,
tubes of lipstick, and two pairs of slippers.
Accompanying her silver gelatin prints were
entries from a diary found in one room ("February 1 at noon: tennis in Nevilly") and observa-
tions by the artist herself ("They have bought
more food: tomatoes, ham, two kinds of cheese,
bread, a bottle of water, two bottles of wine. Their
diary is gone").

Food and drink: *Intimate and charmingly worn, Café
Noir (32 Grand St, 212-431-7910, moderate) offers a
menu of tapas and Mediterranean fare. The bar lends
the sangria-and-cigarette crowd a fitting ambience for
discussing aesthetics.*

Bronx Museum of the Arts

**In a cultural outpost, works of fresh cre-
ativity and innovative diversity are shown
against a multicultural backdrop.**

Map reference: pages 52–53, E2
1040 Grand Concourse, Bronx, NY 10456-3999.
Tel: 718-681-6000, www.bxma.org
Subway: B, D or 4 to 161st St-Yankee Stadium.
*Bus: Bx1, Bx2 or BxM 4 Liberty Express to
165th St and Grand Concourse.*
Wed noon–9pm, Thurs–Sun noon–6pm.
*Admission fee, museum store, performances,
lectures, workshops, wheelchair access.*

It may be far from Fifth Avenue's chic-to-chic
Museum Mile, but there's first-rate contemporary and 20th-century work exhibited at the
Bronx Museum of the Arts. The building was
originally a synagogue, then was born again as a
cultural shrine in 1971. It's encased in a glass
facade that perfectly suits its latter-day function.

Much of the work is vital and innovative. Permanent holdings include the Burns Collection,
consisting of mid-19th and early-20th-century
photographs of African-American subjects. The
images document momentous occasions of various sorts (infancy, weddings, death), and choice
work like the anonymous *Portrait of a Young
Woman* reflects great sensitivity and warmth.

Mexico's Taller de Gráfica Popular movement
(TGP) is also well represented in the collection.
TGP was a print workshop and artistic movement
that had its origins in the late 1930s in pre-revo-
lutionary Mexico. Its artists broke with academic

tradition, arriving at a style close to that of muralist Diego Rivera. Works include prints by that other master muralist, José Clemente Orozco, famous for his festive skeletons inspired by Mexico's Day of the Dead. TGP also inspired Puerto Rican printmakers, and the Museum's holdings encompass radical graphics from the 1970s.

Another highlight is contemporary art from Argentina. Architect and painter Luis F. Benedit is represented by *La Penúltima Conversatión*, an expressionistic painting of the dialogue between an old man and an enormous, disembodied head. The Museum also owns contemporary work by American artists, including pieces by Willie Cole. Cole works with household objects, often imbuing them with a kind of ritual function. For example, he used the burn marks of an iron to create the floor plan of a slave ship, and he superimposed the shape of an iron over the faces of African-Americans in photographs to create the illusion of African masks.

The collection also encompasses potent work by Adrian Piper, who addresses social issues affecting people of color with photomontages and drawings. Recent exhibitions have included a humorous project entitled *(un)Shop: An Installation*, by Lisa Levy. In a glass display case she exhibits *Proof of Their Love*, the objects that were given to her by former boyfriends between 1986 and 1997. These include teddy bears, cards, squirt guns and other items that are all available for sale. After an item has been sold, its photograph is taken with the new owner, and this photo is placed where the item had been in the display case.

One Planet Under a Groove: Hip Hop and Contemporary Art is a recent exhibition that explores the influence of hip-hop music on the arts. Hip-hop was born in the Bronx in the 1970s and its corollary "attitudes" in the form of Grafitti Art, rapping and break dancing attained international popularity. Its influence on Jean-Michel Basquiat, David Hammons, Keith Haring and other latter-day cultural luminaries is examined.

Food and drink: There's no café at the Museum, so consider bringing a bag lunch. Otherwise, take a 10-minute bus ride to Arthur Avenue, where you'll find several good Italian restaurants, including Ann and Tony's (2407 Arthur Ave, 718-933-1469, moderate), a favorite for Neapolitan specialties.

Dia Center for the Arts

Conceptual art takes the spotlight at this Chelsea pioneer and at installations elsewhere in the city and beyond.

Map reference: pages 48–49, C1
548 W. 22nd St (at 11th Ave), 10011.
Tel: 212-989-5566, www.diacenter.org
Subway: C or E to 23rd St. Bus: M23 to 11th Ave.
Mid-Sept–mid-June Wed–Sun noon–6pm, closed in summer.
Admission fee, café, lectures, readings, workshops, wheelchair access.

Dia means *through* in Greek. The idea behind the Dia Center for the Arts, founded in 1974, is to facilitate projects by contemporary artists. The center's founders, Philippa de Menil and Heiner Friederich, were particularly interested in conceptual art in the 1970s and spent hundreds of thousands of dollars to fund outsider creativity like *Lightning Field*. That project, by Walter De Maria, consists of 400 lightning rods that stand on a barren plain in west-central New Mexico and draw lightning bolts during a storm.

Unlike corporate America, Dia was happy to fund difficult art in remote places. A former warehouse in Manhattan's Chelsea neighborhood was renovated and opened to the public in 1987 as the Dia Center for the Arts. Since then, the Museum has been host to some of the most intriguing exhibitions of contemporary art in New York. One of them was

Jorge Pardo's *Project*, a design for the Dia Center's bookshop, lobby and gallery.

A gallery at the New Museum of Contemporary Art, a venue for cutting-edge and experimental work.

Robert Irwin's *Excursus: Homage to the Square*, which involved partitioning a floor of the building into 18 diaphanous cubicles of scrim. Natural and artificial light passed through the partitions to create an atmosphere conducive to meditation – and was used for that purpose on at least one occasion by a woman of obvious Buddhist orientation.

Dia was the spearhead for a large exodus of art galleries from the SoHo district to Manhattan's west Chelsea neighborhood, with restaurants and boutiques following in their wake. Those who enjoy contemporary art will find the area around Dia a good place for gallery-hopping. Printed guides to places in the area will be found at any of the larger galleries.

Long-term installations elsewhere in the city include two works by Walter De Maria: *The Broken Kilometer*, a conceptual piece composed of 500 polished brass rods arranged in three rows on the floor of a SoHo loft at 393 West Broadway, and the *New York Earth Room* which, true to its name, is a room at 141 Wooster Street filled with 250 cubic yards of soil.

Food and drink: Dia has a video lounge café in a little penthouse on the roof. Visitors can enjoy coffee and croissants while watching a video work by Joseph Beuys or Mariko Mori. Over at 214 Tenth Ave is Don Giovanni Ristorante (212-242-9054, moderate) favored by pizza lovers for its tasty brick-oven pies.

New Museum of Contemporary Art

A SoHo trailblazer stays on the cutting edge with thought-provoking art from around the world.

Map reference: pages 48–49, D4
583 Broadway (between Houston and Prince Sts), 10012.
Tel: 212-219-1222, www.newmuseum.org
Subway: N or R to Prince St, 6 to Spring St, F or S to Broadway-Lafayette St. Bus: M1, M5, M6 or M21 to Broadway and Houston St.
Tues–Sun noon–6.30pm, Thurs noon–8pm.
Admission fee, museum shop, talks, workshops, film and video screenings, music events, performances, digital media presentations, wheelchair access.

It wasn't easy showing the work of living artists in any of New York's museums, which frustrated Whitney Museum curator Marcia Tucker. So to remedy the situation she founded the New Museum in 1977. Its first showplace was a gallery in the New School for Social Research, that progressive institution of higher learning in Greenwich Village. There the New Museum exhibited avant-garde works by such luminaries as Dennis Oppenheim and Elizabeth Murray.

Since 1983 the New Museum has been operating in SoHo, the loft-filled downtown district that became such a lively place for budding artists. There it draws a mixed public – students, artists, literati, designers, architects, tourists. From Broadway, passersby are drawn to the Museum's window displays, which often feature installations by emerging artists.

In 1987, these windows featured the now famous neon sign *Silence=Death* by the artists' collective Grand Fury. Curators of the New Museum have always been sensitive to minority voices in the arts, and past exhibitions have included *Extended Sensibilities: Homosexual Presence in Contemporary Art* and *Out There: Marginalization and Contemporary Cultures.* Politics – sexual, civic and otherwise – are rarely far from the surface, as in the recent *Picturing the Modern Amazon*, which explored images of strong women in art and pop culture. There were cartoons by R. Crumb and John Howard of muscular nude women and photos of a lithe, oiled Kim Chizevsky, woman body-builder. The show dealt with issues of feminine pleasure, strength and social power in a fresh way that avoided any didactic or heavy-handed spin.

Part of the Museum's mission is to take a global view of contemporary art and build relationships with like-minded artists and institutions around the world. To that end, curators in recent years have mounted surveys of 20th-century African Art and presented works created by the World View program, a residency for international artists who were provided studio space in the World Trade Center prior to the disaster of September 11, 2001.

The New Museum has also taken a strong interest in the expressive potential of interactive technology and digital media. In 2000, the Museum opened the slick Media Z Lounge. Visitors can enjoy interactive programming online at multimedia stations and play cutting-edge video games that are projected against a white wall.

Don't overlook the wonderful bookstore, which offers hard-to-find publications and a selection of design objects, jewelry and other unusual gifts.

Food and drink: Just a few steps away, Balthazar (80 Spring St, 212-965-1414, moderate), a French brasserie, offers aromatic breads, pastries and strong coffee as well as a tantalizing selection of entrees. Zoe (90 Prince St, 212-966-6722, expensive) is nice for New American cuisine coupled with a worthy choice of American wines and served in a bright dining room with an open kitchen.

P.S.1 Contemporary Art Center

In an old schoolhouse in Queens, an unusual showcase off the beaten museum track displays works of vibrant expression.

Map reference: pages 52–53, D4
22-25 Jackson Ave at 46th Ave, Long Island City, New York 11101.
Tel: 718-784-2084, www.ps1.org
Subway: E or F to 23rd St-Ely Ave (weekdays only), 7 to 45 Rd-Court House Sq; or G to Court Sq. Bus: Q67 to Jackson and 46th Aves or B61 to 46th Ave.
Wed–Sun noon–6pm.
Admission fee, museum shop, café, workshops, performances, limited wheelchair access.

A former schoolyard at P.S.1 is used for outdoor events.

This is an affiliate of the Museum of Modern Art, and it's a building with an interesting history. It started out life as Public School 1. Patrick "Battle Ax" Gleason, the mayor of Long Island City, lavishly doled out contracts for its construction, which began in 1888. Within two years public funds had been dissipated, Gleason was voted out of office, records vanished, and to this day no one knows who the architect of P.S.1

was. What was finally built was a handsome Romanesque revival structure that eventually accommodated 2,000 students, but P.S.1 fell into disuse and the school closed in 1963.

The old schoolhouse was transformed by Alanna Heiss into a contemporary art center that is one of the most inspired, funky exhibition spaces in the Western world. There's a "crypt" downstairs that once housed the boiler room and physical plant and now provides atmospheric galleries for contemporary art – one exhibition featured books in vitrines that seemed to suggest P.S.1's past life.

A renovation project knocked out the floor of one large classroom, creating a deep, pit-like space. Visitors peer down into the sunken chamber where accomplished artists install site-specific artwork. Three floors of former classrooms form a labyrinth of spaces, which differ greatly in size and lighting conditions, depending on the artwork they house at any given moment.

P.S.1 has captured the imagination of European curators and foreign ministries, and the international community has contributed to its growth. A recent example is *Minimalia*, a survey of Italian contemporary art in which curator Achille Bonito Oliva explored a reductive tendency in his country's creative works and broadened viewers' understanding of its nature.

Alanna Heiss' vision was not limited to a simple museum. Under her stewardship, P.S.1 offered artists the chance to compete for exhibiting here and at the Clocktower Gallery in lower Manhattan. A number of foreign and American artists participate in the program each year. In 2001, P.S.1 sponsored a summer frolic inside its renovated courtyard. Freestanding hammocks and low beach chairs appeared beneath misting machines. A wall covered with some 50 oscillating fans created an artificial sea breeze. DJs spun new music while visitors danced, imbibed Brooklyn beer and lounged before a make-believe beach.

Food and drink: What was once a drab school cafeteria has been transformed into a stylish café unlike any other in New York City. It has a "taxi cab" theme. Tables and chairs are made from rubber tires ingeniously cut, woven and fitted into something resembling rattan. Walls are papered with taxi cartoons, and real taxi roofs hang suspended from the ceiling. Available are sandwiches, desserts and beverages.

Luis Castro's *Ese Bolero es Mio* at Wave Hill, with a view of the Hudson River palisades.

Wave Hill

Amid gardens overlooking the Hudson River is a program of visual arts on the cutting edge of creativity.

Map reference: pages 52–53, E1
675 W. 252nd St, Bronx, NY 10471.
Tel: 718-549-3200, www.wavehill.org
Bus: BX7 or BX10 to 252nd St (about a 10-minute walk).

Apr 15–Aug 14 Tues–Sun 9am–5.30pm, Oct 15–Apr 14 Tues–Sun 9am–4.30pm.
Admission fee (free Tues, Sat 9am–noon, and every day Nov 15–Mar 14), museum shop, café, lectures, classes, music, wheelchair access.

Wave Hill was built in 1848 on a picturesque headland of the Hudson River. It was a private place for more than a century before its owners decided to invite the public at large, and today some 100,000 ordinary people stop by each year to visit its beautiful gardens and check out the indoor and outdoor exhibitions of contemporary art.

You should consider spending an afternoon here, dividing your time between art-viewing and garden-hopping. Here you can dine above the Hudson River, with its special light and colors, on tables outside the Wave Hill House. One early guest at Wave Hill was Charles Darwin, and young Theodore Roosevelt spent the summers of 1870 and 1871 here with his family. Teddy loved the natural setting, and when he got to the White House he saw to it that millions of acres of land were set aside as wilderness areas and parks for the public good.

Another famous visitor was Mark Twain, who actually lived here from 1901 to 1903 and created a tree house salon atop the branches of a chestnut. He wrote of winter storms at Wave Hill, "they sing their hoarse song through the big tree-tops with a splendid energy that thrills me and stirs me and uplifts me and makes me want to live always." The 28-acre (11-hectare) estate was once owned by George W. Perkins, a partner of the financier J. P. Morgan. Among other residents were maestro Arturo Toscanini and British delegates to the United Nations.

Wave Hill's buildings and grounds were deeded to the City of New York in the 1960s, and it was opened as a public garden and cultural center in 1965. Special gardens include herbs, wildflowers, shade plants and alpine flowers. The Aquatic Garden features water plants, including a beautiful slate-blue water lily called the Star of Siam. But what makes Wave Hill a world-class museum is the programming of visual arts curator Jennifer McGregor. She's long been interested in the relationship between art and nature that she explores in the woods, outdoor spaces and two galleries on the property.

Verging on the Real, a recent exhibition at Glyndor Gallery, examined artists' memories and interpretations of nature. *Course of Empire*, a

The Return of the Flaming Butterfly, 2000, Ming Fay.

piece by artist Mick O'Shea, addressed the theme of taming nature through use of an electric train that weaves its way through suburban homes, cut-out stars and potted plants. Peter Edlund exhibited paintings that inject social meaning into the Hudson River School style that was so famous in the latter part of the 19th century. His landscapes transform the old colors into unnatural shades of green, red and purple. In one such painting an escaped slave is depicted, and we are reminded how human greed and cruelty can cast their grim shadow on the realm of nature.

In *Sensing the Forest*, another recent show, artist Alyson Shotz exhibited documentation of her performance *Untitled (Reflective Mimicry)*. In it she moved through the forest in a costume covered with mirror tiles, reflecting the green around her in much the same way we all project finite and subjective ideas of nature.

Food and drink: The Wave Hill Café serves soup, salad, sandwiches and other light fare. A terrace affords glorious views of the Hudson River and Palisades.

Whitney Museum at Philip Morris

Even the Surgeon General would approve of this artistic outpost at a corporate tower in bustling midtown Manhattan.

Map reference: pages 50–51, C7
120 Park Ave at 42nd St, 10017.
Tel: 917-663-2453.
Subway: S, 4, 5, 6 or 7 to Grand Central-42nd St. Bus: M1, M2, M3, M4 to 42nd St.
Gallery: Mon–Fri 11am–6pm, Thurs to 7.30pm; Sculpture Court: Mon–Sat 7.30am–9.30pm, Sun 11am–7pm.
Free admission, café, performances, tours.

The Whitney Museum has been branching out, and this is one of the branches, down in the depths of the Philip Morris skyscraper right across from Grand Central Terminal.

The building has a glass-enclosed atrium, which allows sunlight to stream into a sculpture garden on the ground floor. Inside, visitors can peruse the exhibition, sip coffee from an espresso bar, and watch the endless parade of commuters going in and out of the landmark train station. Not wanting to be upstaged by all the hustle and bustle, the curators tend to exhibit big, eye-catching installations, such as the recent *Pastoral Pop!*, which featured colorful forms inspired by nature – cartoon-like trees and bushes, plastic foliage, and clay dioramas complete with Lilliputian animals. Equally arresting were the bright blue-and-white streamers resembling giant inflatable rafts with which Lee Boroson festooned the hall in *Underpass*.

Glass doors open to a small gallery that presents five shows each year. Most are dedicated to emerging or mid-career artists, though it's not unusual to find an intriguing selection of works from the Whitney's permanent collection. Dance, music and theater are occasionally presented in the sculpture court.

All in all, it's a welcome oasis in hectic midtown, and you couldn't ask for a better place to pass an hour or two while waiting for a train.

Food and drink: An espresso bar in the sculpture garden serves up soups, salads and other light fare. For something more substantial, slurp down a few oysters or a bowl of hearty seafood stew at the classic Oyster Bar and Restaurant in the lower level of Grand Central Terminal (212-490-6650, moderate).

ABOVE: Wave Hill's hemlock grove is the setting for Sylvia Benitez's *Beneath the Bark, Under Leaf and Log.*

BELOW: *Some/One*, a site-specific piece by Do-Ho Suh, at the Whitney Museum at Philip Morris. The work consists of more than 100,000 military dog tags.

Photography, Film and Broadcasting

The medium is indeed the message at three New York museums dedicated to the development of modern communications in their various forms – film, video, radio, television and still photography

American Museum of the Moving Image

Artifacts relating to the development of film and television tell the artistic and technological story of the moving image.

Map reference: pages 52–53, E4
35th Ave at 36th St, Astoria, NY 11106.
Tel: 718-784-0077; www.ammi.org
Subway: G, R to Steinway St or N, W to Broadway. Bus: Q101 to 35th Ave.
Tues–Fri noon–5pm, Sat–Sun 11am–6pm, screenings Sat–Sun 6.30pm.
Admission fee, gift shop, highlight tours, films, lectures, education programs, wheelchair access.

Situated in a former movie studio built by Paramount in 1920 and later employed for purposes as diverse as producing Army training films and *The Cosby Show*, the American Museum of the Moving Image houses a collection of some 95,000 objects related to American film and television. This is not an archive of film and videotape but a treasury of what curators call the "material culture" of the moving image – still photographs (more than 38,000); motion picture cameras and projectors; video recorders and television sets (including the oldest in existence, made in 1927); models, props, costumes, makeup and special-effects paraphernalia; and related items such as toys, dolls, fan magazines and soundtrack recordings.

A few notable items include Don Johnson's Armani suits from *Miami Vice*; the original Yellow Brick Road from the 1939 film *The Wizard of Oz*; the anchor desk used by Tom Brokaw in the 1990s on *NBC Nightly News*; and a collection of TV and movie character lunchboxes.

The Museum's core exhibit is *Behind the Screen: Making Motion Pictures and Television*, an in-depth look at the art, science and business of producing moving images and bringing them to market. The exhibit uses 1,200 artifacts from the permanent collection, along with more than five hours of audiovisual presentations and 13 computer-based interactive experiences like "Automated Dialogue Replacement," in which visitors dub their own voices over those of actors in famous movie scenes.

Another innovative facet of the Museum's educational program is "eDocent," which lets visitors access text, photos and audio clips via wireless hand-held devices, then retrieve the same material, as well as related information, over the Internet on their home computers.

More than 400 film and video screenings are offered each year in the 200-seat Riklis Theater. Only the best available prints are shown, and silent films are always accompanied by live music. Classic serials are presented in Tut's Fever Movie Palace, a takeoff on the Egyptian-themed movie houses of the Art Deco era.

Special programs include the Pinewood Dialogues, informal discussions featuring a varied roster of distinguished guests who have included Sidney Poitier, Chuck Jones, Liv Ullmann, John Waters and Edward James Olmos. A series of changing exhibits in the William Fox Gallery explores the evolution of computer-based entertainment, including items from the Museum's extensive collection of home and arcade computer games.

ABOVE: Vintage television sets at the American Museum of the Moving Image.

OPPOSITE: Mass media is the subject of three city museums.

Food and drink: *The small, family-run S'Agapo (34-21 34th Ave, 718-626-0303, moderate) serves traditional Greek cuisine, including delicious homemade olive bread, spinach pie, and meat turnovers. There's a delightful outdoor porch for warm-weather dining. The Café Bar (3290 36th St, 718-204-5273, inexpensive) serves delicious baked goods, coffee drinks, sandwiches and salads, as well as beer, wine and liquor in an arty, Bohemian atmosphere.*

International Center of Photography

A collection of some 55,000 photographs is featured in a series of exhibitions at the ICP's spacious new galleries.

Map reference: pages 50–51, B6
1133 Avenue of the Americas (Sixth Ave) at 43rd St, 10036.
Tel: 212-860-1777, www.icp.org
Subway: Sixth Ave B, D, F, S to 42nd St. Bus: M5, M6, M7 to 42nd St.
Tues–Thurs 10am–5pm, Fri 10am–8pm, Sat–Sun 10am–6pm.
Admission fee, museum store, café, education programs, wheelchair access.

The Critic, 1943, by Weegee (Arthur Felig), a street photographer with a "sixth sense" for finding news-worthy photos.

ICP had its genesis more than a quarter century ago, when *Life* magazine photographer Cornell Capa created a repository for images captured by his brother, celebrated photojournalist Robert Capa, killed by a landmine in Indochina in 1954. Since then, the center has amassed some of the finest work of scores of photojournalists, documentarians and art photographers. The collection's growth culminated in a 2001 relocation to a Times Square campus, encompassing a new museum as well as a school, library and archive. It is the city's only museum dedicated solely to photography and is the largest photography museum and school in the world.

The permanent collection covers nearly the entire 165-year history of the medium but is strongest on the work of 20th-century photographers such as Capa, Henri Cartier-Bresson, Margaret Bourke-White, Weegee, Berenice Abbott, W. Eugene Smith, Edward Weston and Diane Arbus. The institution's library, open to the public by appointment, holds 11,000 books, 2,000 biographical files, and some 6,000 issues of photography magazines and journals.

Since its founding, ICP has mounted more than 450 exhibitions, featuring the work of 2,500 photographers and artists in related media. Recent presentations have included *Another Vietnam*, a survey of war photos by North Vietnamese photographers; *Helmut Newton: Work*, an overview of four decades in the career of the provocative fashion photographer; and *The First Snapshots*, a look at the ways in which amateur photographers made use of George Eastman's early Kodak cameras in the closing years of the 19th century.

Food and drink: *The elegant Art Deco dining room of Restaurant Charlotte (145 W. 44th St, 212-768-4400, expensive) is a delightful spot to enjoy well-prepared Continental fare and great, homemade desserts such as macadamia cake with caramelized fresh bananas. The folksy, informal Virgil's Real Barbecue (152 W. 44th St, 212-921-9494, moderate) serves up hickory-smoked, Southern style barbecue, including pork, grilled catfish, shrimp and ribs.*

Museum of Television and Radio

The sounds and images of more than eight decades of broadcasting find a home in this temple to television and radio.

Map reference: pages 50–51, C5
25 W. 52 St, between Fifth and Sixth Aves, 10019.
Tel: 212-621-6800, www.mtr.org
Subway: E, F to Fifth Ave; B, D, F, S to 47th-50th Sts-Rockefeller Center. Bus: M1, M2, M3, M4, M5, M6, M7 to 52nd St.
Tues–Sun noon–6pm, Thurs to 8pm, Fri to 9pm (theaters only).
Admission fee, museum shop, tours, seminars, wheelchair access.

The Fab Four make a momentous appearance on the Ed Sullivan Show, 1964.

The Museum of Television and Radio was established by the legendary William S. Paley, longtime CBS chairman, who began collecting tapes of radio and television programs in 1975 under the auspices of what was then called the Museum of Broadcasting. The archive has grown enormously since Paley's death in 1990 (it now encompasses more than 100,000 programs) but its mission remains the same: to collect, preserve and interpret television and radio programming, and to make the tapes available for the education and enjoyment of the public.

The Museum covers every period of broadcasting, from the earliest days of radio (the first commercial broadcast went over the airwaves in Pittsburgh in 1920) to the present.

Among the radio programs preserved are a 1920 broadcast by vice-presidential candidate Franklin D. Roosevelt; an eyewitness account of the Hindenburg disaster of 1937; Adolf Hitler's 1939 address to the Reichstag; and Humphrey Bogart and Lauren Bacall performing an adaptation of *To Have and Have Not* for Lux Radio Theatre. Television programming includes the infamous 1991 Rodney King video; segments of the children's TV show *Howdy Doody*; performances by the Beatles and Elvis Presley; masterful comedy sequences by Sid Caesar, Jack Benny, Ernie Kovacs and Jackie Gleason; and Arturo Toscanini conducting Verdi's *Hymn of the Nations* in an early broadcast by the NBC Symphony in 1944.

Each program in the collection has been chosen for its artistic, cultural and historical significance and is catalogued in a computerized library. Visitors entering the Museum make a reservation for an individual viewing or listening console, then search the computer database for TV or radio shows of their choice.

Programs are also presented daily in two screening rooms and two main theaters: daily schedules are available at the John E. Fetzer lobby. Radio programs are aired in the Ralph Guild Radio Listening Room on the fifth floor, which also presents live and taped radio broadcasts by stations from around the country who send representatives here to record programs.

The Museum hosts a year-round series of changing exhibitions, seminars and special programs as well as weekend workshops for children. Recent offerings have included selected short films from 25 years of *Saturday Night Live*, a tribute to the late Jim Henson of Muppets fame, and a retrospective of pilots, premieres and final episodes of television series that went on to become part of American cultural history. "Re-creating Radio" workshops for families with children nine years of age and older are held on Saturday mornings. Seminars bring together broadcasting executives, performers, journalists and government officials for public discussions of a variety of topical issues.

Food and drink: *The stock market appears to be forever rising at the famed "21" Club (21 W. 52nd St, 212-582-7200, expensive), where well-heeled businesspeople enjoy $25 hamburgers and other solid, American fare in one of the city's most renowned dining rooms. The upscale Bombay Palace Restaurant (30 W. 52nd St, between Fifth and Sixth Aves, 212-541-7777, moderate) serves an all-you-can eat lunchtime buffet as well as traditional Indian dishes.*

History and Society

The American experience is the focus of museums that illuminate the historic trends that have shaped the nation and the world – with a special emphasis on New York's role as a port of entry for millions of immigrants

Ellis Island Immigration Museum

Between 1892 and 1954, 12 million people from around the world passed through Ellis Island before entering the United States. The museum tells their story, as well as the story of American immigration.

Map reference: pages 52–53, C6
Ellis Island, New York, NY 10004.
Tel: 212-363-3206, www.ellisisland.org
Subway to ferry: 4 or 5 to Bowling Green. Bus to ferry: M15 to Battery Park. Ferry: Statue of Liberty & Ellis Island Ferry from Battery Park (212-269-5755) or Liberty State Park, N.J. (201-435-9499). Ferry tickets are sold on a first-come, first-served basis.
Daily 9.30am–5pm, extended summer hours
Free admission, cafeteria, gift shop, research library, audio tour, wheelchair access.

The "huddled masses yearning to be free" – more than 12 million people who crossed the Atlantic during the great age of American immigration in the late 19th and early 20th centuries – could only complete their journey after first submitting to a rigorous screening process on 27-acre (11-hectare) Ellis Island in New York Harbor. Designed to weed out the infirm, the mentally incompetent, and the criminal, the screening allowed the vast majority to pass through; others were forced to sail back from whence they came.

Today, more than 100 million Americans are descendants of those intrepid immigrants who landed at what was often called the "Island of Tears." Allowed to fall into ruin after it was closed in 1954, the 100,000-square-foot (9,000-sq-meter) main building on Ellis Island was restored with $156 million in private funds, and in September 1990 it opened as the Ellis Island Immigration Museum under the auspices of the National Park Service.

Island history

Called Kioshk, or Gull Island, by Native Americans, Ellis Island was originally just 3 acres (1.2 hectares). Colonial governors purchased it from the natives and renamed it Little Oyster Island for its primary – in fact its only – crop. During the

1700s it was dubbed Gibbet Island, as it was the site of the gallows used to hang criminals. During the American Revolution, most of the island became the property of Samuel Ellis, who tried unsuccessfully to sell it off.

Recognizing its strategic location, the state of New York leased a small portion of the island after the Revolution with the intention of building a fort on it. To avoid legal difficulties, the state purchased the island in 1808 for "no less than $10,000," then sold it to the federal government, which immediately began construction of Fort Gibson. Completed just before the War of 1812, the fort had 13 guns and a garrison of 182, but was never called into action.

In 1890, Ellis Island was chosen as the site of a new Immigration Station for the Port of New York. When it opened in 1892, a staff of more than 500 – including guards, interpreters, watchmen, gardeners and cooks – was on hand to help process the immigrants.

The tide of newcomers ebbed and flowed over the ensuing years. In 1892 the Island handled almost a half million immigrants. By the turn of the century, due to stricter immigration laws and an economic depression, the number had dwindled to under 200,000 a year. In 1897 a devastating fire gutted the buildings (and destroyed most of the immigration records dating to 1855), and set the stage for a major rebuilding campaign.

On December 17, 1900, the day the newly constructed $1.5 million facility opened, 2,251

OPPOSITE: **A tile ceiling, the work of Spanish immigrant Rafael Guastavino, arches over Ellis Island's Great Hall.**

BELOW: **An Italian family reaches the New World, about 1910.**

immigrants passed through the island's new, fire-proof centerpiece: the red brick Main Building, 338 feet (103 meters) long and 168 feet (51 meters) wide, with four domed, neo-Baroque towers. The first floor was used as a baggage room and rail-road ticket office; the second floor was the Reg-istry Room. In 1918 the vaulted, tiled ceiling (see sidebar) was installed to replace the one destroyed two years earlier when ammunition stored in a railroad yard on the nearby New Jersey shore was blown up by saboteurs. By 1910, landfill from ship ballast and, it is believed, earth from the con-struction of the subway system, were added to the original parcel for hospital wards and an isolation facility for immigrants with contagious diseases.

More than 70 percent of the immigrants who came to America between 1892 and 1954 landed in New York, and all of those who arrived in steerage passed through Ellis Island. At its peak, in 1907, approximately 1¼ million people were processed at a center designed to handle half a million a year. During World War I, however, immigration to America ground to a halt, and the Island was used as an internment center for Ger-man sailors and suspected "aliens and spies." A 1921 law greatly restricted immigration; three

years later, another law established a quota system and required potential immigrants to be inspected at the American consular office in their countries of origin. These changes in policy served to stanch the human flow, and, by the end of 1954, only 21,500 immigrants had passed through dur-ing the preceding year. In March 1955, the gov-ernment declared Ellis Island "surplus property."

A landmark reborn

A battered and forlorn Ellis Island was open to the public on a limited basis as part of the Statue of Liberty National Monument between 1976 and 1984. In 1982 Lee Iacocca, chairman of the board of Chrysler Corporation, launched a drive to raise $230 million to restore the Statue of Liberty and Ellis Island. More than 20 million Americans contributed to the largest historic restoration in the country's history, and, on September 10, 1990, Ellis Island was opened as a National Monument.

Today, visitors arrive on the 27½-acre (11-hectare) island by boat at the same ferry slip their ancestors did and, like them, proceed to the Main Building's baggage room, filled with hundreds of antique trunks, suitcases and baskets once used to carry the scant belongings of families leaving

Sightseers disembark from ferries near the front of the Main Building, just as immigrants did more than a century ago.

Immigrants await final discharge, 1902.

eye disorder. The 20 percent who failed were marked with chalk and detained in dormitories overlooking the Great Hall, sometimes for as long as several months. Although most were eventually granted passage, approximately two percent had to return to their country of origin. Those who passed the inspection descended the "staircase of separation" and boarded ferries to New York or New Jersey.

Another exhibit on the second floor, the 10-room *Peak Immigration Years 1880–1924*, is a broad look at the immigrant experience – how each individual left a homeland, journeyed to America, and became part of what was later dubbed the "great melting pot."

On the third floor is perhaps the most moving exhibit, *Treasures from Home*, a collection of more than 1,000 artifacts and photographs the immigrants carried across the sea to their new home. *Ellis Island Chronicles* gives an overview of the island's history. *Restoring a Landmark*, along with the photography exhibit *Silent Voices*, documents the restoration of the building after

their old homes forever. The main exhibit on this floor, in the former railroad ticket office, is *The Peopling of America: 400 Years of U.S. Immigration History*, which relates how immigration has impacted the country over the years. At listening posts interspersed throughout the exhibits, visitors can hear the recorded reminiscences of immigrants. These are part of an oral history project in which immigrants or their descendants from throughout the nation were interviewed.

After their arrival, immigrants would walk up the stairs into the second-floor Registry Room, also known as the Great Hall. This was where, until 1911, they wove their way through a maze of iron railings from one inspection station to the next beneath the 60-foot-high (18-meter) ceiling. (The iron pens were subsequently replaced by wooden benches.)

Station to station

The main exhibit on this floor, in 14 rooms restored to the 1918–24 period, is *Through America's Gate: Processing at Ellis Island 1892–1924*, utilizing photographs, artifacts, personal papers and audio recordings to recreate each grueling step in a process that often took up to five hours. Immigrants moved from table to table. First, they went to the Personal Documents station to make sure their identification papers were in order. The next stop was the Education and Occupation Station; then the Character Station, where, for a while, literacy tests were administered.

It was the next stop, the Health Check, that the immigrants feared most. U.S. Public Health Service doctors checked for "loathsome and contagious diseases," including trachoma, an infectious

TILE MASTER

Visitors to the Great Hall at Ellis Island often marvel at the beauty of the tiled vaulted ceiling. This was the legacy of a man who himself was an immigrant to the United States, and who left his mark on many of the finest public buildings of his day.

Rafael Guastavino (1842-1908) was a native of Catalonia, in northeastern Spain, where he had achieved renown as an architect and builder before his 1881 departure for America. His specialty was a technique called Catalan vaulting, an ancient system of creating curved horizontal surfaces by carefully layering ceramic tiles in a matrix of mortar. The result is a surface of great strength and complex geometric beauty.

Working with distinguished architects such as Richard Morris Hunt and Cass Gilbert, Guastavino's firm executed nearly 400 commissions in New York alone. These included the tiled components of St. Paul's Chapel at Columbia University (1904), Pennsylvania Station (1910) and Grand Central Terminal (1913). In this last building, it is the vaulted ceiling of the Oyster Bar that exhibits Guastavino's genius with tile.

Guastavino's son supervised the Ellis Island project and carried on the business until 1950, by which time labor-intensive Catalan vaulting was increasingly unable to compete with steel and reinforced concrete. The firm closed in 1962, but its craftsmanship lives on – when the Great Hall was restored in the 1980s, only a scant handful of tiles needed replacement.

30 years of dereliction. Immigrants often spent long nights in this dormitory waiting to find out if they would be allowed to enter the United States or have to return to their homeland.

Two theaters in the Museum screen *Island of Hopes/Island of Tears*, a half-hour film produced by Oscar-winning filmmaker Charles Guggenheim. Seating is on a first-come, first-served basis. In one of the theaters, the film is preceded by a 15-minute talk by a park ranger.

In the immigration library and oral history center, open by appointment only, visitors can listen to taped reminiscences of Ellis Island immigrants and employees.

Immigration History Center

In April 2001, the Statue of Liberty–Ellis Island Foundation and the National Park Service officially opened its newest facility, an electronic database with information on 22 million immigrants, passengers and crew members who entered this country through the Port of New York between 1892 and 1924.

The data, culled from microfilms of passenger manifests, were compiled by the Church of Jesus Christ of Latter-day Saints. The records represent the work of 12,000 volunteers who donated 5.6 million hours of their time to collect and organize the information. It is available on the Internet (www.ellisislandrecords.org), or can be accessed on site for a $5 entrance fee.

Visitors can first enter their ancestors' names into the computer base to see if their arrival records are in the History Center in the Museum's West Wing. If they are, visitors will receive 11 specific pieces of information, including the ship their ancestors crossed on, their ethnicity, date of arrival, last residence, port of departure, ages, and marital status. They can also check the ship's manifest, which may tell of their ancestor's destination and occupation, and the names of other relatives who accompanied them.

Visitors who opt to pay $45 or more to become a member of The Statue of Liberty–Ellis Island Foundation can use one of the center's 10 private work studios, equipped with a computer, color scanner, digital camera and audio equipment, to create a Family History Scrapbook. The scrapbook might include documents from the center as well as family papers from home, small three-dimensional objects such as military medals, and photographs. The scrapbook can be printed on special archival paper or saved on a CD-ROM.

Reservations for the center are recommended

between May and Labor Day, and can be made online at www.ellisislandrecords.org or by calling 212-883-1986. Visitors do not need computer experience to do research or create a scrapbook.

Outside the Museum, the American Immigrant Wall of Honor, overlooking the Statue of Liberty and the New York skyline, commemorates 600,000 individuals or families whose descendants paid $100 to help in the island's restoration. The longest wall of names in the world, it will continue to grow as more contributions are received.

Food and drink: The Ellis Island Café offers no-frills cafeteria fare. An outdoor terrace has views of the Statue of Liberty and lower Manhattan.

Fraunces Tavern Museum

An old gathering place relives the special moments that followed the blood, sweat and tears of a revolution and the birth of a nation.

Map reference: pages 48–49, B8
54 Pearl St (at Broad St), 10004.
Tel. 212-425-1778.
Subway: 4, 5 to Bowling Green; N, R to White-hall St; J, M, Z to Broad St. Bus: M15 to Broad St.
Tues–Fri 10am–4.45pm, Sat noon–4pm.
Admission fee, museum store, restaurant, limited wheelchair access.

George Washington ate here. Several times. Never more memorably than on December 4, 1783. Late on that morning he and 40 or so of his officers met in an upstairs room at Fraunces Tavern to schmooze for auld lang syne, before the General headed south into retirement. Toasts were proposed and spirits flowed. Washington spoke briefly: "With a heart full of love and gratitude, I now take leave of you," he began. He embraced each comrade, many a tear being suppressed around the room, as the scene was recalled. Soldiers escorted him to a waiting boat and off he went. He returned only six years later, hand on a Bible, taking the oath of office at nearby Federal Hall.

Fraunces Tavern, near Manhattan's southern tip, was launched in 1763 as the Queen's Head Tavern. Due to mounting anti-British sentiment, however, owner Samuel Fraunces changed the name. The building had been erected in or about 1719 as a mansion for Samuel De Lancey. The tavern was also popular with British officers when they occupied the city. The place was sold in 1785 and used for offices – State, Treasury, War – early in Washington's first administration (Samuel Fraunces became Washington's steward and chief of household).

The property suffered fire and neglect until it was purchased in 1904 by the Sons of the Revolution and restored. Only a fragment of wall survives from the original structure. The Fraunces Tavern Museum occupies the second and third floors of the building; the restaurant downstairs is a separate operation. Museum exhibits and memorabilia illustrate the setting for Washington's leave-taking and other facets of early New York, including Fraunces and his tavern, the history of the building, and American social and political development during the Federal period.

Besides the Long Room, with its bar, tables, chairs and other furnishings, the second floor also accommodates the Clinton Room, honoring New York's first home-grown governor, George Clinton. He was the host for an earlier Fraunces Tavern reception honoring Washington. That was on November 24, when the Brits went home for good. Spirits also flowed at that "Evacuation Day" dinner, including 133 bottles of the Madeira wine so favored by Washington and colonial America.

Food and drink: Downstairs in the Fraunces Tavern Restaurant (212-269-0014, expensive) the menu includes Maryland crab cakes, an old favorite here, along with West Indies mussels, New England clam chowder and much else. A large-scale renovation was carried out to modernize the kitchen and the several dining rooms and to upgrade the cuisine.

The Clinton Room is named after Governor George Clinton, who gave George Washington a banquet to celebrate the British evacuation of New York.

George Gustav Heye Center of the National Museum of the American Indian

A branch of the Smithsonian highlights Native American cultures in a landmark building at the southern tip of Manhattan.

Map reference: pages 48–49, B8
One Bowling Green (at Battery Park), 10004.
Tel: 212-514-3700, www.nmai.si.edu
Subway: 4, 5 to Bowling Green or N, R to
Whitehall St. Bus: M15 to Battery Park.
Daily 10am–5pm, Thurs to 8pm.
Free admission, store, films, workshops,
performances, wheelchair access.

ABOVE: The Museum is housed in the former U.S. Customs House, an architectural masterpiece designed by Cass Gilbert.

RIGHT: A child's shirt fashioned by Seminole Indians.

Once upon a time – actually from 1922 to 1994 – there was a Museum of the American Indian in the far reaches of northern Manhattan. Hardly anyone visited it by the early 1990s, even though it contained thousands of rare and beautiful items, including Tuscarora wampum belts, Aztec figurines, Sioux medicine bundles and huge Inuit totem poles, all of which had been collected by the Museum's founder and original director, George Gustav Heye.

Heye, an investment banker and oil heir who died in 1957, began amassing anything related to Indian cultures as early as 1897. Initially stored in his Madison Avenue apartment, the results of his obsession – which grew to between 800,000 and a million objects – were either housed in the original museum at 155th Street or crammed into a Bronx warehouse. "George was what we call a boxcar collector," an associate told *The New Yorker* in 1960. "He felt he couldn't conscientiously leave a reservation until its entire population was practically naked."

On the other hand, during a great drought in 1938 he returned a sacred medicine bundle that belonged to the Hidatsa people of North Dakota. Acquired by a missionary in 1907, it was one of Heye's prized possessions, but he didn't hesitate to give it back to the tribe's elders when they asked. Shortly afterwards, it rained.

"If Heye hadn't collected those things back then, we would not have them today to look at. Now, more than 100 years later, my people can see what we had, and it is not lost," remarked Linda Poolaw, Delaware grand chief, when the new George Gustav Heye Center of the Museum of the American Indian opened in lower Manhattan in the fall of 1994.

One of three facilities that now make up the Smithsonian's National Museum of the American Indian, the Heye Center occupies the first two floors of the Alexander Hamilton U.S. Customs House. Facing historic Bowling Green (the country's first public park), its location, somewhat ironically, is also pretty much the spot where Fort Amsterdam once stood and where Dutch governor Peter Stuyvesant "purchased" the island of Manhattan from unsuspecting locals.

The bulk of Heye's collection – the largest of its kind in the world – is being transferred to the Smithsonian's new Cultural Resources Center in Maryland, which includes an extensive research library. From there, objects will be routinely selected for exhibition in New York and at the new National Museum of the American Indian, scheduled to open on the National Mall in Washington, D.C., in 2004.

The Museum's New York branch, meanwhile, offers a particularly intimate glimpse into a rich cultural and artistic tradition, in an unmatched historical setting. Many staff members are Native Americans, from tribal groups across the hemisphere, and their firsthand knowledge (and willingness to impart it) is a far cry from the typical museum experience.

Temple of commerce

Also atypical is the Museum's setting, in what is generally considered the city's finest example of Beaux-Arts architecture. Designed by Cass Gilbert and completed in 1907, this seven-story palace of commerce was built as the U.S. Customs House in an era when government revenue was dependent upon the customs duties garnered from incoming ships at the port of New York.

Appropriately, the exterior features 44 columns decorated with the head of Mercury, the god of commerce. Atop them a set of 12 statues represent the sea powers of the ancient and modern worlds. Even more impressive – and more easily viewed from street level – are the four massive sculptures by Daniel Chester French, who created the even larger statue of Abraham Lincoln for Washington's Lincoln Memorial, in which the four continents are depicted as seated female figures. (In another ironic twist, an Indian peers from behind the figure representing America.)

The building's nautical theme continues inside the grand main entrance, at the top of a set of steep granite steps, where the lobby is awash with marble pillars and monumental arches leading to a central rotunda topped by a spectacular elliptical skylight. Around the ceiling is a circle of WPA murals of the city's seafaring past that were painted in 1937 by New York artist Reginald Marsh.

A collection with spirit

On either side of the rotunda are twin sets of galleries, with a third at the far end that, until recently, was home to *All Roads Are Good: Native Voices on Life and Culture*. Along with 300 objects selected for their spiritual as well as artistic significance, the exhibit included a poignant "Circle of Moccasins" made of more than 100 pairs of vintage beaded, fringed, laced and quilled footwear from almost as many tribal groups.

Although *All Roads Are Good* was removed in April 2002, the Heye Center continues to offer short- and long-term exhibits imbued by the same powerful sense of creative spirituality. In recent years these have ranged from a magnificent collection of 19th- and early 20th-century Plains Indian shirts to rare Navajo weavings and a remarkable display of Iroquois beadwork from upstate New York and Canada. Through March

Moccasins from dozens of tribes represent the diversity and unity of native cultures.

2003, the Heye Center is also sponsoring *Great Masters of Mexican Folk Art*, in which more than 100 artists from all parts of Mexico have used ancestral traditions to create works in clay, wood, straw, leather, silk, feathers, metal and stone.

A permanent highlight, however, is the opportunity to learn more about Native American life in general, thanks to the Resource Center located to the left of the main entrance. In what was the old Cashier's Office (gleaming brass grille still intact), visitors can use computer technology to learn about the Lenni Lenape people who first lived on Manhattan island, or browse through the *Choctaw Community News* and similar publications for a glimpse of more contemporary issues. An adjacent research area holds over 5,000 books on various related subjects, from Mayan textiles to early New York history.

In addition to its ongoing exhibits, the George Gustav Heye Center hosts musicians, dancers, artists and elders in informal programs that allow them to share their cultural heritage with the public. Visiting artists in recent years have included Navajo sandpainters, Inuit wood carvers and Arapaho beadworkers. Along with a regular series of film and video productions (either directed by Native Americans or with Native American stars), they're presented in the basement level's 314-seat auditorium. For details, call 212-514-3869.

After nearly 30 years of service, the U.S.S. *Intrepid* serves as a museum.

Food and drink: Pret a Manger (60 Broad St, 212-825-0412, inexpensive) offers sandwiches, sushi and other light bites, without preservatives or additives. Those with hardier appetites can repair to Fraunces Tavern, which is historic in two ways – as the site of George Washington's farewell address and an outpost of the beef-and-martini lunch.

Intrepid Sea Air Space Museum

A ship that served the nation valiantly in war and peace continues to stand tall for public inspection.

Map reference: pages 52–53, C4
Pier 86 at W. 46th St and Twelfth Ave, 10036.
Tel: 212-245-0072, www.intrepidmuseum.com
Subway: A, C, E to 42nd St-Port Authority Bus Terminal; walk west to Twelfth St, then north to Pier 86. Bus: M50 to Pier 86 or M42 to Pier 83.
Apr–Sept Mon–Fri 10am–5pm, Sat–Sun 10am–7pm; Oct–March Tues–Sun 10am–5pm. Admission fee (except for those on active military duty), museum store, cafeteria, children's programs, wheelchair access.

The U.S.S. *Intrepid* was rescued from the junkyard in 1976 and granted a new life. Having served the nation faithfully in war and peace for nearly three decades, the old aircraft carrier was about to be born again – as a floating museum anchored off the Hudson River in New York, where the great old transatlantic liners used to tie up.

It was launched on its new mission on the first Saturday in August 1982, when patriotic-minded visitors began invading Intrepid Square at Pier 86 and swarming aboard the big ship. They're still coming, well over half a million a year, standing atop her immense 900-foot-long (275-meter) Flight Deck and trying to imagine what it was like when bomb-laden Navy planes took off for the skies of Tokyo, back when Japan was the United States' mortal enemy. They climb to the bridge, where officers once steered a course and looked for trouble. And they go below to the Hangar Deck, where there is a range of exhibits showcasing aircraft, military and scientific equipment, and various memorabilia.

Launched in 1943, the *Intrepid* (the fourth ship by that name in U.S. Navy history) was one of 24 speedy carriers of a type known as the Essex Class. She was kept busy in World War II, enduring Japanese bombs, torpedoes and kamikaze attacks to such a degree that she began to seem jinxed. Eleven crewmen were killed

when a torpedo struck in February 1944, then another 10 in October in the first of the kamikaze assaults. She participated in much action, including the great battle at Leyte Gulf in the Philippines, and her pilots sank two battleships and downed hundreds of enemy aircraft.

Her worst day came in November 1944, two days after Thanksgiving, when a kamikaze attack – the second of two only minutes apart – ignited a hellish fire that caused 69 deaths and scores of serious injuries. Another suicidal assault off Okinawa in April 1945 took 20 more lives and wrought heavy damage. Patched up once again, the *Intrepid* launched her last attack of the waning war in August 1945 at Wake Island.

Later she helped blockade Cuba in the missile crisis of October 1962; plucked astronauts from the sea in space recovery missions warming up for the great moon landing of 1969; and undertook three separate tours of duty in the Vietnam War. During the Cold War era, she tracked Soviet submarines, then wound up her career as a Bicentennial Exposition ship in 1976. Her reincarnation as the world's largest naval museum was championed by the late New York builder, philanthropist and patriot Zachary Fisher.

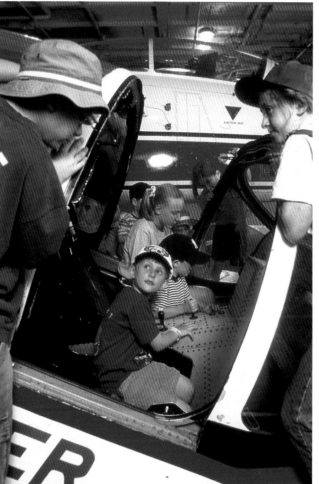

Would-be pilots climb inside the cockpit of a jet fighter.

Focus on the skies

Naval aviation is the chief preoccupation, and various exhibits in the Hangar Deck focus on a great ship's history and development. (Audio devices, supplied to each visitor, provide tape-recorded explanations.) Examples of modern aircraft are on display in Navy Hall. Early aircraft is shown in Pioneer Hall as well as an exhibit on the development of early submarines, including a full sized replica of the *Turtle*, a wooden sub used in New York Harbor during the American Revolution.

Among the exhibits in Technologies Hall is a reproduction of the Gemini space capsule, along with a Sioux helicopter and the cockpit of a Boeing 707. There are continuous showings of films such as *Desert Storm*, *Air Power at Sea* and *Proudly We Serve*, the latter devoted to service by African-Americans in a once segregated Navy and Coast Guard. World War II aircraft are positioned in an area known as Intrepid Hall, which also has illustrations of kamikaze fighters and various dioramas.

On display up above on the Flight Deck – the carrier was refitted in 1956 with an angled rather than straight deck – are several aircraft, including an A-12 Blackbird, a reconnaissance plane from the 1960s; a Grumman F-11 Tiger jet fighter; a Grumman anti-submarine plane; and several helicopters. The ship's fantail provides a bird's-eye view of the Hudson River shoreline. Strong winds, rain and inclement weather can make the Flight Deck inhospitable and subject to shutdown.

Along the other side of Pier 86 are two additional vessels: the USS *Growler* SSG-577 and the USS *Edson* DD-946. Visitors to the *Growler* submarine see torpedo rooms and a center for attack operations, handling guided missiles, that at one time were highly secret and strictly off-limits to public view. Physical limitations inherent in such a vessel, with its cramped quarters, are responsible for long waits in an adjoining tent before successive visitors can enter. Children under the age of six are not permitted aboard the sub. Guided tours aboard the *Edson* also provide a glimpse of life at sea for America's sailors.

A new visitor center, built at a cost of $5.5 million, was opened in June 2000. It contains a McDonald's restaurant and souvenir shop offering a wide range of items with patriotic, New York City and other themes.

Food and drink: *Among nearby restaurants in this Hell's Kitchen area are the Landmark Tavern (626 Eleventh Ave at 46th St, 212-757-8595, moderate), an old-style pub and, for something completely different, Zen Palate (663 Ninth Ave at 46th St, 212-582-1669, inexpensive), a vegetarian spot inspired by the cuisine and tranquil atmosphere of a Buddhist monastery.*

Goldfish Vendor, 1928, by Reuven Rubin, from Culture and Continuity: The Jewish Journey *at the Jewish Museum.*

Jewish Museum

A people's long history is celebrated at this repository of Judaica inside a grand old mansion along New York's Museum Mile.

Map reference: pages 50–51, F1
1109 Fifth Ave (at 92nd St).
Tel: 212-423-3200, www.jewishmuseum.org
Subway: 6 to 96th St. Bus: M1, M2, M3, M4 to 92nd St.
Sun 10am–5.45pm, Mon–Wed 11am–5.45pm, Thurs 11am–8pm, Fri 11am–3pm.
Admission fee, museum store, café, guided tours, wheelchair access.

The varieties of Jewish experience are cataloged in this fine old French Renaissance mansion on Fifth Avenue that was built around 1908 for banker-philanthropist Felix Warburg. The designer of this New York landmark was Charles Gilbert, son of the even more renowned architect Cass Gilbert, and inside is one of the world's greatest collections of Judaica – art, artifacts and antiques that tell the story of Jewish persistence in an age-old struggle for survival.

Such an important collection is only to be expected in a great city on which Jews have left their indelible cultural imprint, from whatever their starting point – Middle Eastern, Sephardic, German, East European. Founded in 1904 in the library of the Jewish Theological Seminary of America, of which Warburg was a trustee, the Museum has amassed more than 28,000 ceremonial objects, works of art that include contemporary painting and sculpture, photographs, ethnographic material and much more. It mounts special exhibitions drawing on its own holdings and on material lent by public and private sources in the United States, Europe and Israel. Recent shows have included an exhibition for children exploring life in ancient Israel and a highly controversial display of conceptual works employing Nazi imagery.

In 1944, Warburg's widow, Frieda Schiff Warburg, donated her home to the Seminary for use as a museum. It opened three years later. A sculpture garden was installed in 1959, an annex was built in 1963, and exhibition space was doubled in another extensive expansion (completed in 1993) that cost $36 million. The collection includes paintings by such luminaries as Marc Chagall and Ben Shahn as well as a plaster cast of George Segal's *The Holocaust* that depicts a sole survivor against a backdrop of corpses. There is also a broadcasting archive that preserves highlights of classic, characteristic Jewish comedy.

The centerpiece of the collection is a permanent exhibition, mounted on two floors, entitled *Culture and Continuity: The Jewish Journey* that illuminates cultural history and values extending back more than 4,000 years, with four basic themes that point up a people's resilience in the face of historical circumstance and frequent social oppression.

"Forging an Identity" deals with early times during which separate customs were created and Israelites were transformed into Jews bearing a distinct cultural consciousness. Illustrating the segment are a variety of artifacts – Hanukkah lamps, vessels, agricultural tools, ritual objects, ancient coins and other items.

The three main branches of Judaism are the focal point of the second segment, "Interpreting a Tradition." Those branches are Middle Eastern, Sephardic and Ashkenazi. Later historical circumstances involving Jewish migration and resettlement are dealt with in "Confronting Modernity," while "Realizing a Future" is the overall theme for ongoing exhibitions devoted to contemporary art.

There is an interactive computer program centering on the Talmud, a separate gallery for Torah-related objects, and classrooms and gallery space designed to teach children about Jewish heritage. There are also frequent special exhibitions, including the first comprehensive showing of 20th century Russian and Soviet Jewish artists. Another, entitled *The Emergence of Jewish Artists in Nineteenth-Century Europe*, displayed 70 works by 21 painters, including the Impressionist master Camille Pissarro, Gauguin's friend Jacob Meyer de Haan, Max Lieberman and Jozef Israels. Still another exhibited the illustrations and set designs of Ben Katchor, creator of the comic-strip novel *The Jews of New York* and other work.

Food and drink: Kosher cuisine is served in the Museum's own artfully decorated Café Weissman, on the lower level. There's a selection of soups, salads and sandwiches, plus desserts and beverages, in a stained-glass ambience.

Lower East Side Tenement Museum

The immigrant experience of a century ago is brought vividly to life in this preserved tenement building, with apartments kept exactly as their inhabitants left them.

Map reference: pages 48–49, E6
90 Orchard St (at Broome St), 10002.
Tel: 212-431-0233, www.tenement.org
Subway: F to Delancey St or J, M, Z to Essex St.
Bus: M15 to Grand and Allen Sts.
Daily 11am–5.30pm; call for tour schedule.
Admission fee, museum store, performance series, wheelchair access at visitor center only.

TOP: A selection from the Jewish Museum's renowned collection of Hanukkah lamps.

BOTTOM: *The Holocaust,* 1982, George Segal.

F amilies who sought a new life in the United States during the great era of immigration, about 1880–1920, often found their first American home in a building such as this gaunt, six-story brick tenement on Manhattan's Lower

Above: A typical apartment had three rooms – front, back and kitchen.

Below: Nathalie Gumpertz, a resident of 97 Orchard Street in the 1870s.

East Side. Built in 1863 by Lucas Glockner, a German tailor, 97 Orchard was reasonably comfortable by the standards of the day and attracted renters who fit a lower-middle-class profile of workers and tradesmen rather than that of the impoverished masses depicted living in squalor by chroniclers like Jacob Riis a generation later. Each floor had four apartments of three rooms each; at least one room was lit by the sun. Glockner himself lived on the premises. There was no indoor plumbing – that would have been a luxury in this period – but outdoor privies and a water pump were available behind the building.

The tenement at 97 Orchard predated even the earliest New York housing codes. City-mandated upgrades in the early 1900s included hall toilets on each floor and windows set into interior walls to carry a dim glimpse of daylight to the two inner rooms.

Throughout the 72 years during which the building was inhabited, there was no central heating. The only source of heat in each apartment was the coal-fired kitchen range. Gaslights were installed in the 1890s, but there was no electricity until 1924.

As 97 Orchard grew older, the neighborhood around it grew poorer, more crowded, and more diverse. Around the turn of the 20th century, the Lower East Side was the most densely populated place in the world, with 750 to 1,000 people per acre. The Orchard Street block where No. 97 stands had more than 2,300 inhabitants. Over a span of seven decades, this one building alone housed more than 7,000 people from some 20 countries.

In 1929, a new round of housing codes led the building's owners to forgo further rental of residential space. In 1935, the upstairs apartments were sealed, while the first floor and basement housed retail tenants until 1987. For more than a half century, the apartments stood empty and neglected, their interiors left as an inadvertent time capsule. Then, in 1989, a group of New Yorkers intent on creating a vivid memorial to the American immigrant experience selected 97 Orchard Street as the locus for the Lower East Side Tenement Museum. In 1998, the building was declared a National Historic Landmark.

Tours begin at the visitor center, 90 Orchard Street, where "Gallery 90" includes an open-sided, meticulously detailed six-foot-tall (2-meter) model of the tenement, showing what life inside looked like at two periods – 1870 and 1915. The center also offers slide and video presentations on the immigrant experience, as well as walking tours of the surrounding neighborhood, still heavily populated with recent immigrants.

At the tenement itself, guides recount stories culled from the lives of former residents and escort visitors through the apartments in which they lived. One flat has been left exactly as it was found when the building was reopened, while others have been furnished as they would have been when they were inhabited. The shadowy halls and stairways still reveal panels of "lincrusta," a leathery synthetic material stamped to look like low-relief ornamental plasterwork.

Window on the past

In the "ruin apartment," time stands still, frozen at the moment when the last tenants moved out and the apartment was sealed. Plaster lies where it fell from the cracked ceiling, and smudged walls still bear the inventory notations left by garment workers when the space was used for storage. The "ruin" reveals the task that awaited researchers and restorers after the tenement was chosen for its current function. Along with decay, museum personnel found an enormous trove of artifacts, some 1,500 in all, including kitchen equipment, toys, bottles, newspapers and letters, bits of fabric, buttons and even a ouija board.

The objects helped researchers reconstruct not only the furnishings of several apartments but some of the details of life in the building. In the apartment of the German Jewish Gumpertz family, residents in the 1870s and 1880s, 21 layers of wallpaper were removed to reveal the pattern familiar to the Gumpertzes themselves. The apartment is furnished as it was when Nathalie Gumpertz, who had been abandoned by her husband Julius, ran a seamstress shop in the front room with her daughters, making dresses for women in the neighborhood.

Other apartments that have been restored and furnished to reflect the lives of their inhabitants include those of the Rogarshevskys, Eastern European Jews (ca. 1900); the Baldizzis, a Sicilian family that was among the last 1930s tenants at 97 Orchard; and the Confinos, Turkish Sephardic Jews who lived here around 1916. A special aspect of the Confino apartment tour, especially geared towards children, is a visit with 14-year-old Victoria Confino, portrayed by an adult actress. The immigrant girl talks about her family's arrival in the United States, and the challenges of assimilation – all with the assumption that her young visitors, too, are recent arrivals needing advice on how to adjust to life in New York. In this apartment, children can touch everything – and can listen to recorded simulations of the street sounds of Victoria Confino's time.

A total of five apartments are open to the public, and work is under way on the re-creation of an 1893 sweatshop and the Civil War-era living quarters of an Irish immigrant family. Another project involves the revival of Schneider's, a ground-floor German beer parlor that thrived more than a century ago, and an effort is being made to acquire and preserve the adjoining tenement for a much-needed expansion.

Food and drink: Katz's Deli (205 E. Houston St, 212-254-2246, inexpensive), a Lower East Side institution, has a busy cafeteria atmosphere and features overstuffed corned beef, pastrami and salami sandwiches. Grotta Azzurra (387 Broome St, 212-925-8775, expensive) in Little Italy is the place to go for lobster fra diavolo and a big selection of other southern Italian favorites.

A mural greets museum visitors.

Museum of American Financial History

Set in the heart of New York's financial district, this affiliate of the Smithsonian Institution tells the story of the free-market system in America.

Map reference: pages 48–49, B8
28 Broadway (at Bowling Green), 10004.
Tel: 212-908-4110, www.financialhistory.org
Subway: 4, 5 to Bowling Green. Bus: M15 to Whitehall St.
Tues–Sat 10am–4pm.
Admission fee, museum shop, wheelchair access.

The Museum of American Financial History stands on one of the business world's most hallowed addresses. Alexander Hamilton, father of the Bank of New York, once kept a law office here, and the building itself housed the offices of John D. Rockefeller's Standard Oil Company. Drawing on an archive of some 10,000 artifacts and documents, the Museum focuses on the rise of capital markets in New York and the nation since the days when securities were traded beneath a buttonwood tree on Wall Street by the men who founded the New York Stock Exchange.

Drawing on its proximity to Wall Street and the surrounding financial district, the Museum has assembled a collection that documents the increasing speed and technological sophistication with which capital moves throughout the global economy. An 1880 stock ticker, one of Thomas Edison's early inventions, represents what was once the state of the art in tracking and reporting quotations – and in providing the raw material for New York's famous "ticker tape parades."

An assortment of artifacts are exhibited at the Museum of Chinese in the Americas.

To provide a sense of what stock trading was like on the cusp of the electronic age, the Museum displays a brokerage trading desk from the early 1960s, complete with rotary dial phone, mechanical quote board, and a push-button Quotron machine that prefigured today's computerized stock price monitoring. Other highlights from the permanent collection include letters from Alexander Hamilton to the Bank of New York, a U.S. bond owned and signed by George Washington while he was president, and a ticker tape from the morning of October 29, 1929 – better known as Black Tuesday – recording the stock market crash that set off the Great Depression.

The Museum mounts a series of special exhibits, among which have been recent presentations on J. P. Morgan, John D. Rockefeller, the development of financial journalism and, on the lighter side, the history of the "piggy bank." In addition, there are weekly walking tours of Wall Street and the financial district on Friday at 10am.

Food and drink: *Traders pack the Wall Street Kitchen & Bar (70 Broad St, 212-797-7070, inexpensive), housed in a handsome old bank building just a block and a half from the New York Stock Exchange. The selection of bar food and beer is right on the money.*

Museum of Chinese in the Americas

The Asian experience is summed up in words, images and artifacts at a modest museum in Chinatown.

Map reference: pages 48–49, D6
70 Mulberry St (at Bayard St).
Tel: 212-619-4784,
www.chinatownweb.com/moca
Tues–Sat 10am–5pm.
Subway: N, J, R, 6 to Canal St. Bus: M1, M103 to Canal St.
Admission fee, neighborhood walking tours, no wheelchair access.

This small repository once known as the Chinatown History Museum pays tribute to the countless numbers of migrants, especially from Asia, who have added their distinctive flavor to the American melting pot – as best exemplified by multicultural New York. Founded in 1980, the Museum of Chinese in the Americas (or, as it likes to call itself, MoCA) is on the second floor of what for many years was a public school, P.S. 122, that served Italian, Jewish and a lot of other kids.

Only the Chinatown in San Francisco rivals New York's, at least in public awareness. Actually, New York's population of Chinese descent, from the mid-19th century on, wasn't all that gigantic – until really taking off after 1965. It now constitutes the largest number (about 300,000) of any Chinatown in the Western Hemisphere.

The Museum has a gallery of thousands of photos and illustrations, plus old maps, immigration documents and other memorabilia that recount the experience of a vibrant community that is one of the most densely populated sections of the city. A file of oral histories is kept, and the Museum rates as an important archival source for researchers. Guided walking tours of the area are also arranged here.

Among other special displays that have been held here were *In the Shadow of Liberty: Graphics of Chinese Exclusion, 1870s–1890s*, laying bare the forms of discrimination faced by Asians, and *Gateway to Gold Mountain*, a traveling exhibit that chronicled the immigration experience of thousands of Asians who came to America between 1910 and 1940. "Gold Mountain" was the term applied by Chinese to the largely illusory land of their dreams.

Another exhibition displayed the hand-crafted work of illegal immigrants from China whose ship ran aground off New York, work they turned out while being detained as captive aliens. The incident drew wide attention to the great numbers of would-be settlers.

A large collection of books dealing with the Chinese-American experience is kept, and there are costumes, musical instruments and memorabilia.

Food and drink: The neighborhood is rich in dining opportunities, with an estimated 300 restaurants serving a variety of regional cuisine, not to mention the portable food carts on Canal Street. The no-frills Bo-Ky (80 Bayard St, between Mott and Mulberry, 212-406-2292, inexpensive) is Chinese-Vietnamese, has savory soups and oodles of noodles. Also inexpensive, especially for lunch, is Shanghai Cuisine (89 Bayard St at Mulberry, 212-732-8988). Try the braised pork in brown sauce.

Museum of Jewish Heritage

This living memorial to the Holocaust also recounts the story of Jewish life and culture from the late 1880s to the present.

Map reference: pages 48–49, A8
18 First Place (at Battery Place), 10004-1484.
Tel: 212-509-6130, www.mjhnyc.org
Subway: N, R to Rector St or 4, 5 to Bowling Green. Bus: M15 to Battery Park.
Sun–Wed 9am–5pm, Thurs 9am–8pm, Fri 9am–5pm.
Admission fee, museum shop, kosher café, audio tours, wheelchair access.

The Museum of Jewish Heritage is housed in a distinctive hexagonal building on the landscaped grounds of Battery Place.

The Museum of Jewish Heritage opened its doors in 1997, in view of the Statue of Liberty and Ellis Island and close to the spot where the first Jews set foot in North America in 1654. The shape of the three-level, 30,000-square-foot (2,800-sq-meter) granite building with a steep, louvered roof is symbolic: there are six sides to honor the 6 million who died in the

Holocaust, as well as to evoke the Star of David.

Exhibits are organized into three broad sections and draw from a rich pool of personal histories, artifacts and images to present the story of the Jewish people in the 20th century. The presentations weave together themes of joy, tradition, tragedy and horror, putting the Holocaust into the larger context of Jewish history.

On the first floor, *Jewish Life a Century Ago* traces the rich traditions and cultures of Jews throughout the world – their differences as well as their similarities and shared experiences. The exhibit frames the diaspora of the Jews within the larger history of the changing world around them. Among exhibits focusing on customs and traditions are a hand-painted sukkah canvas created in the 1920s and '30s in Budapest, Hungary, and videos of religious festivals around the world.

On the second floor, *The War Against the Jews* recounts the persecution and isolation of European Jewry in the 1930s and '40s before and during the Holocaust, once again drawing on first-person accounts as well as artifacts and photographs. The focus here is on people's humanity, dignity and spirit when faced with brutality and extinction.

On the third floor, *Jewish Renewal* looks at contemporary Judaism throughout the world, focusing primarily on the United States and Israel. Exhibits address the present as well as the future of the Jewish religion in today's society, and include the means by which the Jewish people have reacted to injustice and intolerance since World War II. A particularly poignant artifact among the third-floor exhibits is the Czech Torah, once the treasure of the synagogue in Domazlice in what is now the Czech Republic. Stolen by the Nazis and warehoused for eventual display in a museum they planned to create after their triumph, the scroll was rescued by Holocaust survivors after the war and preserved by the Memorial Scrolls Trust in London.

Sight and sound

The Museum draws from its unique collection of 800 historical and cultural artifacts, more than 2,000 photographs and 15,000 objects to create its exhibits. Many were donated by Holocaust survivors and their families, as well as by liberators, and by immigrants to the United States and their families. This is one of only five institutions in the world that has access to the video testimonies compiled by Steven Spielberg's Survivors of the Shoah Visual History Foundation. Twenty-four original films from this series are interspersed throughout the Museum, which also presents footage from its own video archives. The Spielberg project and the Museum's own films have as their object the first-person explanation of what Jewish life in Europe was like prior to the Hitler era, the personal and collective devastation of the Holocaust, and the efforts to rebuild private lives and the world Jewish community over the past half-century.

Visitors can take an audio tour recorded by actress Meryl Streep and violinist Itzhak Perlman. A "core" tour highlights the central exhibition; the "random access" tour features specific artifacts, such as a copy of Hitler's *Mein Kampf* annotated by Gestapo chief Heinrich Himmler. Both tours are approximately 90 minutes long.

A new East Wing, scheduled to open in the fall of 2003, will offer opportunities for interactive exhibits and house a state-of-the-art theater and special exhibition galleries, as well as a memorial garden and café. The addition is part of the Museum's ongoing mission to teach the legacy of the Holocaust as well as Jewish life around the world in the years since World War II.

The Museum sponsors a year-round roster of special exhibitions and events, including music, lectures, films and holiday celebrations. Family programs are offered on Sunday.

Food and drink: It's a short walk through the Financial District to Mangia (40 Wall St, 212-425-4040, inexpensive), a gourmet cafeteria with a delectable variety of goodies, from fresh salads, soups and hot entrees to a habit-forming selection of pastries and other sweets.

The *Ambrose Lightship*, now moored at South Street Seaport, guided vessels into New York Harbor in the early 1900s.

South Street Seaport Museum

Past and present meet at a historic water-front that was America's front door in the great age of sailing ships.

Map reference: pages 48–49, C8
12-14 Fulton St, 10024.
Tel: 212-748-8600, www.southstseaport.org
Subway: A, C, 1, 2, 4, 5 to Fulton St-Broadway Nassau. Bus: M15 to Fulton St.
Daily 10am–6pm (to 5pm mid-Sept–mid-May). Admission fee, shops, restaurants, educational programs, performers, limited wheelchair access.

The first non-local to discover New York's five-star harbor, with its easy access from the sea and ample deepwater docking space, was Giovanni da Verrazano, who came by in April 1524. The place was called New Amsterdam until the Dutch were muscled aside by the English, who knew a good port when they saw one.

By the 19th century there were so many vessels lined up at the East River waterfront that the main drag (South Street, eventually) would come to be known as the "Street of Ships." It was a jungle of tall masts, bowsprits that arched over the street, a relentless wave of immigrants, and a motley crew of dock hangers-on. By 1860, two-thirds of all imports into the U.S. entered here, a commerce that enriched New York and its gatekeepers and made a lot of history.

But steamships found more suitable berths on the Hudson River, and by the 20th century the glory days were over for the old seaport on the Lower East Side – until 1967. That's when the South Street Seaport Museum was created, saving the area from the certain fate of high-rise development. Renovation completed in the early 1980s produced a historic district that mixed ships and shops in a generally winning way. The reinvigorated Seaport, spiced with open-air concerts and other forms of entertainment, added a festive ambience that helped boost the entire downtown Manhattan area.

Cobbled streets and restored buildings recall the heyday of 19th-century seafaring.

Sails and sales

Old ships are the chief historic attraction of the 11-block Museum district. They are tied up at Piers 15 and 16. Nearby is the Pier 17 Pavilion, with its stores, cafés and third-floor food court

provide one at great profit. Currently a $15 million renovation of the Schermerhorn complex is under way. It will include, in addition to its shops and offices, a permanent exhibition entitled *World Port New York* that will illustrate the port's historic significance in the nation's development.

Three of the historic vessels on permanent exhibit may be boarded by the public: the *Wavertree*, the *Peking* and the *Ambrose Lightship*. The *Wavertree* was the first vessel acquired by the Museum. Built in England in 1885, it is one of the last large sailing ships made of wrought iron. It has four masts and some 45,000 square feet (4,200 sq. meters) of sail and in her time plied the oceans from Europe to India to South America with various cargo.

The *Peking*, a bark built in 1911 in Hamburg, Germany, also has four masts, the tallest standing 18 stories high. On its return trips after bearing cargo from Europe to South America it regularly transported nitrates for fertilizer purposes. It was used as a training vessel in England for 40 years and was acquired by the Museum in 1975.

The *Ambrose Lightship* was parked in 1908 at the entrance to New York Harbor to serve as a beacon guiding ships safely in from the Atlantic Ocean. It was replaced in 1932 by an actual beacon tower and ultimately donated to the Museum by the U.S. Coast Guard.

Three operational vessels are used for sail training programs and other purposes, and are available for private charter: the *Pioneer*, a cargo schooner built in 1885; the *Lettie G. Howard*, an old (1893) fishing schooner that brought back many a catch to Gloucester, South Street and other places; and the tugboat *W. O. Decker*. There is also a Pilot House on Pier 16 that was once part of a steam tugboat that ferried passengers across the harbor waters.

On Pier 15 is a Maritime Crafts Center in which craft specialists demonstrate the techniques

ABOVE: The four-masted, steel-hulled *Peking* is one of the largest sailing vessels ever built.

RIGHT: A Cunard poster from the Museum's Der Scutt collection of models and memorabilia.

offering appropriately democratic vistas of the nearby Brooklyn Bridge. Altogether, the Seaport district has more than 50 shops and some 30 food emporiums.

Also nearby is the Fulton Fish Market, oldest of its kind, and, across Fulton Street, the equally venerable Schermerhorn Row, built in 1810–12 to house maritime offices and warehouses.

Fish has been sold here continuously since the early years of the 19th century, and in a structure of corrugated metal known as the Tin Building starting in 1907. Now, however, the business is shifting to the large Hunts Point food center in the Bronx. The market, with its busy midnight-to-dawn operation, was unique in the life of the city.

Ship owner Peter Schermerhorn's row of buildings was constructed in a distinctive Georgian Federal style on land reclaimed from the East River. The timing was fortuitous, since in 1814 operators of a new ferry service from Brooklyn – it became the famous Fulton Ferry – needed a terminal location, and Schermerhorn was able to

of carving and model ship making. Over at the intersection of Fulton and Water Streets is the Titanic Memorial Lighthouse; it commemorates the huge loss of life that occurred when the *Titanic* rammed an iceberg in 1912.

Water Street has several galleries devoted to maritime topics and local history, exhibiting ship models, paintings, prints, watercolors, books and memorabilia, and accommodating lectures, tours and a range of special programs. Bowne & Co., Stationers, at 211 Water Street, has printing presses from early periods. The Chandlery at 209 Water Street has books on ships and local history.

The Museum also runs New York Unearthed, an off-site archaeology center where visitors can examine artifacts documenting some 6,000 years of New York history and watch archaeologists and conservators at work in a glass-enclosed lab.

Food and drink: Most visitors browse in the food court, though there are several good places within a few minutes of the waterfront. Try the North Star Pub (93 South St, 212-509-6757, inexpensive) for shepherd's pie, fish and chips, and other pub grub. Wash it down with a pint of Guinness or a single-malt scotch. Overlooking the Seaport, the Yankee Clipper (170 John St, 212-344-5959, expensive) serves up fresh seafood, including crab cakes, lobster ravioli and a delicious New England clam chowder. Non-fish meals are also available.

Statue of Liberty

Perhaps the most famous sculpture in the world, Lady Liberty has stood watch over New York Harbor for more than a century.

Map reference: pages 52–53, B6
Liberty Island, NY 10004.
Tel: 212-363-3200, www.nps.gov/stli
Subway to ferry: 4 or 5 to Bowling Green. Bus to ferry: M15 to Battery Park. Ferry: Statue of Liberty & Ellis Island Ferry from Battery Park (212-269-5755) or Liberty State Park, N.J. (201-435-9499). Tickets sold on a first-come, first-served basis. Daily 9am-5pm.
Free admission, museum store, café, wheelchair access to 10th floor observation area only.

I t was one of the most festive days in the history of New York City. On July 4, 1986, the streets and piers along the harbor were packed with an estimated 2 million people, among them President Ronald Reagan, all of whom were gathered to watch a majestic parade of modern warships and ancient windjammers – and, after dark, to witness a stupendous pyrotechnic display of more than 40,000 shells. "We expected

The Seaport's resident woodcarver works at the Maritime Craft Center, Pier 16.

the best fireworks since Nero set Rome on fire," said New York Mayor Edward Koch, "and we got them."

The occasion was no ordinary Fourth of July but the rededication of the Statue of Liberty, splendidly restored in honor of the 100th anniversary of its original unveiling at a similar fireworks celebration attended by President Grover Cleveland. During that first century in which it had stood on Liberty Island (formerly Bedloes Island), the statue had become far more than the symbol of international friendship it was originally intended to be. It had become, and remains, a national icon – a touchstone for the very best things America represents. Even today, when most immigrants to the United States arrive by air, the Statue of Liberty looms in the popular imagination as a sort of goddess of welcome, as she was for the steamship-borne multitudes who arrived when she was new.

The Statue of Liberty – its formal name, as a work of sculpture, is *Liberty Enlightening the World* – was a gift to the United States from the people of France. It was conceived by a French admirer of American democracy named Edouard-René Lefebvre de Laboulaye, who conveyed his enthusiasm to the sculptor Frédéric-Auguste Bartholdi. Bartholdi not only designed the monument (using as his inspiration a combination of Delacroix's painting *Liberty Leading the People to the Barricades* and the stern visage of his own mother), he also took a leading role in raising funds for its construction.

Bartholdi raised 1 million francs – worth about $400,000 at the time – and began with a clay model of his statue, enlarging it in three stages until the copper segments of its outer surface were ready to be assembled. The iron frame was designed by Alexandre-Gustave Eiffel, the engineer who later created the Eiffel Tower. On July 4, 1884, the finished work was formally presented to the United States at a ceremony in Paris. It remained for the statue to be dismantled, shipped to New York, and re-assembled. The U.S. government had already donated the island, which had outlived its military usefulness, but little had been done beyond laying the cornerstone and 15 feet (5 meters) of masonry for the statue's massive pedestal, designed by Richard Morris Hunt. In what might be taken as ingratitude or at least indifference to France's monumental gift, fundraising for the pedestal had slowed to a trickle.

To the rescue came a prominent New Yorker who was himself an immigrant. He was the owner and publisher of the *New York World*, Joseph Pulitzer by name, and with a zeal that quadrupled the circulation of his newspaper while pulling in thousands of modest pledges for the statue's cause, he raised more than $100,000 to put Liberty on her pedestal. The dedication was celebrated on October 28, 1886 (construction couldn't be completed by July 4, the date which has figured so prominently in the statue's history), and the monument soon became a major tourist attraction.

Later, in 1903, a plaque inscribed with Emma Lazarus's sonnet *The New Colossus* was installed in the pedestal. Written for a fund-raiser, the poem concludes with the now-famous lines, "Give me your tired, your poor,/Your huddled masses yearning to breathe free,/The wretched refuse of your teeming shore,/Send these, the homeless, tempest-tost to me,/I lift my lamp beside the golden door!"

Big-boned gal

The statue, depicting Liberty in the allegorical figure of a woman stepping free from broken shackles, stands 151 feet (46 meters) from the bottom of her sandals to the tip of her torch. The granite pedestal, including the star-shaped base that was originally part of the bastions of Fort Wood, adds another 142 feet (43 meters) to the statue's height. The width of the head is 10 feet (3 meters), and each eye is 2½ feet (80 cm) across. The upraised arm bearing the torch is 42 feet long (13 meters) and reaches a height (torch included) of more than 300 feet (92 meters) above sea level. The statue's waist is 35 feet (11 meters) in diameter. In the left hand is a tablet, variously described as representing a book of law or the Declaration of Independence, inscribed "July 4, 1776."

The 225-ton statue is made of hammered copper less than an eighth of an inch (3 mm) thick. Like all untreated copper exposed to the elements, it has acquired a green patina called verdigris. This copper skin weathered remarkably well over the statue's first century, but serious problems had developed with Eiffel's interior trusswork. Corrosion of the iron strapping threatened the integrity of the entire monument. The upraised right arm was in particular danger; it had been swaying for more than 60 years, and visitors had long been barred from the torch viewing platform accessible via a narrow staircase inside the arm.

The four-year restoration, which was undertaken in conjunction with the refurbishing of nearby Ellis Island and which cost $66 million for the statue alone, involved replacing the entire system of iron strapping with stainless steel. Access to the viewing platform in Liberty's crown is still via a spiral staircase that wraps around the central pylon, although interior views are more dramatic now that the staircase's old wire mesh enclosure has been removed to reveal the intricate folds of the statue's copper "robe." The torch, which remains inaccessible, was another focus of renovation. Its flame had originally been composed of curving panels of glass, lit from within. These have been replaced with a flame of gold leaf – Bartholdi's original intention – which shines brilliantly in sunlight.

Head rush

Now that exhibits pertaining to immigration history are concentrated at Ellis Island, the small museum at the Statue of Liberty is devoted primarily to the history of the monument itself. Located in the base, the museum displays photographs, plans, tools and models that trace the construction of Bartholdi's heroically-scaled project, and of the 1980s restoration. There are also films, photos and recordings that relate the role of the statue as an icon for immigrants, and its status as a symbol of American ideals.

Visitors wishing to ascend to the statue's crown should keep in mind that this is a slow and sometimes uncomfortable process. On especially busy days, the combined wait and stairway ascent can take two to three hours, and summer temperatures inside the statue can reach 110°F (43°C). Even if the climb to the crown proves impossible or inconvenient, visitors can reach the 10th floor observation deck via elevator.

Food and drink: There's a small cafeteria on Liberty Island with indoor and outdoor dining areas.

Twilight colors the sky behind Lady Liberty, standing some 300 feet above the waters of New York Harbor.

Historic Houses

Lifestyles of the rich and famous and others, too, are examined at several preserved residences. The exhibits give visitors an intimate glimpse into how life was lived once upon a time in New York City

Alice Austen House

"Clear Comfort" is the restored Victorian Gothic home and garden of Alice Austen, one of America's first female documentary photographers.

Map reference: pages 52–53, B8
2 Hylan Blvd, Staten Island, NY 10305.
Tel: 718-816-4506, www.aliceausten.8m.com
Bus: S51 from ferry terminal to Bay St-Hylan Blvd
Thurs–Sun, noon–5pm.
Admission fee, museum shop, limited wheel-chair access (call ahead).

Alice Austen's documentary photographs offer a rare window onto America in the late 19th century. She was one of the first women photographers to work outside a studio and chose among her many subjects the immigrant community and other less genteel aspects of metropolitan life. Clear Comfort, her home overlooking the Narrows at the entrance to New York Harbor, recalls her roots in an older, more comfortable New York.

Now a National Historic Landmark, the extensively restored Carpenter Gothic cottage built around an 18th-century Dutch farmhouse was home to Alice for most of her life (1866–1952). She was introduced to photography here at the age of 10 by her Uncle Oswald, a clipper ship captain. Over the next seven decades, she made approximately 9,000 images.

Financial difficulties and ill health forced Austen into a city poorhouse in 1945. She died seven years later at age 86, her last days made more comfortable by *Life* magazine's rediscovery of her work. When Clear Comfort was threatened with destruction in the 1960s, the Friends of Alice Austen House raised money to save and restore it, using Austen's own photos as a guide. Alice Austen's interest in flowers – she was a founding member of the Staten Island Garden Club – is immediately evident: the lawn and gardens provide a magnificent framework for views of the Verrazano-Narrows Bridge, the Statue of Liberty and Manhattan.

Visitors can tour most rooms, including the formal parlor and the casual middle parlor, Alice's bedroom, and the 18th-century dining room and kitchen. The tiny darkroom where she spent countless hours developing and printing is off limits, but 50 of her photographs are on permanent display in the house.

Food and drink: Good Fella's Old World Brick Oven Pizza (1718 Hylan Blvd, 718-987-2422, moderate) is a traditional pizza parlor with fancy choices like pizza à la vodka.

Dyckman Farmhouse Museum

The only surviving 18th-century farmhouse in Manhattan offers a unique glimpse into an age when farms and orchards dominated the island's northern tip.

Map reference: pages 52–53, E1
4881 Broadway at 204th St, 10034.
Tel: 212-304-9422.
Subway: A or 1 to 207th St. Bus: M100 to 204th St.
Tues–Sun 10am–4pm.
Admission fee, concerts, lectures, children's craft program, no wheelchair access.

William Dyckman, a descendant of the earliest Dutch settlers of northern Manhattan, built his first farmhouse near upper Broadway in 1748. The house was burned during the American Revolution, and Dyckman built the present structure about 1784 in

LEFT:
Alice Austen (standing) and friends.

OPPOSITE:
Edgar Allan Poe lived in the Bronx for three years before his death in 1849.

Built in Dutch style about 1784, the Dyckman Farmhouse reflects the simple comforts of colonial life.

the typical Dutch colonial style, with thick stone walls, a wooden upper story, a gambrel roof, and distinctive split "Dutch" doors. An attached summer kitchen is probably 50 years older than the main house.

The Dyckman house, focal point of one of Manhattan's largest farms, totaling some 450 acres (180 hectares), was still bordered by apple orchards a century ago. In 1915, much of the property was purchased by sisters Mary Alice Dyckman Dean and Fannie Frederika Dyckman Welch, descendants of the original owners. They restored the building and its landscaping, and presented the property to the City of New York.

Although not original to the Dyckman family, furnishings in the house are typical of the late 18th and early 19th centuries. The kitchen hearth is equipped with iron cranes for suspending cooking utensils and the full complement of pots, skillets and a reflector oven necessary for preparing meals over an open fire. The parlor and dining room are more formally furnished in a style befitting a comfortable, though not wealthy, landowning family of the era. (The dining chairs once belonged to the father of Samuel F. B. Morse.) A "relic room" displays artifacts of everyday early American life excavated in the vicinity.

Visitors are reminded of Manhattan's role in the early campaigns of the American Revolution by a replica of a log Hessian Officers' Hut, built in 1916 in adjacent Dyckman Park. An herb and vegetable garden, smokehouse and formal boxwood garden planted with heirloom flowers add to the period character.

Food and drink: The airy, oak-paneled New Leaf Café (1 Margaret Corbin Dr, 212-568-5323, moderate) at the southern entrance to nearby Fort Tryon Park, uses Hudson Valley ingredients to turn out creative salads, sandwiches, and beef and chicken dishes.

Edgar Allan Poe Cottage

The Bronx home of Edgar Allan Poe recalls one of the few settled periods in the author's troubled life.

Map reference: pages 52–53, E1
Grand Concourse and East Kingsbridge Rd, Bronx, NY 10458.
Tel: 718-881-8900.
Subway: D or 4 to Kingsbridge Rd. Bus: BX1, BX2, BX32 to Kingsbridge Rd; BX12 or BX24 to Grand Concourse; BX15 or BX17 to Fordham

Plaza; BX9, BX26, BX28 or BX34 to 194th St.
Sat 10am–4pm, Sun 1pm–4pm.
Admission fee, gift shop, no wheelchair access.

Poet, critic and short story writer Edgar Allan Poe moved to this wooden farmhouse in 1846 with his young wife Virginia and her mother, Maria Clemm. Poe, who had lived in Manhattan during the preceding two years, vainly hoped that the quaint surroundings and country air of what was then the village of Fordham would help Virginia recover from tuberculosis. Alas, she died in 1847, after which the disconsolate author remained at the cottage to write his grief-inspired poem "Annabel Lee" as well as "Ulalume" and "The Bells." This was Poe's last home; he died in Baltimore during a lecture tour in 1849.

Built about 1812, the Poe Cottage was moved to the present location in Poe Park from its original site in 1913. Administered by the Bronx Historical Society, it has been restored to its 1840s appearance and includes several items associated with the author, including his rocking chair and Virginia's deathbed. Admission to the cottage includes a film about Poe's life and his contributions to American literature.

Food and drink: *You'll find decent diner food at Poe Coffee Shop (2432 Grand Concourse, 718-365-6717, inexpensive).*

Merchant's House Museum

Little has changed at this downtown residence after a century of ownership by a single family.

Map reference: pages 48–49, E4
29 E. 4th St (at Lafayette), 10003.
Tel: 212-777-1089, www.merchantshouse.com
Subway: N or R to 8th St, 6 to Astor Place, F to Broadway-Lafayette. Bus: M1, M5, M6 to 4th St.
Thurs–Mon 1pm–5pm.
Admission fee, shop, no wheelchair access.

In 1835, wealthy merchant Seabury Tredwell moved with his wife and seven children into a three-year-old brick and marble row house in an upscale "suburb" to the north of burgeoning lower Manhattan. Although his office was some distance away, near today's South Street Seaport, Tredwell was able to hop aboard an omnibus each morning along with other pioneering Manhattan commuters.

The Tredwells' home, with handsome dormer windows and a fanlight above the front entrance, was similar to many of the late Federal-era row houses that lined the streets in the then-fashionable area. It was fitted out with all of the latest technological conveniences, including gas lights, a 4,000-gallon (15,000-liter) cistern, and a system of bells for summoning four live-in servants. Formal parlors done in the new Greek Revival style had matching black-and-gold marble mantelpieces and mahogany pocket doors. Special touches included a magnificent Ionic double-column screen and matching plaster ceiling medallions. The Tredwells furnished the rooms with pieces made by renowned New York artisans,

ABOVE: The Poe Cottage's sparse interior; though the poet had achieved some critical success, his finances remained shaky.

LEFT: The Merchant's House is a fashionable residence of the mid-19th century.

including Duncan Phyfe and Joseph Meeks.

As the Tredwell family grew – Gertrude, the youngest, was born in 1840 – the neighborhood changed at a typically relentless New York pace. By the end of the Civil War, businesses had moved into many of the row houses that had been left vacant as their owners moved to more desirable uptown neighborhoods. Over the next 20 years, many homes were replaced by workshops and factories.

Through all the changes, the Tredwells remained in their home until Gertrude, who never married and who made few alterations to the house and its contents (including such personal items as gloves, hats and parasols), died there in 1933. Three years later, the house opened as a museum. Today this National Historic Landmark is once again in the middle of an upscale neighborhood: the area, called NoHo (North of Houston), has recently experienced a rebirth and is filled with chic bistros, theaters and fashionable shops.

Seven rooms on three floors, along with the Tredwells' "secret" garden, are open to the public for self-guided tours. A free self-guided walking tour of the neighborhood is also available; guided walking tours are offered on weekends.

A portrait of the family matriarch, Eliza Parker Tredwell, hangs in the front parlor.

Food and drink: After visiting one museum, have a sandwich and an ale at another. McSorley's Old Ale House (15 E. 7th St, 212-473-9148, inexpensive), founded in 1854, is New York's oldest watering hole and looks it. Proprietors have taken pains not to change anything, from the potbellied stove to the dusty paraphernalia hanging on the walls. An old-time favorite is the ploughman's lunch of cheese, crackers and onions accompanied, of course, by the house brew, which comes cheaper if you buy two mugs at a time.

Morris-Jumel Mansion

This old house in upper Manhattan has connections to some of the leading historic figures of the 18th and 19th centuries.

Map reference: pages 52–53, D2
65 Jumel Terrace (between W. 160th and W. 162nd Sts), 10032.
Tel: 212-923-8008.
Subway: C to 163rd St. Bus: M3, M18 or M101 to 160th St.
Wed–Sun 10am–4pm.
Admission fee, limited wheelchair access.

Two rich, beautiful women figure in the story of the Morris-Jumel Mansion, the oldest surviving residence in Manhattan. One was the well-bred Mary Philipse Morris, first lady of the house when it was built in 1765. The other was

the not so well-bred Eliza Bowen Jumel, an eccentric old recluse when she died there exactly a century later.

Mary Philipse is thought to have been the object of the young George Washington's affections. Whether true or not, the man she chose to marry in 1758 was his onetime fellow officer, the English-born Colonel Roger Morris. The Morrises intended the Palladian-style Georgian mansion as a country villa in Harlem Heights (now Washington Heights) a dozen miles from their residence in downtown Manhattan. Built of brick encased in wood siding, it originally had 19 rooms on its two floors plus a garret for the servants.

The Morrises were unsympathetic to the Revolution, so their mansion was confiscated and used for a time in 1776 as a base of operations for General Washington – its high elevation afforded a commanding view of upper Manhattan – but it was seized by British forces and became wartime headquarters for General Henry Clinton. Washington returned there as president in 1790 for a dinner with his Cabinet, including Alexander Hamilton, then Secretary of the Treasury. The property was neglected until its purchase in 1810 by French merchant Stephen Jumel.

His wife – and erstwhile mistress – Eliza Bowen Jumel saw to it that the property was modernized and its furnishings upgraded in lavish style. But past dalliances caused her to be shunned by New York society and the Jumels moved to France in 1815, finding greater acceptance there as well as a relationship with Napoleon Bonaparte, newly deposed as emperor. Upon her husband's death in New York in 1832, "Madame Jumel" inherited the mansion, and there in 1833 she married Aaron Burr, an old acquaintance (and Hamilton's fatal adversary). It was a practical union for Burr, who was more interested in the Jumel fortune (which he quickly squandered) than the madame herself, and divorce soon followed. Madame Jumel died in her nineties at the mansion in 1865.

The mansion was acquired by the City of New York in 1903, and extensive restoration has been conducted in recent years. Points of interest include the front parlor in which Burr and Madame Jumel were married. The room contains Burr's drop-lid desk, made about 1820. The dining room has a complement of 12 chairs and a settee by the famed New York cabinetmaker Duncan

Phyfe. The mansion's octagonal room, used for entertaining, was unique to the American colonies at the time the house was built. The room is decorated with a distinctive hand-painted wallpaper.

On the second floor, the wide hall has a large portrait of Madame Jumel and her two grandchildren (through adoption). Notable among the furnishings in Madame Jumel's bedroom is a mahogany sleigh bed that reputedly had been used by Napoleon. There is a strong flavor of French Empire influence. Aaron Burr's bedroom is on display as well, as is the second-floor office thought to have been used by Washington.

The Morris-Jumel Mansion (top), built in 1765, is a masterpiece of Georgian architecture. The dining room (bottom) is decorated in the style of the 1790s.

Food and drink: A picnic lunch can be enjoyed in nearby Roger Morris Park.

The "Ladies' Parlor" at the Mount Vernon Hotel Museum.

Mount Vernon Hotel Museum and Garden

Popular as a country hotel some 175 years ago, the Mount Vernon offers a glimpse of a vanished rural Manhattan.

Map reference: pages 50–51, F5
421 E. 61st St (between First Ave and York), 10021.
Tel: 212-838-6878.
Subway: N or R to Lexington Ave, 4, 5 or 6 to 59th St. Bus: M15 or M31 to 61st St, M57 to 60th St and York Ave.
Tues–Sun 11am–4pm, Tues to 9pm June and July. Admission fee, guided tour, concerts, lectures, youth programs, limited wheelchair access.

During the 1820s and 1830s, the area that encompasses today's Upper East Side was an outer suburb of New York City. Among the popular institutions of that era were "day hotels," places that offered overnight lodging but were patronized primarily as restaurants and taverns by the fashionable set during their country excursions. The stone hotel was originally constructed in 1799 as a carriage house on the estate of Colonel William Stephen Smith and his wife Abigail Adams Smith, daughter of President John Adams. After the main house was destroyed by fire in 1826, the carriage house was converted into a hotel, as its location made it accessible to travelers arriving either by carriage or by boat on the East River.

The hotel operated only until 1833, after which the building remained in private hands until it was purchased by the Colonial Dames of America and opened to the public (originally as the Abigail Adams Smith Museum) in 1939. Restored to its appearance as a day hotel, the Mount Vernon is furnished with more than 1,000 works of art and decorative objects from the period, including numerous articles of furniture made by 19th-century New York craftsmen. Nine rooms are included in the museum tour.

The museum garden, a secluded spot in the midst of the bustling neighborhood that now occupies the old Smith estate, is planted in the Dutch style popular in New York at the time. It features species common to gardens of that era, including Hawthorn trees, rhododendron, wisteria, wild cherry, grape hyacinth and crocus.

Food and drink: Angel's (1135 First Ave between 62nd and 63rd Sts, 212-980-3131, moderate) serves satisfying portions of home-cooked Italian pasta, chicken and seafood. The international menu at the casual East Side Café (189 E. Broadway, 212-387-0366, moderate) includes everything from gyros and lasagna to corned beef sandwiches.

Theodore Roosevelt Birthplace

A replica of the 26th president's birthplace and boyhood home, this brownstone recalls upper-middle-class life in the mid-19th century and houses memorabilia of Roosevelt's political career.

Map reference: pages 48–49, E2
28 E. 20th St (between Broadway and Park Ave), 10003.
Tel: 212-260-1616, www.nps.gov/thrb/
Subway: N, R or 6 to 23rd St. Bus: M1, M2, M3, M6 or M7 to 20th St.
Wed–Sun 9am–5pm.
Admission fee, guided tours on the hour (last tour at 4pm), no wheelchair access.

In 1854, wealthy New York importer Cornelius Roosevelt purchased a pair of three-story brownstone houses in what was then a residential neighborhood as gifts for his sons, Robert and Theodore. Four years later, Theodore's wife, Martha Bulloch Roosevelt, gave birth to Theodore Roosevelt, Jr., at the East 20th Street address. The future president and his family lived here until he was 14, when, after a yearlong trip to Europe, they moved to a newly fashionable West 57th Street address.

In 1916, the owners of the building on East 20th Street had it demolished and replaced with a nondescript two-story commercial structure. Three years later, following the ex-president's death, a committee of prominent citizens purchased the site, removed the new building, and faithfully replicated the Roosevelt home. With adjacent museum galleries on the site of the Robert Roosevelt house, the birthplace – now the property of the National Park Service – has been open to the public since 1923.

Nearly half of the furnishings at the site belonged to the family during their residence here. They are displayed in an interior that re-creates the appearance of the house following an 1865 redecoration and fourth-floor addition. On the main floor, the formal parlor, library and dining room are furnished in the Rococo Revival furniture that typified upper-middle-class taste in the 1860s; in the library is a small red velvet chair used by Roosevelt as a boy, and a pair of mantelpiece obelisks purchased during the family's 1872 visit to Egypt.

Upstairs is the master bedroom, with Roosevelt's parents' original rosewood and satinwood furnishings and an oil portrait of his mother; the nursery, with a chair and crib that belonged to the president; and the little gymnasium where he exercised as a child to improve his precarious health.

Food and drink: Gramercy Tavern (42 E. 20th St, 212-477-0777, expensive) has a superb wine list, exquisite decor and continental fare, including lamb, chicken and seafood. Nearby, the herb- and flower-filled garden at the elegant Verbena (54 Irving Place, 212-260-5454, expensive) is a lovely spot to enjoy American fare prepared with a Mediterranean influence. Tapas are served in a small bar.

Theodore Roosevelt was born and raised in a three-story brownstone near Gramercy Park.

The plant kingdom and how it blooms is the theme at
New York's major botanical parks, while at a third center
visitors get a hands-on opportunity to explore scientific
principles with a variety of interactive exhibits

Brooklyn Botanic Garden

A tree – and much else – grows in Brooklyn at this urban oasis with more than 12,000 carefully nurtured plants and flowers.

Map reference: pages 52–53, D6
1000 Washington Ave, Brooklyn, NY 11225.
Tel: 718-623-7200, www.bbg.org
Subway: S, Q to Prospect Park or 1, 2 to Eastern
Pkwy-Brooklyn Museum. Bus: B41, B43, B48 and
B71 to Flatbush Ave or Eastern Pkwy entrances.
Tues–Fri 8am–4.30pm, Sat–Sun 10am–4.30pm,
until 6pm Apr–Sep.
Admission fee (except Tues–Sat morning Nov to
mid-March), café, gift shop, guided tours,
education programs, concerts, wheelchair access.

Despite an ignominious start as an ash dump, the Brooklyn Botanic Garden has become one of the country's finest examples of urban gardening and horticultural display. Opened to the public on July 1, 1910, it was originally laid out by two sons of Frederick Law Olmsted, the co-creator of adjacent Prospect Park. The design was subsequently perfected by longtime (1912–45) staff landscape architect Harold Caparn, who conceived Magnolia Plaza and the Cranford Rose Garden, among other floral delights.

Today the Brooklyn Botanic Garden is renowned for its many specialty gardens and extensive research and educational programs. Plants, trees and flowers from around the world are displayed on the 52-acre (21-hectare) grounds and in the Steinhardt Conservatory. With regular concerts, festivals and special events, the garden is also a mainstay of the city's cultural landscape, offering visitors and residents alike a place to stop, unwind and "smell the roses."

Entering from Eastern Parkway, a path leads to the Osborne Garden – a vision of sweeping green edged by walkways that pass beneath wisteria-draped pergolas. The adjoining terrace, reached by gradual granite steps, has a cascading fountain made from a single piece of limestone, and fluted columns modeled after those of the Boboli Garden in Florence.

All this romantic formality ends farther south, where the Native Flora Garden includes a bog, a meadow, pine trees and wildflowers common to the New York region. But order is restored at the Cranford Rose Garden, where climbers and ramblers tumble over arches, and hybrid teas and old garden roses bloom in immaculately tended beds. Beginning in early June, more than 5,000 rosebushes of over a thousand cultivars fill the air with intoxicating sweetness.

On the other side of the rose garden, the Cherry Esplanade's double-flowering Japanese cherry trees and the equally splendid specimens along neighboring Cherry Walk are a major attraction beginning in early April. (Check the Garden's Web site for updates on blossoming time.)

The adjacent Japanese Hill and Pond Garden is one of New York's most popular oases of tranquility. A viewing pavilion, pond, waterfall and graceful bridges combine with dreamy, Zen-like landscapes that are as lovely in winter, when snow drifts over stone lanterns, as in spring, when the pond fills with the blurry pink-cloud reflections of the surrounding cherry trees.

Leading to the Beaux-Arts administration building designed by McKim, Mead & White, the pink, ivory and purple blossoms of Magnolia Plaza, first planted in 1932 by Harold Caparn, are another spring attraction. They begin to bloom in late March in tandem with the daffodils on a nearby hill, and some last through early June.

Formal ponds filled with water lilies front the adjacent Steinhardt Conservatory, which contains tropical, temperate and desert pavilions, starting with a large, lush rainforest with its own waterfall and streams. Before leaving, follow the Trail of Evolution tracing the development of the natural world over billions of years, and marvel at the

OPPOSITE:
Spring at the New York Botanical Garden.

BELOW: The Japanese Garden at the Brooklyn Botanic Garden.

the Immortal Bard's plays. Nearby is the start of the Celebrity Path, along which names of famous Brooklynites such as Barbra Streisand and Mae West have been immortalized in stone. Meandering through thickets of Austrian pines and rhododendrons, it ends at the Alfred T. White Memorial, a shady hillside concert spot which honors the local philanthropist who, in 1909, donated $25,000 to make the Brooklyn Botanic Garden a reality.

Next to the Conservatory, the Garden Gift Shop sells everything from plants, seeds, soil and containers to stationery, posters and gardening

The Cherry Esplanade (above) and lily pond (below) at the Brooklyn Botanic Garden.

century-old bonsai trees on display in the C. V. Starr Bonsai Museum. The Aquatic House features orchids and tropical water plants, and there's an art gallery with exhibitions of botanical and nature-inspired works.

Other must-sees include the children's Discovery Garden, near the Flatbush Avenue entrance, and the small but delightful Herb Garden, Fragrance Garden and Shakespeare Garden clustered along Washington Avenue. Reminiscent of an English cottage garden, the Shakespeare Garden features more than 80 plants mentioned in

books. The Garden Visitor Center, located in the administration building, has maps, brochures and information about special events. Free guided tours are offered at 1pm on weekends, except major holidays.

Food and drink: The Terrace Café by the Steinhardt Conservatory is open year-round for lunch, with seating outside from spring to early fall, and inside the Conservatory in late fall and winter. The menu changes seasonally and includes salads, homemade soups, smoked turkey sandwiches, veggie burgers and chicken pot pies, as well as assorted beverages and desserts.

New York Botanical Garden

One of the world's premier botanical centers features miles of idyllic pathways, an array of specialty gardens, and a magnificent conservatory.

Map reference: pages 52–53, F1
200th St and Southern Blvd, Bronx, NY 10458.
Tel: 718-817-8700, www.nybg.org
Subway: 4, D, B to Bedford Park Blvd (transfer to Bx26 bus or walk 8 blocks east); Metro-North Railroad from Grand Central to Botanical Garden. Bus: Shuttle from Metropolitan Museum of Art (82nd St and Fifth Ave) Fri–Sun (Sat only Nov–Dec); call 718-817-8700 for reservations. Tues–Sun 10am–4pm (to 6pm Apr–Oct). Admission fee, café, gift shop, guided tours, special shows and exhibitions, educational programs, wheelchair access.

Three of New York's power brokers reached into their deep pockets, pulled out $250,000 between them and came up with the seed money for the New York Botanical Garden. The year was 1891, the money-men were Cornelius Vanderbilt, Andrew Carnegie and J. P. Morgan, and the funds went to purchase a 250-acre (100-hectare) parcel of what was then Bronx Park.

But it was a fourth man who was the project's guiding light and its first director-in-chief: Nathaniel Lord Britton, a botanist at Columbia University. Actually, he always gave credit for the garden's creation to his wife, Elizabeth. A distinguished botanist in her own right, it was she who suggested, after the Brittons had toured London's Kew Gardens in 1888, that a botanical garden be established on this side of the Atlantic.

Most important to Mr. Britton was the establishment of a scientific research center, a function the garden still serves. More than a century after the botanical garden's founding, the new International Plant Science Center is ranked among the top herbaria in the world and currently holds more than a dozen federal research grants. There's also a Beaux-Arts-style Library Building with galleries and a lecture hall, and a renowned educational program with classes for beginners right up to graduate students.

For the casual visitor, however, its main claim to fame are the 48 specialty gardens and plant collections that offer welcome sanctuary from the frenetic pace of city life only 20 minutes by train from midtown Manhattan. In spring, colorful drifts of daffodils, tulips, azaleas, magnolias and cherry trees resemble nothing so much as an Impressionist painting. In summer, the intoxicating scent of 2,700 blooming roses fills the Peggy Rockefeller Rose Garden, while the eye is tantalized by hibiscus, bold Shasta daisies and delicate wisteria. In fall, goldenrod, native witch hazel and autumn foliage brighten the view along forest paths and around the terrace of the picturesque Snuff Mill, built about 1840.

Winter brings its own delights, including a pristine vision of snow on deep-green pines, spruces and ornamental conifers.

A year-round attraction, especially on rainy days, the Enid A. Haupt Conservatory, a National Historic Landmark, contains a wealth of beautiful specimens from around the globe. Inside, a permanent exhibition called *A World of Plants* surveys the plant kingdom from lush tropical rain forests to the deserts of the American Southwest.

The Haupt Conservatory (top) and springtime bulbs (bottom) at the New York Botanical Garden.

A family outing at the Botanical Garden; an Adventure Garden and a series of educational programs are designed with children in mind.

Numerous special exhibits are also held here, including the annual Japanese garden, with an interior bonsai display and an adjacent demonstration garden of exquisite late-blooming chrysanthemums.

Not far away, the Everett Children's Adventure Garden has been a major attraction since opening in 1998. A 12-acre (5-hectare) indoor/outdoor nature discovery experience, it features a kid's herbarium and lab, a waterfall to splash around in, and two separate mazes: one of boulders, the other of hedges and ivy-covered arches. Children can even conduct their own experiments – including building a giant bird's nest.

Adventures of a different sort await visitors to the 40-acre (16-hectare) Forest, where raccoons and skunks might be spotted in the underbrush, and red-tailed hawks occasionally swoop overhead. The majestic oaks, beech and surviving hemlocks are among the last remnants of the wilderness that once blanketed the metropolitan area. Below well-marked paths, the Bronx River tumbles through a deep gorge banked by craggy outcroppings and spills over a 6-foot (2-meter) dam built in the 19th century to supply power to nearby Snuff Mill.

Like much of the surrounding land, the mill was originally owned by the descendants of Pierre Lorillard, a successful Manhattan tobacconist. His sons moved the family business to the Bronx in 1792, and the mill was kept in operation mixing rose petals and tobacco until 1870. In 1884, the building was acquired by the city, along with the property that eventually became the New York Botanical Garden.

The best place to start a tour of the garden is the Information Plaza just inside the main Conservatory Gate entrance off Southern Boulevard. Useful maps and information about weekend events and guided tours can be picked up here, as well as at the kiosk seasonally located inside the Mosholu Gate entrance, across from the Metro-North train station. Next to the Conservatory, there's also a well-stocked gift shop with an extensive array of gardening and garden-related gifts.

Food and drink: Lunch and snacks are available in the Garden Café, near the Mosholu Gate entrance. It's open year-round, and the menu includes soups, salads, sandwiches, hamburgers and hot entrees (weekdays only), along with sweets and beverages. There are picnic tables near the Everett Children's Adventure Garden, the Snuff Mill and on the Snuff Mill River Terrace.

New York Hall of Science

A hands-on science center explores the worlds of physics, chemistry and biology and their relation to everyday life.

Map reference: pages 52–53, F4
47-01 111th St (Flushing Meadows Corona Park), Queens, NY 11368.
Tel: 718-699-0005, www.nyhallsci.org
Subway: 7 to 111th St (walk south on 111th St to park entrance at 49th Ave). Bus: Q48 to Roosevelt Ave and 111 St, Q23 or Q58 to Corona Ave and 51st Ave.
Tues–Wed 9.30am–2pm (to 5pm in summer), Thurs–Sun 9.30am–5pm.
Admission fee (free Sept–June Thurs–Fri 2pm–5pm), museum shop, wheelchair access.

At the New York Hall of Science, visitors learn what makes roses red, how mold gets on Roquefort cheese, and why atoms behave as they do. The best part is that it's all fun: kids may not even realize that this is a serious museum devoted to teaching how the world works.

The interactive exhibits permit visitors to explore scientific principles at their own pace. The new Pfizer Foundation Biochemistry Discovery Lab, the first hands-on lab of its type in the world, is devoted entirely to biochemistry. Here visitors can measure, mix and mash to explore the chemistry of living things. In *Hidden Kingdoms: The Worlds of Microbes*, visitors step through the eye of a giant 12-foot-tall (4-meter) sewing needle into the world of microorganisms to learn how these tiny creatures affect our health and environment.

Other exhibits include *Marvelous Molecules*, where an infrared camera maps out the hottest spots in a person's body and guests can build their own hands-on molecular models. *Realm of the Atom* features a moving three-dimensional model of an atom magnified one billion times. *Seeing the Light*, with 91 hands-on exhibits, allows visitors to experiment with the properties of color, light and visual perception. *Sound Sensations* takes the mystery out of everyday audio devices such as CDs and tape recorders. In *Feedback*, a wide variety of mechanical and biological systems explore how machines and living things sense and adapt to changes in their

environment. In a room designed by composer Ron Kuivila, visitors use their shadows to compose computer-controlled synthesized music.

The *Living Carpet* draws on imagery inspired by the Greek myth of Theseus, Ariadne and the Minotaur to give visitors an "immersion experience." Their footsteps on 200 hidden floor sensors create a "ballet of human images," causing projected images to metamorphose. Every few minutes the installation transforms into another dream phase, creating a new mythical world of feelings, dreams and emotions. In the Technology Gallery, *Gateway to Cyberspace* offers visitors unlimited Internet access.

The Science Playground, open from April through November, weather permitting (additional fee), is designed for active bodies and inquisitive minds. The 30,000-square-foot (2,800-sq-meter) outdoor laboratory invites total physical immersion, with exhibits such as a giant spider web designed for climbing, oversized slides, windmills and a water play area with exhibits such as Archimedes' Screw, a contraption that causes water to flow uphill.

"Explainers" are on hand to help visitors get the most out of each exhibit, and an audio tour is available to rent in the lobby.

The museum is on the grounds of 1,125-acre (455-hectare) Corona Park, site of the 1964–65 World's Fair, and was built as a Fair pavilion. The park's centerpiece is the 140-foot-high (43-meter), 380-ton steel *Unisphere*.

Food and drink: Stroll over to Lemon Ice King (52-02 108th St, 718-699-5133, inexpensive) for a genuine Italian ice. They come in a variety of flavors, including a few unusual choices like cantaloupe and peanut butter.

The New York Hall of Science, originally a pavilion at the 1964 World's Fair, features more than 200 interactive exhibits.

Books, Prints and Special Collections

Coins, manuscripts, Bibles and Fabergé eggs are among the hodgepodge of precious objects and curiosities contained in a number of specialized holdings, many reflecting the passions and eccentricities of their collectors

American Numismatic Society

Money is the subject of this uptown museum and a satellite exhibition in the Financial District.

Map reference: pages 52–53, D2
Audubon Terrace, Broadway at 155th St, 10032.
Tel: 212-234-3130, www.amnumsoc.org
Subway: 1 to 157th St. Bus: M4 or M5 to Broadway and 155th St.
Tues–Fri 9am–4.30pm.
Free admission, no wheelchair access.

Founded in 1858, the American Numismatic Society houses one of the world's most extensive collections of coins, medals and paper money. There are about a million objects in all, from nearly every culture and historic period one cares to imagine, as well as a reference library with some 100,000 books, pamphlets, manuscripts, auction catalogues and more.

The collection is especially strong in coinage from ancient Greece and Rome, the Near and Middle East after the rise of Islam, the Far East (particularly China), Latin America and the American colonial period, and a wide variety of private coinages. About 2,000 of the pieces are on display in two galleries at Society headquarters on Audubon Terrace in Harlem.

The exhibition *World of Coins* traces the history of coinage beginning in about 500 B.C. but is more than a mere survey. Instead, it draws connections between the style and composition of money and the economic, political and cultural context in which it was used. Serious coin collectors will be enthralled, but even visitors with a casual interest will find the display enlightening.

If schlepping uptown isn't in your travel plans, consider seeing the Society's downtown show, *Drachmas, Doubloons and Dollars: The History of Money*, a special, five-year exhibition at the Federal Reserve Bank of New York, 33 Liberty Street, in the Financial District. More than 800 of the Society's most valuable coins and medals are on display. Among the most noteworthy are a Brasher doubloon, a Confederate States half-dollar and a 20-dollar "Walking Liberty" gold piece designed by sculptor Augustus Saint-Gaudens, considered by some connoisseurs to be the most beautiful American coin ever minted. The exhibit is open Mon–Fri, 10am–4pm.

The Society's plans to move its headquarters to the Financial District have been delayed indefinitely due to the World Trade Center disaster of September 11, 2001. Visitors are advised to call ahead to make sure of the current location.

Food and drink: Options are limited in this area, so consider packing a lunch. ALCA Pizzeria (Broadway at 157th St, 212-491-4300, inexpensive) serves pizza and other Italian specialties. Sandwiches, meatloaf, burgers and other diner standbys are on the menu at Coral's Diner (Broadway at 159th St, 212-927-7545, inexpensive).

Cooper-Hewitt, National Design Museum

Housed in Andrew Carnegie's handsome Upper East Side mansion, this branch of the Smithsonian Institution showcases centuries of achievement in the art of design.

Map reference: pages 50–51, F1
2 E. 91st St (at Fifth Ave), 10128.
Tel: 212-849-8400, www.si.edu/ndm/
Subway: 4, 5, 6 to 86th St or 6 to 96th St.
Bus: M1, M2, M3 or M4 to 91st St.
Tues 10am–9pm, Wed–Sat 10am–5pm, Sun noon–5pm.
Admission fee, museum store, lectures, classes, workshops, wheelchair access (call ahead).

As the Smithsonian's National Design Museum, Cooper-Hewitt maintains comprehensive collections of decorative and applied arts and industrial design, fulfilling its original mission as a "visual library" chronicling the history of style. The founding of the Museum, and the gathering of its initial resources, was the accomplishment of Sarah, Eleanor and Amy Hewitt, granddaughters of industrialist and Cooper Union founder Peter Cooper. Initially housed at Cooper Union, the distinguished school of art and design located in Manhattan's East Village, the collection became a part of the Smithsonian Institution in 1963 and has been housed in the former Carnegie mansion since 1976.

Cooper-Hewitt's holdings are divided into four broad

OPPOSITE: A portrait of J. P. Morgan, Jr., hangs in the lavishly appointed West Room of the Morgan Library.

BELOW: A bandbox of cardboard and block-printed paper, made about 1830, from the Cooper-Hewitt collection.

The Cooper-Hewitt was originally the New York home of steel magnate Andrew Carnegie.

categories. The Department of Applied Arts and Industrial Design focuses on three-dimensional objects. Some 40,000 individual items are in the collection, ranging from antiquity through the 20th century. Many of the articles were hand-crafted or manufactured for use in the home and provide a fascinating chronicle of domestic life and taste, both popular and sophisticated, through the ages. Chairs, lighting fixtures, tableware and architectural elements are all represented in historical depth and breadth of style, as are ceramics, glassware, appliances, tools and even Christmas-tree ornaments. Specialized groupings include the Metzenberg Collection of Historic Cutlery; the Brener Collection of Matchsafes; and the Shapiro Collection of 20th-century Soviet porcelains.

The Drue Heinz Center for Drawings and Prints is the Museum's repository for more than 160,000 works on paper. The focus is design: graphic, architectural, interior, industrial, textile, landscape, theatrical and virtually any other creative pursuit that requires preliminary drawings. The collection is particularly strong in 17th-through 19th-century French and Italian drawings and prints created by architects and decorative artists, and in 20th-century architectural, industrial and graphic design.

Textiles have been a major part of the Cooper-Hewitt mission since its inception, when J. P.

Morgan assisted the Hewitt sisters by donating three of his European textile collections. Today, the 30,000 pieces in the institution's holdings represent cultures as diverse as Han Dynasty China (206 B.C.–A.D. 221), pre-Columbian America, and 18th- and 19th-century Europe. Virtually every technique used to create and give color to textiles is represented – among them hand and machine weaving, knitting, crocheting, quilting, silk screening, tie-dyeing and more.

Cooper-Hewitt's fourth great collection is the nation's largest assemblage of wall coverings – more than 10,000 specimens in all. Early block-printed wallpapers made for modest American homes are represented, as are the exquisitely detailed papers manufactured in France in the early 19th century. The collection traces the influence of designers such as William Morris in late-19th-century England, the visionaries of Germany's 1920s Bauhaus, and Frank Lloyd Wright.

Cooper-Hewitt's public exhibition rooms can hold only a selective representation of the Museum's vast holdings and are also used for special exhibits drawn from collections at other institutions. Visitors can, however, make appointments for more in-depth visits to the four curatorial departments, as well as to Cooper-Hewitt's 60,000-volume library and its archives, which include the papers of prominent designers. No academic or professional credentials are necessary.

Modest mansion

The home of Cooper-Hewitt for the past quarter-century is itself a fine expression of a particular period in the history of American design and technology. The mansion was designed for Andrew Carnegie by the firm of Babb, Cook and Willard. Construction took four years (1898–1902) and cost $1.5 million – a tiny fraction of Carnegie's steel fortune, the vast majority of which he gave away in a broad range of philanthropies. The property tax was $1 million per year.

Almost as if in anticipation of his great house and the ultimate use to which it would be put, Carnegie had earlier written in his essay *Wealth* that "It is well, nay, essential, for the progress of the race that the houses of some should be homes for all that is highest and best in literature and the arts, and for the refinements of civilization." Although the mansion could hardly be called modest, Carnegie – never a pretentious or extravagant man – wanted his New York City seat to stand in clear distinction to the baronial palaces and faux chateaux raised by many of his robber-baron contemporaries. He wanted a house, as he put it, that was big but not "vulgar or ostentatious," and for its location he chose a site far north of fashionable midtown Manhattan.

Carnegie's architects gave him a sedate Georgian Revival structure, four stories in height and with three basements. There were 64 rooms in all, served by systems that were a marvel of technology for their day. This was the first private home in New York with a steel frame and an Otis passenger elevator. It also boasted a rudimentary air-conditioning system in which air was drawn by fans over tanks of cool water in the attic. The three great boilers in the sub-basement were fired by two tons of coal a day during cold weather.

The Museum's exhibition spaces still convey much of the character of Carnegie's home and include a sunny breakfast room overlooking his beloved garden, and a study where the philanthropist worked at a massive desk surrounded by inspirational mottoes carved in the wood paneling.

Food and drink: *Creative, contemporary French-American fare is the specialty at Table d'Hôte (44 E. 92nd St between Madison and Park Aves, 212-348-8125, expensive), a nook of a place just right for intimate dining. The early-bird special, until 6.30pm, is a wonderful bargain. The Bistro du Nord (1312 Madison Ave at 93rd St, 212-289-0997, expensive) is equally snug, but it's a fine spot to enjoy a bowl of steamed mussels, a plate of escargot or a fragrant bowl of French onion soup.*

Forbes Magazine Galleries

Malcolm Forbes, publisher and socialite, created this museum to house an eclectic trove, ranging from Fabergé eggs to presidential papers.

Map reference: pages 48–49, D2
62 Fifth Ave at W. 12th St, 10011.
Tel: 212-206-5548.
Subway: F to 14th St or 1, 2, 3 to 14th St. Bus: M2, M3, M5 to 12th St.
Tues–Wed, Fri–Sat 10am–4pm.
Free admission, museum store, wheelchair access.

The collection of *Forbes* magazine reflects the broad range of interests, at turns serious and playful, of the late publisher Malcolm S. Forbes. Although known as an avid balloonist, motorcyclist and party giver, the always-ebullient Forbes was also an inveterate collector.

Forbes' most celebrated acquisitions were the creations of the Franco-Russian jeweler Peter Carl Fabergé, many of which were commissioned by the last three Romanov czars – Alexander II, Alexander III and Nicholas II. The 400-item Forbes Fabergé collection includes 12 of the splendid eggs presented as Easter gifts by Alexander III and Nicholas II. Crafted of gold, enamel, and precious and semiprecious stones, the eggs are renowned not only for their flawless work-

On the Beach, by Winslow Homer, one of the notable American works in the Forbes Collection.

manship but for the "surprises" that many of them conceal. The Coronation Egg, presented by Nicholas II to Czarina Alexandra in 1897, opens to reveal a tiny golden replica of the coach Alexandra rode on the way to her coronation ceremonies. Another, the Chanticleer Egg, given by Nicholas to his mother the Dowager Empress Marie in 1903, contains an enameled rooster adorned with diamonds that rises on the hour to flap its wings and crow.

Eclectic, eccentric

Two galleries reveal an entirely different acquisitive inclination of Malcolm Forbes and his sons. They contain a rotating exhibit of items from the Forbes Collection of American Presidential Manuscripts, which comprises over 4,000 items written by or relating to every U.S. president. Diary excerpts, drafts of speeches, letters and notes reflect presidential character and characteristics. The papers include a manuscript containing Harry Truman's famous line, "If you can't stand the heat, get out of the kitchen"; Gerald Ford's humble self-appraisal, "I am a Ford – not a Lincoln"; and thoughts on Vietnam by Richard Nixon.

Toy soldiers were another Forbes passion. The On Parade gallery exhibits some 10,000, arrayed in a variety of historical battle scenes. The theme of history in miniature continues in a collection of scale-model rooms depicting Washington's headquarters at Yorktown, Thomas Jefferson's bedroom

and study at Monticello, and several other haunts of the famous.

The Ships Ahoy gallery features more than 500 antique toy boats, as well as models of Malcolm Forbes' own special toys – his five successive *Highlander* yachts, each more sumptuous than the previous one. *Highlander V*, launched in 1985, carried a helicopter, two speedboats, and two Harley-Davidson motorcycles. A series of gold leaf panels, reverse-painted on glass, are a relic of the great liner *Normandie*.

The eclectic borders on the eccentric in a pair of galleries devoted, respectively, to the history of the board game Monopoly and to a collection of more than 175 trophies illustrating "the mortality of immortality." The trophies were acquired at auction and from pawnbrokers, and honor achievements such as victory in egg-laying contests.

With a bow to the conventional stuff of collecting, there is also a room devoted to selections from the firm's treasury of 19th-century American, British and French paintings.

Food and drink: Since 1991, celebrity chef Bobby Flay has been honing Mesa Grill's (102 Fifth Ave between 15th and 16th Sts, 212-807-7400, expensive) well-earned reputation as the city's hottest spot for innovative Southwestern fare. Specialties such as spice-crusted Black Angus steak and shrimp and roasted garlic corn tamales are served in this sometimes noisy, often crowded, always cheerful restaurant. The weekend brunch is extremely popular.

Morgan Library

A magnificent collection of fine art, historical manuscripts and early books amassed by legendary financier J. P. Morgan graces a library fit for a Renaissance prince.

Map reference: pages 50–51, C7
29 E. 36th St (at Madison Ave), 10016.
Tel: 212-685-0610; www.morganlibrary.org
Subway: 6 to 33rd St; 4, 5, 6, 7 to Grand
Central; B, D, F, Q to 42nd St. Bus: M2, M3,
M4, Q32 to 36th St.
Tues–Thurs 10.30am–5pm, Fri 10.30am–8pm,
Sat 10.30am–6pm, Sun noon–6pm.
Admission fee, museum store, lectures, concerts, guided tours, wheelchair access.

John Pierpont Morgan (1837–1913), the investment banker known for his consolidation of railroad and steel empires and his role in rescuing the American economy during the Panic of 1907, was a master collector whose tastes and vast wealth underlie the considerable resources of the Morgan Library. "As long as he was in active life, and in whatever field he entered, he bought the highest-priced corner lot," wrote his son-in-law and biographer Herbert Satterlee. He added that Morgan's insistence on the best also resulted in his purchasing "the most notable pictures."

Those pictures, and a collection of equally notable manuscripts and books, are Morgan's greatest legacy. Starting with President Millard Fillmore's autograph, which he acquired when he was 14, Morgan went on to collect medieval stained glass, then items as diverse as ancient Egyptian artifacts and majolica. His ambition reached its pinnacle around the turn of the 20th century, when he began outbidding competitors for entire collections brought to his attention by the most prominent art dealers in Europe and the United States. Morgan bought Chinese ceramics, medieval tapestries and Near Eastern antiquities as well as paintings and drawings by the Old Masters. Turning to manuscripts and printed works, he acquired illuminated books of hours, a Gutenberg Bible and handwritten letters by luminaries such as Jefferson, Washington, Napoleon and Elizabeth I. Beginning with Thackeray, Morgan collected manuscripts of works by Dickens, Keats, Milton and other first-rank authors.

By 1900 Morgan's collections had outgrown his New York City house, and he commissioned Charles McKim, partner in the great architectural firm of McKim, Mead and White, to design a proper repository. McKim's response was a building which *New York Times* critic Paul Goldberger described as "the triumphal moment of Italian Renaissance architecture in America." With a 1928 annex and a 1992 conservatory linking the structure to the J. P. Morgan, Jr. mansion, McKim's elegant palazzo is the core of the present Morgan Library.

Opened in 1924, the library is centered around Morgan's enormous and opulent private study, and showcases some of the most valuable treasures in his collection. Here is the finest assemblage of medieval and Renaissance illuminated manuscripts outside Europe; the handwritten originals of Milton's *Paradise Lost*, Dickens's *A Christmas Carol* and Keats' *Endymion*; a 1455 vellum Gutenberg Bible (the library owns three); a 1477 Caxton printing of Chaucer's *The Canterbury Tales*; a working draft of the U.S. Constitution; selections from the largest collection of Rembrandt prints in the United States; and Mozart's first opus, scribed

The grandeur of turn-of-the-century New York is evoked to stunning effect in the East Room of the Morgan Library.

by his father. Acquisitions made after Morgan's death include Albert Einstein's original manuscript outlining the theory of relativity.

The Library also hosts touring exhibitions, as well as theme shows drawn from portions of the collection that aren't often displayed. The latter have included recent exhibitions devoted to photographs of the American West by William Henry Jackson and printed works and manuscripts by Oscar Wilde.

Food and drink: Some of the city's finest brioche and croissants are served alongside cassoulet, steak frites and other bistro staples at Chez Laurence (245 Madison Ave, 212-683-0284, moderate), a casual spot at the corner of 38th Street. For a more ambitious outing, consider the handsomely-furnished Toledo (6 E. 36th St, 212-696-5036, expensive) for rich and flavorful Spanish dishes.

New York Public Library

At the city's vital center is a storehouse of treasures that goes beyond books.

Map reference: pages 50–51, C7
Fifth Ave and 42nd St, 10018.
Tel: 212-661-7220, www.nypl.org
Subway: B, D, F, S to 42nd St. Bus: M1, M2, M3, M4, M5, M42, M104 to Fifth Ave and 42nd St.
Mon–Wed 11am–7.30pm, Thurs–Sat 10am–6pm.
Free admission, library shop, guided tours, wheelchair access.

Patience, one of a pair of marble lions, guards the library stairs.

It was an improbable merger that created the New York Public Library in 1895 out of the legacies of three individuals and bibliophiles: John Jacob Astor, James Lenox and Samuel P. Tilden. Just as improbable, in many ways, was the showplace for their books that emerged in 1911 – a neoclassical jewel in a city full of undistinguished design, on a site that once held millions of gallons of water (Croton Reservoir), at a corner that was fast becoming a world crossroad (Fifth Avenue and 42nd Street).

With its Corinthian columns and white Vermont marble, its palatial staircases and famous sculptured lions (Patience and Fortitude) standing guard out front, the Beaux-Arts-style building is a landmark of its kind, ranking with such select worthies as the Metropolitan Museum of Art, the Morgan Library, and Grand Central Terminal. The building's architects were John Merven Carrère and Thomas Hastings, two Paris-trained partners who triumphed in a design competition. They put their lives into the years-long, $9 million construction project. Sadly, Carrère did not live to see the dedication in May 1911, having died two months earlier in an auto accident.

Not to be missed is the majestic Main Reading Room on the third floor, brilliantly renovated in 1998 at a cost of $15 million, its vast perimeter lined with reference works surrounding lamp-lit desks. Here swarms of readers digest the acres of books summoned with "call slips" from the library's vast hidden recesses, including space under adjacent Bryant Park. No books may leave this building, which is the reference-only Humanities and Social

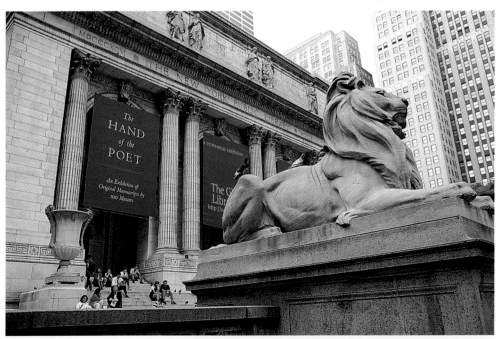

Sciences Library, vital center of a vast municipal system (126 branches, some 18 million books).

Free tours are offered daily from Astor Hall at the library's entrance. Among the books, maps, manuscripts, periodicals, photos and varied items numbering in the millions housed in this building alone are the first Gutenberg Bible brought to America, Columbus' 1493 account of his momentous voyage, Washington's own handwritten Farewell Address and Jefferson's early draft of the Declaration of Independence.

Food and drink: Directly behind the library is the Bryant Park Café (25 W. 40th St, 212-840-6500, moderate), in an area long since reclaimed from drug peddlers and turned into a pleasant midtown oasis. A glass-and-steel pavilion attracts a largely thirty-something crowd eager for food, drink and social merriment. It's especially pleasant in warm weather, and there's a more upscale Bryant Park Grill here as well.

Rose Museum at Carnegie Hall

An illustrated history of New York's legendary concert hall is on display at this hallowed shrine on 57th Street.

Map reference: pages 50–51, C4
154 W. 57th St (at Seventh Ave), 10019.
Tel: 212-903-9629, www.carnegiehall.org
Subway: N, R or Q to 57th St. Bus: M6, M7,
M30, M31 or M57 to Seventh Ave and 57th St.
Thurs–Tues 11am–4.30pm.
Free admission, wheelchair access.

How do you get to Carnegie Hall? Practice, practice, practice. Tchaikovsky was here, so was Toscanini. Here great violinists fiddled, pianists tinkled, Isadora Duncan danced, Billie Holliday sang, Benny Goodman swung. Everybody who was anybody has made it to the place that was known first as the Music Hall, when Tchaikovsky opened it in May 1891, then as Carnegie Hall in honor of the man who had put up the money for it – Andrew Carnegie.

In the 1960s, when Avery Fisher Hall went up over at the glitzy new Lincoln Center, there was a plan to scrap the building, but violinist Isaac Stern orchestrated a public outcry. And in 1991, in time for the hall's centennial celebration, the Rose Museum was opened next to the 2,084-seat

main auditorium to provide a permanent display of this musical landmark's storied history.

Visitors are welcome to stop by and view the memorabilia on display that tells of Carnegie Hall's performance history and the history of the landmark building itself, which has been home to many leading musicians and show-business personalities. The permanent collection is augmented by changing exhibitions of showbills, photos, letters, paintings, books and posters.

The silver trowel with which Mrs. Andrew Carnegie laid the cornerstone in 1890 is here, as is the baton wielded by Arturo Toscanini, Benny Goodman's clarinet, an autographed program of the Beatles' concert of 1964 and much more. An archive was established in 1986, and much of the material it holds was subsequently supplied by Carnegie Hall's devoted corps of music patrons.

Fanciful New World maps and illustrations by the 16th-century German engraver Theodor De Bry, from the library's archive.

Food and drink: Steps away from Carnegie Hall is the renowned, and pricey, Russian Tea Room (150 W. 57th St, 212-974-2111, expensive). Another landmark is the Carnegie Deli, famous for mile-high sandwiches and classic New York attitude (854 Seventh Ave at W. 55th St, 212-757-2245, moderate).

Children's Museums

Fun and games and education, too, are served up at several activity centers designed especially with kids in mind. From art and culture to science and technology, there's a lot to do – and adults can do it, too

Brooklyn Children's Museum

Kids are encouraged to explore the world at a subterranean museum.

Map reference: pages 52–53, D6
145 Brooklyn Ave, Brooklyn, NY 11213.
Tel: 718-735-4400, www.bchildmus.org
Subway: A, C to Nostrand Ave. Bus: B43, B44 to
St. Mark's Ave or B45, B65, B25 to Brooklyn Ave.
Wed–Fri 2pm–5pm (extended Fri hours in
summer), Sat–Sun 10am–5pm.
Admission fee, performances, workshops,
wheelchair access.

Kids know they're in for a good time the moment they enter this 35,000-square-foot (3,250-sq-meter) subterranean museum through a colorful old trolley kiosk in Brower Park. Since it was founded in 1899, the institution has collected almost 27,000 cultural artifacts and natural-history specimens, which have been incorporated into exhibits and programs designed to teach children about the world around them with a maximum of whimsy, amusement and plain old fun.

There are plenty of buttons to push, levers to pull, instruments to pluck, ropes to jump, and a wealth of fascinating objects (such as African masks and a pickled human brain) that are worth studying. Four floors of exhibit space are connected by a huge sewer pipe that's been recycled into a "People Tube."

Among the exhibits are *Together in the City*, which explores how New Yorkers from various cultures play and work together, and *Animals Inside and Out*, which features giant beetles, among other peculiar creatures. *Around the Block* is a play group for early learners and their caregivers that fosters motor coordination and creative play, and *Music Mix* is filled with musical instruments from around the world.

In the Children's Resource Library, young visitors can delve more deeply into subjects of special interest such as butterflies, feathers and coins, using specimens from the Museum's collections, which have been organized into individual study boxes. The Museum presents an ongoing program of daily workshops, classes and weekend multicultural performances.

Food and drink: *Visitors are invited to picnic in the grove behind the Museum.*

Children's Museum of Manhattan

A wonderama of life and how to deal with it is tailored for youngsters at this urban indoor playground, but adults can learn a thing or two as well.

Map reference: pages 50–51, C1
The Tisch Building, 212 W. 83rd St (between
Broadway and Amsterdam Ave), 10024.
Tel: 212-721-1234, www.cmom.org
Subway: 1, 2 to 86th or 79th Sts or B, C to 81st
St. Bus: West Side M7, M11, M104 to 83rd St or
M79, M86 to Broadway.
Wed–Sun 10am–5pm.
Admission fee, gift shop, workshops, classes,
performances, wheelchair access.

Hands-on creativity for kids of all ages is what the Children's Museum of Manhattan is all about. It's in the Tisch Building on the Upper West Side, and it has five floors of interactive exhibits dealing with art, science and nature.

The whole family can get involved in this vibrant and visually exciting place. Climb through a human digestive tract, stop in for a visit to the lungs, and zap body invaders along the way at *Body Odyssey*, just one of the multitude of exhibits. Each is designed to appeal to a specific childhood age group, but adults aren't excluded from the fun.

Activities in the Early Childhood

OPPOSITE AND TOP: Kids get an inside look at the human body at the Children's Museum of Manhattan.

BELOW: A Chinese lute is one of several instruments visitors can play with at *Music Mix*, Brooklyn Children's Museum.

Center and the Family Learning Center are geared toward the younger set and their chaperones. At *WordPlay*, parents with newborns and toddlers explore how language skills develop, crawling and toddling with them through exhibits such as *Baby Bubble*, designed to stimulate babies' brains using words as building blocks. They can climb, slide, paint and join in on group sing-alongs.

Older siblings can take their places in front of the camera as newscasters, or stay behind the scenes as camera operators and/or animators at the fully-equipped Time Media Center. They can patent inventions using digital imaging, scanners, cameras and printers at the HP Inventor Center; and then hop over to the Russell Berrie Art Studio for classes in illustration or drawing.

Founded in 1979 as the Manhattan Laboratory Museum, the center offers an ambitious roster of activities, exhibitions and workshops designed to involve the entire family in an ongoing program of lifelong learning. Nature workshops, puppet shows, films, storytelling and holiday celebrations are all part of the picture.

In the Sussman Environmental Center, visitors can float boats down a 16-foot (5-meter) zigzag water stream at City Splash. Exhibits here focus on environmental issues, with displays such as "Get to Know Your Trash" and "Underground New York"; the latter teaches about the vast and intricate subterranean systems that bring light, power, water and steam to every corner of the city. One of the Museum's highlights, the Urban Tree House, has an outdoor play area with three stories of interactive displays designed to reinforce the environment-friendly themes: Reduce, Reuse, Recycle and Rethink.

On the first Saturday of each month, singer-songwriter and early-childhood educator Louie gets the kids together for singing and dancing. Every Saturday, the youngsters can write and design their own books at the Klutz Book Factory. Some programs and workshops require advance registration; be sure to call ahead if you're interested in a specific activity.

WordPlay, at the Children's Museum of Manhattan, reinforces language skills.

Food and drink: *The "all in one" sandwich at Artie's New York Delicatessen (2290 Broadway at 83rd St, 212-579-5959, inexpensive) is a mountain of turkey, pastrami, roast beef, Swiss cheese, cole slaw and Russian dressing – it's one of the house specials. The hot dogs are homemade, the chopped liver, potato pancakes and knishes are classic deli, and there's plenty of chicken soup.*

Children's Museum of the Arts

A multitude of activities is served up for kids from 18 months to 10 years of age, the goal being to help develop their potential for creativity.

Map reference: pages 48-49, D5
182 Lafayette St, NY 10013.
Tel: 212-941-9198, www.cmany.org
Subway: 6 to Spring St or N, R to Prince St.
Bus: M1, M6 to Broome St.
Wed–Sun noon–5pm (Thurs to 6pm, free admission 4pm–6pm).
Admission fee, gift shop, wheelchair access.

B etween two commercial buildings bordering Chinatown, a zebra statue and brightly painted windows mark the entrance to a space that is part museum and part artist's studio. Here children learn about the visual and performing arts and the creative process by becoming artists on the spot.

Once inside, visitors quickly comprehend that this is a space for children: everything is built half-size. Parents may feel a bit cramped, but the kids are instantly at home, scampering from one work space to another, plunging into fingerpaints, sculpting clay, building collages, and even exploring the world of theater.

Founded in 1988 by artist and educator Kathleen Schneider, the Museum is divided into spaces geared toward different age groups. In the

Creative Play Area, for ages 5 and under, kids can view slides in the Art House and make their own art at the WEE (Wonderous, Experimenting and Exploring) Art Station. Artists from the community work alongside youngsters 5 and older at the Artists' Studio, where there are a variety of creative media to explore. Young thespians will enjoy dressing up in costume in the Actors Studio, where story starters are on hand to help them develop their own scripts.

The Ball Pond, a cushioned area surrounded by murals of Monet's water lilies and filled with brightly colored balls, integrates color, light and textures to evoke a feeling of being surrounded by water. The activity of rolling in the balls is designed to develop motor skills. In Magnetic Masterpieces, children arrange reproductions of classic and contemporary works of art that have been cut up into puzzle pieces. A rotating exhibition of works by children from around the world is spotlighted in the International Children's Art Gallery.

Changing exhibitions focus on multicultural themes and have included works by children in countries at war and from remote cultures. Daily workshops include activities such as beadworking and giant animal sculptures, and special projects geared around specific holidays. The Museum displays pieces it has commissioned to appeal especially to children.

Food and drink: In Chinatown, Ping's Seafood (22 Mott St, 212-602-9988, moderate) serves a large selection of authentic cuisine in a large, crowded, smoke-free room. Kids get a kick out of the fish tanks, out of which chefs scoop your meal.

Sony Wonder Technology Lab

Cutting-edge gadgetry delights kids and adults at Sony's technology playground.

Map reference: pages 50–51, D5
Sony Plaza, 550 Madison Ave, 10022.
Tel: 212-833-8100, wondertechlab.sony.com
Subway: 4, 5, 6 to 59th St or E, F to Fifth Ave.
Bus: M1, M2, M3, M4, M5 to 56th St or M57,

Visitors test products and learn about electronics at the Sony Wonder Technology Lab.

M31 to Madison Ave.
Tues–Sat 10am–6pm (Thurs to 8pm), Sun noon–6pm.
Free admission, films, wheelchair access.

More marketing ploy than museum, the Technology Lab is Sony Corp's attempt at "retail entertainment." Situated at the company's corporate plaza in midtown Manhattan, the Lab guides visitors through four floors of high-tech, interactive exhibits that explore information technology and product design (and, incidentally, pitch Sony products).

Both kids and adults have a great time editing music videos in the Television Production Studio, exploring the human body with ultrasound and endoscopy at the Medical Imaging Lab, recording a song in the Audio Lab, operating a robot at the Factory Automation exhibit, or testing the next generation of video games. It's all presented in a slick neon-lit atmosphere abuzz with computer tones and synthesized voices.

A series of workshops and free film screenings are also available. Admission cannot be guaranteed without a reservation, which should be made at least two weeks in advance. Expect to wait before entering, even with a reservation.

Food and drink: Mars 2112 (1633 Broadway at 51st St, 212-582-2112, moderate) takes theme restaurants to the next level, with spacey rockscapes, laser lights, costumed alien waiters, a simulated spaceship ride and a video arcade. The food's not bad, either.

About New York City

Whatever you call it – Gotham, the Big Apple or just plain New York – this great metropolis has an absorbing history filled with colorful characters and monumental events. These institutions tell the story of the city

Municipal Archives of the City of New York

The archives constitute the institutional memory of New York City, with records dating back to the 17th century.

Map reference: pages 48–49, C7
31 Chambers St, Room 103, 10007.
Tel: 212-788-8580; www.ci.nyc.ny.us/html/doris
Subway: N or R to City Hall. Bus: M1, M6 or
M22 to City Hall.
Mon–Thurs 9am–4.30pm, Fri 9am–1pm.
Free admission, museum store, wheelchair access.

Although not an old city by world standards, New York has a history reaching back nearly 400 years, much of which is documented in the Municipal Archives. While much of the material amassed in the collection is of interest primarily to academic researchers (almshouse records, for instance, reach back to 1758; Manhattan real estate valuations to 1789), amateur historians and New York City buffs have access to a broad range of documents that will help expand an appreciation of the metropolis and its growth.

For instance, the archives house the original construction plans for the Brooklyn Bridge, beginning in 1867 during John Roebling's original survey for the span; Frederick Law Olmsted's plans for Central Park; and photographs, scrapbooks and correspondence relating to New York mayors from 1849 to the present.

The archives provide a comprehensive pictorial record of the city, with photographs depicting municipal buildings, public works, docks and ferries, and special events. One portion of the archives contains photographs assembled for the 1930s WPA Federal Writers' Project guidebook to New York, as well as original manuscripts and research materials for the massive undertaking.

Individuals researching family connections to New York City will find census records, city directories (the oldest Brooklyn directory is from 1796), and records of births, deaths and marriages. Court records dating to 1684 may be of assistance in instances where genealogical research takes an unexpected turn. Of particular interest to those who were born in or have lived in the city are the "tax photographs," taken for property appraisal purposes between 1939 and 1941, of which there

is one for each building in the five boroughs. The photographs may be viewed on microfilm free of charge, or ordered as prints for a fee.

Food and drink: Drift a couple of blocks north to Chinatown for flavorful Chinese, Thai and Vietnamese at places like New York Noodlehouse (28 Bowery at Bayard St, 212-349-0923) and Joe's Shanghai (9 Pell St between Bowery and Mott St, 212-233-8888), where cheap and authentic food makes up for the loud, chaotic atmosphere.

Museum of the City of New York

America's first museum dedicated to the history of a single city encompasses the story of New York from Dutch colonial times to the present.

Map reference: pages 52–53, D3
1220 Fifth Ave at 103rd St, 10029.
Tel: 212-534-1672; www.mcny.org
Subway: 6 to 103rd St or 2, 3 to 110th St. Bus:
M1, M2, M3 or M4 to 103rd St.
Wed–Sat 10am–5pm, Sun noon–5pm.
Free admission (donation suggested), museum shop, lectures, concerts, walking tours, wheelchair access.

Founded in 1923 and originally located in Gracie Mansion, the building now used as the mayor's official residence, the Museum of the City of New York has amassed a collection of more than 1½ million artifacts and artworks related to the city's ever-changing character and phenomenal growth. For an introduction to this

ABOVE:
Brooklyn Bridge, about 1932. Original plans for the bridge can be found at the Municipal Archives.

OPPOSITE:
Colorful banners welcome visitors to the Museum of the City of New York.

protean metropolis, visitors should first view *The Big Apple*, a 22-minute film covering nearly 400 years of history, presented throughout the day.

On the ground level is the Fire Gallery, which features antique fire engines and other firefighting equipment as well as sections of the hollow-log pipes that once carried water beneath the city's streets. Highlights include an Americus Big 6 double-decker fire engine built in 1851, a hose carriage of the type used in the mid-19th century and a chilling depiction of the 1911 Triangle Waist Company fire by self-taught artist Joseph Gatto.

On the second floor you'll find *Painting the Town: Cityscapes of New York*, an exhibition of 70 canvases chronicling the changing landscape of New York from 1809 to 1997. The exhibition captures historic events such as the completion of the Erie Canal in 1886, the Wall Street Panic of 1857

New York impressions: *First Night Game, Yankee Stadium, May 28, 1946,* Paolo Corvino (top), and *Last Clock on Fifth Avenue,* Tom Christopher (below), from *Painting the Town: Cityscapes of New York.*

and the unveiling of the Statue of Liberty in 1886. Featured are the works of such notables as Hudson River School painter Asher B. Durand, American Impressionist Childe Hassam, and urban realists Reginald Marsh and Ben Shahn.

Also on the second floor is a series of period rooms, replicating the domestic environments of wealthy New Yorkers from early colonial times to the Gilded Age. A Dutch Alcove reveals the relatively spartan circumstances of even well-to-do residents of old New Amsterdam, although the Delft china and silver tableware imported from the Netherlands are handsome examples of 17th-century craftsmanship. A parlor and bedroom represent the English colonial period of the 18th century, an era of far greater elegance and sophistication in furniture manufacture. A pair of drawing rooms from homes in lower Manhattan and Brooklyn Heights trace the progression of 19th-

century taste from the simplicity of Federal styles to high Victorian ornamentation, while the opulence – some might say excess – of the Gilded Age is illustrated by a drawing room from the Park Avenue mansion of Harry Harkness Flagler, designed by Richard Morris Hunt.

Adjacent to the period rooms is the J. Clarence Davies Gallery of historic paintings, prints and maps, and a collection of furniture and family portraits that belonged to Alexander Hamilton, who lived at an estate called The Grange in Manhattan's Washington Heights section before he was killed in a duel by Aaron Burr in 1804.

The Marine Gallery, elsewhere on the second floor, celebrates the role New York City played in the development of American shipping and marine technology. A series of 30 dioramas, along with models, maps, paintings and photographs, show how the harbor and the shipping industry evolved over the centuries. Near the gallery entrance stands a 10-foot-tall (3-meter) statue of Robert Fulton, steamboat pioneer and one of the seminal figures in the city's development as a major port.

Toys and treasures

The Museum's third floor houses *New York Toy Stories*, a toy exhibit spanning more than two centuries, and the Dolls' House Gallery, with miniatures accurately portraying period New York homes. On the same floor, an exhibit called *Broadway* chronicles the history of New York's celebrated boulevard from its origin as a thoroughfare linking New Amsterdam with settlements to the north to its heyday as the "Great White Way."

A series of rooms on the fifth floor offers another look at how wealthy New Yorkers furnished their homes during the city's most opulent era. In this instance, however, the chambers on exhibit were once owned by the wealthiest, though hardly the most ostentatious, of New York robber barons. He was John D. Rockefeller, Sr., who lived at the East 54th Street brownstone whose master bedroom and dressing room are preserved here. The bedroom is in the Eastlake style, drawing heavily on Japanese and Near Eastern motifs and making use of stained glass and intricate woodwork. The dressing room has lovely marble fixtures and an elaborate dresser. The Rockefeller townhouse, incidentally, was demolished along with the neighboring mansion belonging to his son, John D. Rockefeller, Jr., when the younger Rockefeller donated the properties to the Museum of Modern Art in 1937.

Statue of Liberty Enlightening the World, by Edward P. Moran, depicts Liberty's unveiling in 1886. The artist may have taken at least one liberty himself: the event actually took place in the rain.

The Museum presents an ambitious series of special exhibits, which recently have ranged from an appreciation of theatrical cartoonist Al Hirschfeld to a retrospective of postcards depicting scenes and structures from a vanished New York.

A pleasant adjunct to a museum visit is a stroll in the Conservatory Garden, a portion of Central Park two blocks north at Fifth Avenue and 105th Street. Located behind gates that once adorned one of the Vanderbilt mansions, the garden includes tree-lined paths, a lily-pad pool, and formal plantings of annuals and roses (daily 8am–dusk, guided tours Sat 11am spring and summer).

A plan is in the works to relocate the Museum downtown to the restored Tweed Courthouse. Cooperation from the city remains problematic, however, and there is no certainty at this writing when – or if – the move is going to happen.

Food and drink: At Jackson Hole (1270 Madison Ave at 91st St, 212-427-2820, inexpensive) the ambience is 1950s diner, the portions are mountainous, and the hamburgers are among the best in the city. The cuisine – and prices – are more rarefied at Bistro du Nord (1312 Madison Ave at 93rd St, 212-289-0997, expensive), a cozy French café and bistro.

New-York Historical Society

A neoclassical edifice houses a repository of American art, history and culture, ranging from the sublime landscapes of the Hudson River School to the quirky accoutrements of the Founding Fathers.

Map reference: pages 50–51, D2
2 W. 77th St (at Central Park West), 10024.
Tel: 212-873-3400, www.nyhistory.org
Tues–Sun 10am–5pm.
Subway: B or C to 81st St. Bus: M10 to 77th St
or M79 to 81st and Central Park West.
Admission fee, museum store, wheelchair access.

No, that's not a typo. New-York (hyphenated) was the accepted spelling of the city's name back in 1804, when the historical society was founded. Like its location – in the heart of a pedestrian's paradise between Central Park and the dignified West 70s – the Society is an island of tranquility. The stately granite building contains a trove of Americana, where the old is often the odd – an illustrious wooden leg, a mesmerizing death mask, a ceramic cockroach trap. Visitors explore New York and American history through a collection of 40,000 objects, including galleries of rare 18th- and 19th-century paintings.

The newest and arguably the best reason to visit the Society is the Henry Luce III Center for the Study of American Culture. Opened in 2000, the fourth-floor center displays objects stored away during the Society's 200-year history. The objects are neatly categorized: Tiffany lamps (132 of them), furniture (from an 18th-century baby walker to George Washington's inaugural armchair), sculpture (famous busts, folk art, a life mask of Lincoln and a death mask of Aaron Burr), toys and amusements (don't miss the 19th-century Noah's ark, with countless pairs of painted-wood animals), personal accessories (handsome canes once used by Benjamin Franklin and other notables, shaving kits, smoking supplies and more), and tools for home and trade.

The Luce Center's mezzanine collections include buttons, badges and souvenirs; coins and medals; archaeological curios; maritime objects; and fire, police and military items. Of special interest are old fire helmets, General Washington's camp cot and a huge bass drum struck by bullets at the Battle of Bull Run. In the Luce Center's painting gallery are thousands of works, among them 435 original watercolors by John James Audubon; New York cityscapes dating back to the mid-1700s; an exotic 1796 portrait of Seneca chief Cornplanter; and a controversial portrait of Edward Hyde, an alleged cross-dresser who governed New York in the early 18th century.

Computer stations enhance the fourth-floor experience, allowing visitors to learn more about even the tiniest objects on display. The free audio tour, crucial to discovering the remarkable history behind many items, features narration from New Yorkers aptly – and amusingly – matched to their subjects.

To visit the second-floor holdings (there are no exhibits on the third floor) is to grasp why the Society remained the

Flags on 57th Street, Winter, 1918, by Childe Hassam, one of America's leading Impressionists. His flag paintings were prompted by the U.S. entry into the First World War.

city's premier art museum for much of the 19th century. In lordly Dexter Hall hang large canvases by members of the Hudson River School, the country's first homegrown art movement. These sublime works include Thomas Cole's *The Vale and Temple of Segestae, Sicily*; Albert Bierstadt's *Donner Lake from the Summit*; and Asher Durand's *Black Mountain From Harbor Islands, Lake George, N.Y.*, between whose clouds and water the mountain sits like a weak chaperone, unable to prevent the union of sky and lake.

The naked truth

Also on view are portraits of such interesting characters as Dred Scott and Commodore William Bainbridge, as well as John Vanderlyn's stunning nude *Ariadne Asleep on the Island of Naxos*, a painting that, according to the gallery plate, caused a commotion in 1814, when few New Yorkers "had ever seen a completely rendered figure, much less a nude woman in apparently post-coital repose." The adjacent Luman Reed Gallery holds colonial and 19th-century portraits, such as Samuel S. Osgood's likeness of Edgar Allan Poe, who sat for the artist in 1845,

the year he wrote "The Raven." The poet's visage exercises a strange hold on viewers – not least because of his long pinched nose, thin wraparound eyebrows and little scratch of a mouth.

The Society mounts up to three temporary exhibits at a time on the first floor. Recent exhibits included *Without Sanctuary: Lynching Photography in America*, *Treasures from Mount Vernon: George Washington Revealed* and *Flophouse: Life on the Bowery*.

Kid City, located on the lower level, gives children the feel of old New York, with a sidewalk, storefronts and a hopscotch course.

Food and drink: You'll find no end of choices a block or two from the Society on Columbus Avenue, Amsterdam Avenue and Broadway. Standouts include Zen Palate (2170 Broadway between 76th and 77th Sts, 212-501-7768, inexpensive), for healthy Japanese-influenced fare in a slick, contemporary environment; Josie's Restaurant & Juice Bar (300 Amsterdam Ave at 74th St, 212-769-1212, inexpensive) for organic, dairy-free specialties; and for those with no fear of cholesterol, Big Nick's Burger Joint (2175 Broadway at 77th St, 212-362-9238, inexpensive), for a selection of first-rate pizzas, burgers, pancakes and other comfort food in a chaotic diner atmosphere.

Thomas Cole's *Consummation*, 1836, is the third in the *Course of Empire* series, a cautionary tale about the rise and fall of civilization.

tools, including a collection of beautiful horse- and hand-drawn pumpers, antique helmets, lanterns, axes, hoses, painted leather buckets and old-fashioned fire call boxes.

Portraits, parade hats and the world's largest collection of fire insurance marks are displayed on the second floor, along with several vintage fire engines like the 1765 Bolton Quick Step. Other paraphernalia dating back to the days of New York's volunteer fire companies include a helmet frontpiece and trumpet that belonged to the young William Marcy Tweed, later known as the notorious "Boss" Tweed.

New York City Fire Museum

An old firehouse contains one of the nation's most comprehensive collections of firefighting artifacts from the 18th century to the present.

Map reference: pages 48–49, C4
278 Spring St, 10013.

ABOVE: Vintage pumpers chronicle firefighting equipment at the New York City Fire Museum.

BELOW: A wood carving depicts a volunteer fireman, about 1857.

Tel: 212-691-1303; www.nycfiremuseum.org
Subway: 1 or 2 to Houston St, C or E to Spring St. Bus: M20 or M21 to Spring St.
Tues–Sat 10am–5pm, Sun 10am–4pm.
Admission fee, museum shop, guided tours with advance reservation, wheelchair accessible.

More than 300 New York City firefighters died in the line of duty as a result of the World Trade Center attack on September 11, 2001. It is estimated that they saved the lives of approximately 25,000 people before they perished. Their proud tradition – one that dates back more than two centuries in New York – is brought to life at the city's Fire Museum, housed in a renovated 1904 firehouse complete with large apparatus doors, housewatch entrance, stone floor, brass sliding pole and hose tower.

Exhibits fill two of the three floors. On the first, a Memorial Exhibit remembers those who died at the World Trade Center on September 11, explains what the firefighters did that day, and documents the tremendous outpouring of public support and appreciation following the tragedy. Other exhibits on this floor chronicle the evolution of firefighting

Food and drink: Seventeen varieties of oysters, a sensational raw bar and a huge variety of fresh fish have helped Aquagrill (210 Spring St at Sixth Ave, 212-274-0505, expensive) earn its reputation as one of the city's finest fish houses; reservations are highly recommended. Students from the French Culinary Institute serve up regional dishes at L'Ecole (462 Broadway at Grand St, 212-219-3300, moderate), a great lunch bargain.

New York City Police Museum

A restored precinct station from the early 1900s chronicles the history of law enforcement in the Big Apple.

Map reference: pages 48–49, B9
100 Old Slip, 10004.
Tel: 212-480-3100, www.nycpolicemuseum.org
Subway: J, M, Z to Broad St or 1, 2 to Wall St. Bus: M15 to Old Slip.
Tues–Sun 10am–6pm.
Admission fee, wheelchair access.

Founded in 1929 to house the crime- and police-related paraphernalia amassed by former detective Alfred J. Young, the New York City Police Museum outgrew its longtime home at the old Police Academy building on 20th Street and recently moved to more spacious quarters in a former financial district precinct house. Its collection, which now exceeds 50,000 items, draws from both sides of the law. Here are the tools of every variety of criminal trade, ranging from switchblades and brass knuckles to a virtual armory of illegal firepower. The machine gun collection alone includes a Thompson (better known as a

force as well as uniforms and caps worn by officers since the 1870s. Uniforms and equipment from around the world fill an international exhibit.

Visitors can get a taste of the split-second, life-or-death decision making that is a crucial part of police work in an interactive exhibit that sets up potentially threatening situations in which the participant, playing the role of an officer on duty, decides whether to "shoot" a perpetrator. After the shot is fired, an instant computer analysis decides if the use of deadly force was justified.

The collection is particularly strong in photographic documentation, with pictures of police at work over a century of the city's history. The crimes that kept them busy are documented in a collection of "police blotters," the day-to-day reports processed and committed to record at precinct houses. One portion of the exhibit area is devoted to forensic DNA work, one of the latest tools of investigation and criminal identification, and a "Hall of Heroes" honors New York City police personnel who lost their lives in the line of duty.

LEFT: A cop on the beat, 1907.

BELOW: A squad of New York's finest in front of a station house, 1909.

Tommy gun) that once belonged to Al Capone as well as the first submachine gun used in a New York City murder. There are also modern weapons like 9mm Uzis, which are far lighter and faster than their cumbersome, wooden-stock antecedents.

The "good guys" portion of the collection includes examples of every style of New York City Police badge since the 1845 founding of the

Food and drink: It's a short walk through the Financial District to Mangia (40 Wall St, 212-425-4040, inexpensive), an upscale cafeteria with gourmet chow, and the Wall Street Kitchen & Bar (70 Broad St, 212-797-7070, inexpensive), where traders go for bar food and a great selection of beer.

Farther Afield

Numerous places of more than passing interest await the unsuspecting traveler outside the city. Featured are artistic treasures, a state-of-the-art science center, a historic seaport and a legendary collection of "curiosities"

Barnum Museum

A flamboyant landmark is devoted to the life and times of P. T. Barnum, legendary museum and circus owner, and "the patron saint of promoters."

Map reference: pages 52–53, F1
820 Main St, Bridgeport, CT 06604.
Tel: 203-331-1104, www.barnum-museum.org
Public transit: Metro-North and Amtrak trains
to Bridgeport Transportation Station, and Grey-
hound bus to Bridgeport Bus Terminal. From
either, cross Water Street, walk two blocks to
Main Street, turn left and walk another two
blocks. Car: I-95 north to Exit 27 (Lafayette Blvd),
continue to fifth traffic light, left on Main St.
Tues–Sat 10am–4.30pm, Sun noon–4.30pm.
Admission fee, performances, wheelchair access.

Phineas Taylor Barnum, who coined the phrase "every crowd has a silver lining," was born in Connecticut in 1810 and began his career by touring the countryside with a woman who claimed to be George Washington's nurse. Subsequent triumphs ranged from the famously tiny Tom Thumb (only 25 inches/64 cm in his teens), to Jumbo, an elephant so imposing his name became synonymous with "big."

Famous for his hoaxes, the 1842 opening of Barnum's wildly popular American Museum of Curiosities in New York proved that even signs could be profitable. One that promised THIS WAY TO THE EGRESS caused unwary crowds to tumble out an exit, thus forcing payment of a second entrance fee.

At the age of 60 the "Prince of Humbugs" went on to create the forerunner of today's Ringling Brothers and Barnum & Bailey Circus, still known as The Greatest Show on Earth. Bridgeport, the circus's summer home until 1929, was also Barnum's adopted city, where he not only served a term as mayor but also created the striking red sandstone museum (and national landmark) that bears his name.

Opened three years after his death (as the Bridgeport Scientific and the Fairfield County Historical Societies), the Barnum Museum – its exterior a fantastic blend of Romanesque, Gothic, Byzantine and Islamic motifs – remains a fitting legacy for the Great Showman.

The three floors of exhibits start in the main lobby with a mounted 700-pound (318 kg) elephant, and continue in the main gallery where *Barnum and Bridgeport* includes a recreation of the library from one of his local mansions.

A Victorian Picture Gallery shares the second floor with an exploration of Bridgeport's history as a 19th-century manufacturing center. But it's the third floor where you'll find a facsimile of the infamous Feejee Mermaid (actually a wizened monkey attached to a fish tail), "General" Tom Thumb's carriages, and memorabilia from the 1850 tour by "Swedish Nightingale" Jenny Lind, which grossed over $700,000.

There's also a perfect miniature five-ring circus, consisting of 3,000 pieces carved by a Connecticut artist and, back on the first floor, a gift shop with fittingly Barnumesque souvenirs.

Food and drink: You'll find lasagna Bolognese, polenta, veal and other homestyle Italian dishes at Ralph 'n Rich's (121 Wall St, 203-366-3597, moderate). The atmosphere is casual enough for families, romantic enough for a date.

OPPOSITE: *Child in Sunlight*, 1915, by Willard Metcalf, from the Florence Griswold Museum at Old Lyme, Connecticut.

BELOW: P. T. Barnum and "General" Tom Thumb.

Bruce Museum

Art, science and anthropology are featured at this small museum, which attracts more than 100,000 visitors a year and presents exclusive regional showings of major art exhibitions.

Map reference: pages 52–53, F1
One Museum Dr, Greenwich, CT 06830.
Tel: 203-869-0376, www.brucemuseum.org
Train: From Grand Central Terminal to the Greenwich Metro-North railroad station. The museum is one block south. Car: I-95 to Exit 3 (Arch St), bear right and follow signs.
Tues–Sat 10am–5pm, Sun 1pm–5pm.
Admission fee (except Tues), lectures, gallery tours, children's programs, museum shop, handicapped access.

Set on a tree-covered hill, the Bruce Museum of Arts and Science in suburban Greenwich, Connecticut, is one of the metropolitan area's gems. Donated to the town as a museum by textile manufacturer Robert Bruce in 1908, the original Gothic 19th-century stone mansion was transformed in 1993 by an extensive renovation that added 7,000 climate-controlled square feet (650 sq meters). However, an eclectic Victorian heart still beats somewhere inside the now creamy and classical-style edifice, which hosts an average of 16 annual exhibitions and installations.

In recent years these have included rock-and-roll photographs by Linda McCartney; an edgy look at post-World War II Russian art; a magnificent collection of treasures from the Ottoman Empire; and an in-depth exhibit on the American West, in which works by Frederic Remington and Albert Bierstadt were juxtaposed with those by contemporary Native American artists.

The Museum's permanent art collection, meanwhile, spans vintage French couture, Tiffany glass and Connecticut Impressionists like Childe Hassam and Emil Carlsen, who were part of the famed Cos Cob colony that thrived in Greenwich at the turn of the 20th century. And its mission – to bridge the arts and sciences, foster learning and preserve the past for the future – means you're as likely to find a bronze cast of Rodin's *The Kiss* on display as a well-preserved timber wolf or pre-Columbian pottery vessel.

An emphasis on the natural heritage of New England also encompasses ongoing exhibits like *Changes in Our Land*, an interactive visual display on the local environment, including a woodland habitat and a marine "touch tank." A corresponding focus on public programs includes nature workshops for children and teachers, along with a regular series of films, concerts and other special events. The Bruce also sponsors two annual outdoor festivals, one for fine arts and one for ceramics, jewelry and other crafts, which take place, respectively, in October and May.

Food and drink: The Bruce is a short walk from Greenwich Avenue, where Thataway Café (409 Greenwich Ave, 203-622-0947, moderate) serves up hamburgers, nachos, salads and pasta in a casual setting. Nearby, Abis (381 Greenwich Ave, 203-862-9100, moderate) specializes in tempura, seafood, noodles and other Japanese specialties. Mediterraneo (366 Greenwich Ave, 203-629-4747, moderate) offers upscale Italian, and Le Figaro Café (372 Greenwich Ave, 203-622-0018, expensive) has authentic French bistro-style cuisine.

American Indian Gothic, 1983, David Bradley, from a show of contemporary Native American art at the Bruce Museum.

Florence Griswold Museum

A favored country retreat of American Impressionist painters now houses a rich sampling of their work.

Map reference: pages 52–53, F1
96 Lyme St, Old Lyme, CT 06371.
Tel: 860-434-5542, www.flogris.org

Clark Vorhees House, 1914, Matilda Browne, from the Florence Griswold House.

Apr–Dec Tues–Sat 10am–5pm, Sun 1pm–5pm; Jan–Mar Wed–Sun 1pm–5pm.
Admission fee, museum shop, workshops, concerts, children's programs, wheelchair access.

The Florence Griswold Museum recalls an era when Old Lyme was the home of a major artists' colony. The town's popularity with painters began when Henry Ward Ranger, a devotee of the French Barbizon School, came to the spacious Georgian home of Florence Griswold in 1899 to ask if he might rent a room for the summer. Miss Griswold welcomed Ranger, and other painters soon followed. The artists were attracted to the subtle, seasonally changing tones of the semirural landscape around Old Lyme. Ranger's movement, called Tonalism, favored deep colors and the use of glazes that lent paintings a translucent quality. The painters kept coming back, in large part, because of Miss Griswold's hospitality and the camaraderie and encouragement they provided each other.

In 1903 Childe Hassam joined the coterie, and under his influence the Lyme Art Colony became increasingly identified with the American Impressionist movement. Heading off each day into Miss Griswold's garden and across the farm fields and salt marshes that bordered the Lieutenant River, and working directly from nature in the mode of the French Impressionists, Miss Griswold's boarders created canvases filled with the light and character of the New England countryside. The painters also left their mark on the house itself, collaborating on a delightful series of 41 painted panels on the doors and dining room walls.

Today, the Griswold house is the centerpiece of a museum exhibiting a fine collection of locally-created Tonalist and Impressionist canvases. Artists represented include Ranger and Hassam, as well as some 135 other Lyme Art Colony painters. In all, more than 400 paintings and 2,000 drawings, watercolors and prints make up a permanent collection housed in the mansion and in a riverside gallery.

Food and drink: Lunch at the 1756 Colonial Bee & Thistle Inn (100 Lyme St, 860-434-1667, expensive) is elegantly casual: a roaring fireplace, linens and creative American fare, including Maryland-style crab cakes, smoked turkey and artichoke turnovers, lobster ravioli and filet of sole. Sunday brunch is a treat.

Liberty Science Center

Just across the Hudson River from lower Manhattan, this vast science center features hundreds of hands-on exhibits and the nation's largest IMAX Dome Theater.

Map reference: pages 52–53, B5
Liberty State Park, Jersey City, NJ 07305.
Tel: 201-200-1000, www.lsc.org
Feb–Aug daily 9.30am–5.30pm, Sept–Jan
Tues–Sun 9.30am–5.30pm.
Admission fee, cafeteria, museum store,
wheelchair access.

The idea behind Liberty Science Center is that learning is an individual process and that it should be fun. To this end, the Center's designers have assembled more than 250 hands-on activities. Exhibits on each of three theme floors are presented in an imaginative and accessible manner, allowing visitors of all ages to proceed at their own pace. Each floor has a Discovery Room guided by staff and volunteers and a Science Demonstration Stage where shows are presented throughout the day.

Opened in 1993, the 170,000-square-foot (16,000-sq-meter) center houses the nation's largest IMAX Dome Theater and a 170-foot (52-meter) observation tower overlooking Manhattan, Ellis Island and the Statue of Liberty. Just inside the front door, the center's signature exhibit, Chuck Hoberman's 700-pound (320-kg) aluminum geodesic globe, suspended from the soaring 90-foot (30-m) atrium, is animated by motorized cables that open and close the structure. The Hoberman Sphere expands from 4.5 feet (1.4 meters) to 18 feet (5.5 meters) in diameter every 20 minutes. Another first floor attrac-

The Science Center's geodesic dome houses the nation's largest IMAX theater.

tion is a three-dimensional laser show (separate admission fee required) presented in the Joseph D. Williams Science Theater.

On the Health Floor, visitors learn about the human body and health issues. Highlights here include a 100-foot-long (30-meter), totally dark Touch Tunnel; Perception Alley's hall of mirrors; a thermography camera that shows the body's "hot spots"; a medical imaging station; and a cardiac surgery area, where visitors can "suture an incision." In the Cardiac Classroom, they can view periodic real-time presentations of cardiac surgery being performed at nearby Atlantic Health Care System hospitals.

Exhibits on the Environment Floor focus on the Earth, with emphasis on the atmosphere, the planet's remarkable variety of life forms (there's an exhibit of live reptiles and insects), and geology. *E-Quest*, a $1 million exhibit funded by Exxon-Mobil, takes visitors on an interactive journey encompassing the five major sources of world energy. There's also a 20-foot (6-meter) Rock Wall, studded with fossils to climb; a solar telescope; a touch tank filled with starfish, horseshoe crabs, sea urchins and other sea creatures; and, in the Atmosphere area, an exhibit about air pressure and the weather.

The Invention Floor is all about structures and engineered systems. In the USAF Flight Simulator, a combat pilot training device donated by the U.S. Air Force, visitors can soar over the Statue of Liberty and the Brooklyn Bridge. Other highlights include Virtual Sports, pitting players against "virtual" opponents in basketball, ping pong or soccer; a Digital Darkroom; a laser light and sound display; and "Invention Central," where visitors are invited to roll up their sleeves and create their own inventions.

The IMAX theater, under a 125-foot-high (38-meter) aluminum geodesic dome, has an impressive 88-foot-wide (27-meter) screen that ranks as the largest in the nation. The theater presents a changing roster of specially-produced films such as *Africa: The Serengeti*, *The Human Body*, *Ocean Oasis*, and *Journey into Amazing Caves*.

The museum hosts an ongoing program of science demonstrations, traveling exhibits from other science centers throughout North America and special programs for local schools. At weekend "Camp-Ins," children in first through eighth grades stay overnight at the Center, explore the exhibits, and watch a laser show and IMAX film.

The George
Inness Gallery
at the
Montclair Art
Museum.

On the museum grounds, adjacent to Liberty State Park, there are several interactive exhibits as well as "Solar Babies," tall, slender solar and wind-activated sculptures. Several outdoor decks and a picnic area afford spectacular views of New York City and its harbor.

Food and drink: The cafeteria offers sandwiches, pizza, hot dogs and other child-friendly food.

Montclair Art Museum

A suburban museum features a first-class collection of American art.

Map reference: pages 52–53, A4
3 S. Montclair Ave (at Bloomfield Ave), Montclair, NJ 07042
Tel: 973-746-5555, www.montclair-art.com
Tues–Sun 11am–5pm, Thurs to 9pm
Bus: From midtown Manhattan, take DeCamp Bus 33 from Port Authority terminal to Bloomfield and South Mountain Aves in Montclair.
Admission fee (except Sat 11am–2pm), museum store, wheelchair accessible.

Montclair is one of those outlying towns transformed by the railroad mania of the 19th century into highly desirable main-line suburbs. With the businessmen commuters who flocked to Montclair came a bevy of artists. One of the trendsetters in that regard was George Inness, the master American landscapist. Inevitably the need for an art center was felt, and by 1914 the Montclair Art Museum was up and running.

The collection is especially strong in American art – realistic portraits dating as far back as the early years of the 18th century, romantic landscapes typical of the 19th century, art and objects by Native Americans. And enhancing it all now is the Museum's renovated quarters in upper Montclair, reopened in early 2002 after a $14.5-million face lift.

Floor space was virtually doubled in the physical makeover, which added a wing and several galleries, a glass-roofed Great Hall nearly two stories high, a glass-encased staircase and up-graded administrative facilities. Inness, who lived the last decade of his life in Montclair, is now honored with a gallery of his own. The Museum owns 17 of his paintings, two watercolors and an etching. One of his earlier masterpieces,

Queensborough Bridge, 1927, Elsie Driggs, from the Montclair Art Museum.

(ca. 1884–86). There are two masterful works by Joseph Blackburn, and Robert Henri, mentor of American realists of Ashcan School notoriety, is represented by the vibrantly youthful *Jimmy O'D*, painted about 1925 during Henri's visit to Ireland.

The serene *Early Morning at Cold Spring* (1850) is by that other New Jersey landscape master, *Asher B. Durand* (he lived in what is now Maplewood). There are works, too, by Thomas Cole, William Merritt Chase, Stuart Davis, Edward Hopper and many more, including later 20th-century modernists such as Josef Albers, Arshile Gorky, Robert Motherwell and Andy Warhol. The sculpture ranges from works by Augustus Saint-Gaudens and Daniel Chester French to Chaim Gross, Theodore Roszak, Louise Nevelson and George Segal (*Girl on a Chair*, 1970).

The Museum also has more than 3,500 drawings, watercolors, prints and photos. The print collection contains works by some of the major figures in that endeavor, including Currier & Ives, John James Audubon, George Catlin, Childe Hassam and James A. M. Whistler. The Native American collection was stimulated by an early benefactor's intense interest in Indian art and artifacts.

Special exhibitions are numerous. One recent showing, for example, was *Primal Vision: Albert Bierstadt "Discovers" America*, centered on that artist's racially problematic conception of Columbus's grandiose arrival among awed natives. Exhibitions over the years have included *The Eight and Their Generation*, *The American Character Revealed in Art* and *Two Hundred Years of American Masterpieces*, to name a few at random.

Delaware Water Gap (1857), shows the clear influence of the Hudson River School and its exterior grandeur. By contrast, *Winter Morning, Montclair*, and *Early Autumn, Montclair*, painted in the 1880s, show the spiritual intensity that marked Inness' later, impressionist-like work.

George Washington posed for both Gilbert Stuart and Charles Willson Peale, both of whom are represented in the collection; the Museum owns Peale's *General George Washington*, done in 1783. Later portraits include Thomas Sully's *Samson Levy, Jr.*, and Thomas Eakins' painting of his art dealer, *Charles Haseltine* (ca. 1901). John Singer Sargent is here, too, with *Ernest-Ange Duez*

Food and drink: A varied selection of cuisine is available just steps away from the Museum at restaurants along Bloomfield Avenue. They include the Chelsea Grille (973-509-3444), A Taste of Asia (973-744-3525), Taj Palace (973-744-1909) and Top Notch (973-746-5699), all moderately priced with a casual atmosphere. Directly across the street, for coffee lovers, is a Starbucks café.

Mystic Seaport

The days of America's long-ago dalliance with the sea are brought to life again in a restored village on the Connecticut shore.

Map reference: pages 52–53, F1
50 Greenmanville Ave, Mystic, CT 06355-0990.
Tel: 860-572-5315, www.mysticseaport.org
By car: Interstate 95 to Exit 90, then 1 mile
south to Seaport.
Museum grounds: daily 9am–6pm; ships and
exhibits: 9am–5pm.
Admission fee, museum stores, restaurants,
educational programs, limited wheelchair access.

A two-hour drive north on I-95 will deliver you from the pressing crowds of New York's asphalt jungle to the cobblestone walkways and leisurely ambience of Mystic Seaport. Here you are invited to imagine what it was like living on the edge of maritime America in olden days. It's a mini-village with ships and shops that bills itself as "the Museum of America and the Sea" and evokes the storied age of sail.

It was not exactly a major seaport. Nor were any big battles fought off shore. Its major activity was shipbuilding. The village sits at the mouth of the Mystic River, which flows into Long Island Sound. The name Mystic derives from the Algonquin *missituk* – "great tidal river." English settlers showed up in 1654, and before long they were cobbling together vessels for the coastal trade and the busy West Indian market. Pretty soon, a whole lot of shipbuilding was going on – in the 19th century more than 800 vessels were launched here, including the fast-moving clippers.

Shipbuilding times were good from about 1820 to 1860. And whaling was big, too. Mystic's seafarers, like those next door in New London and Stonington, took up the pursuit of whales that kept countinghouses humming. Eventually, however, Mystic's shipyards went out of business as wood and sail lost out to steel and steam. Little went on here until well into the 20th century, when Mystic emerged as a resort community stocked up on maritime memorabilia and much pride in its past.

The first steps in that direction were taken in 1929 with formation of the Marine Historical Association, but it was not until 1941 and the arrival of the venerable *Charles W. Morgan* that the past really began to come alive for the seaport and its patrons. Reeking with history, the *Morgan* was a hangover from the golden age of whaling, a full-rigged ship that was being decked out in New Bedford even as Herman Melville and Frederick Douglass, runaway slave turned ship caulker, stopped by. The *Morgan* went forth to chase whales and sperm oil across the oceans for 37 long voyages and 80 remarkable years before slipping into its final resting place at Mystic at the neat age of 100.

Now she's a national historic landmark, ever the centerpiece for all the tourists who keep stepping aboard to check out deck, forecastle, booby hatch, blubber room and all the trappings of an improbable long-ago encounter between man and mammal. There are other ships to visit, too. The *L. A. Dunton* is a fishing schooner built in 1921 that worked the Grand Banks and brought back many a load of cod to Gloucester in its time. Even older (1882) is the full-rigged training ship *Joseph Conrad*. Built in Copenhagen, it went down in 1905 with the loss of 22 Danish cadets, then was raised and repaired and added to the Mystic fold in 1947.

Altogether there are some 400 vessels at Mystic, mostly small craft, in a wide-ranging maritime collection that is said to be the largest in the world. Among them is a two-masted coasting schooner, the *Australia*, captured off Georgia in 1863 trying to slip past the Union blockade. Mystic also had the privilege of launching, in March 2000, a born-again version of one of the most notorious ships in American history: the *Amistad*, focal point of a raging controversy over slavery in 1839–41. Besides being the place where the *Amistad* replica was constructed, Mystic Seaport's quaint appearance made it an apt

The 1882 training vessel *Joseph Conrad* is one of several historic tall ships at Mystic Seaport.

setting for several scenes in Steven Spielberg's 1997 movie inspired by the shipboard slave rebellion and the ensuing legal battle. It was doubly apt since the *Amistad* and its rebels had actually been brought close by, to New London, in the first step to their eventual freedom.

Covering 17 acres (7 hectares), the seaport is the nation's largest maritime museum. It has more than 60 historic homes, buildings and waterfront industries, with "interpreters" – sometimes in costume – explaining the various facets of building and rigging the old ships. There are exhibits on sailmaking, rope handling, ship carving and other activities, a large number of ship figureheads and scrimshaw (whalemen's carvings from baleen or ivory), and unparalleled collections of marine photography and of models of clipper ships. Incomparable, too, is the G. W. Blunt White Library with the thousands of books, manuscripts, ship registers, logbooks, charts, maps and other material that make it a font of maritime data.

Food and drink: Three restaurants offer a choice of dining experiences: the Seamen's Inne (expensive), Schaefer's Spouter Tavern (moderate) and the Galley (inexpensive).

Newark Museum

An oasis of art and exotica awaits the unsuspecting visitor to the center of New Jersey's largest city.

Map reference: pages 52–53, A4
49 Washington St, Newark, NJ 07101.
Tel: 973-596-6550, www.newarkmuseum.org
Subway: From Manhattan, take the PATH train at 33rd St to Penn Station in Newark, then a NJ Transit Loop bus to the museum.
Wed–Sun noon–5pm, Thurs to 8.30pm.
Free admission (except planetarium), museum shop, café, guided tours, art workshops, films, concerts, wheelchair access.

Three famous Newark names – Dana, Bamberger and Ballantine – are bound up with the Newark Museum. Oddly enough, all were born elsewhere – Dana in Vermont, Bamberger in Baltimore, Ballantine in Albany, New York.

John Cotton Dana founded the Museum in 1909 as an offshoot of his legendary effort in making the Newark Public Library a user-friendly place with a thoroughly democratic mission. The Museum was housed on the library's fourth floor until 1926, when it moved into a home of its own courtesy of Louis Bamberger, owner of one of the country's great department stores.

The $750,000, three-story museum was designed by the Chicago architect Jarvis Hunt. Added to it in 1937 was an adjacent mansion that had been built for brewery magnate John Holme Ballantine. Used for museum offices, the Ballantine House was restored in 1976 to its Victorian splendor. A planetarium was opened in 1953. One more major undertaking – a four-year renovation, under architect Michael Grave, that was completed in 1989 – has thrust the Newark Museum into newfound public favor as a gem of its kind and a contributing factor in the city's own reawakening from its long night of urban depression.

Asia, Egypt, America

The Museum has 80 galleries brimming with artifacts of art and science, old and new. It has long been most famous for its Tibetan collection, a circumstance that arose from a chance encounter between two men aboard a steamship out of Yokohama in 1910. One was a museum trustee, Edward N. Crane, and the other a missionary who collected Asian objects. The missionary, Dr. Albert L. Shelton, lent his collection for display in Newark, and eventually the collection, much augmented, wound up in the Museum's hands. The centerpiece is a Buddhist altar that was consecrated in 1990 by the Dalai Lama on a visit to Newark.

The Tibetan objects are part of an Asian Collection that includes a wide range of artifacts spanning the centuries – porcelain and calligraphy from Korea, stone and wood sculpture from India, enamels and lacquer ware from China, *netsuke* and prints from various Japanese periods, and all manner of bowls, vessels and textiles.

A highlight of the holdings from ancient Egypt and the Mediterranean is the 3,000-year-old painted *Coffin Lid of Henet-Mer*, the so-called Songstress of Amun, created for her burial across the Nile River from Thebes. The lid was discovered in 1926 minus its mummy, removed by tomb robbers in ancient times. From the 1st century A.D. is a glass-and-bronze *Oil Flask* of a type Romans took with them to the public baths, and from the same time and place is a marble *Portrait of Roman Lady* in elaborate hairstyle à la Faustina the elder, wife of Antoninus Pius.

Newark's ancestral ties to New England and its Federalist underpinnings are reflected in its collection of American paintings and decorative arts. A walnut *High Chest of Drawers* in stately Queen Anne style from 1740–50, its creator unknown, suggests the rise of both colonial and British fortunes. It was a time when gleaming portraits of self-confident subjects were going up in front halls and parlors, an outstanding example being John Singleton Copley's *Portrait of Mrs. Joseph Scott*, painted about 1765. Later, when the Revolution ignited, the Loyalist-minded Scotts fled to England. Copley was already one step ahead of them.

There are notable works by later portraitists, among them John Singer Sargent's rendering of *Mrs. Charles Thursby* (1898–98), and Oliver Tarbell Eddy's *Portrait of the Four Youngest Children of William Rankin, Sr.* (1838), in addition to paintings by Hudson River School luminaries, American Impressionists such as Mary Cassatt and Childe Hassam, and African-American artists Romare Bearden, Jacob Lawrence and others.

The other half

The Ballantine House offers a discrete charm of its own in depicting how the upper half lived once upon a time. The brick mansion was erected by Newark's polyglot labor force of Irish, Scots, Germans, Italians, Poles and other newcomers and completed in 1885. The living quarters were sumptuous and included a parlor, reception area, library, dining room, music room and a place for billiards, while the second floor contained bedrooms for John and Jeannette Ballantine – portraits of each were painted by Benjamin Constant for $4,000 apiece – and daughter Alice, plus a boudoir for the missus. Family life and the servants' view are illustrated in *Upstairs, Downstairs* fashion by printed guide information largely pitched to visiting schoolchildren, an approach in keeping with Dana's belief that public facilities of this kind should reach out to the wider community and serve primarily as a means of education. The Museum also has a Mini Zoo, a sculpture garden, a schoolhouse and the Alice and Leonard Dreyfuss Planetarium.

Food and drink: A café is situated in the Charles Engelhard Court on the main floor, the center of much social activity at the Museum, including summer jazz concerts in the garden and in the court itself.

From Brooklyn Heights, 1925, George Copeland Ault, Newark Museum.

The Gravenor Family, ca. 1754, Thomas Gainsborough, from the Yale Center for British Art.

Yale University Museums

An Ivy League institution offers a three-in-one museum experience.

Map reference: pages 52–53, F1

Peabody Museum of Natural History
170 Whitney Ave (at Sachem St), New Haven, CT.
Tel: 203-432-5050, www.peabody.yale.edu
By car: I-91, Exit 3. The museum is five blocks northeast of New Haven Green.
Mon–Sat 10am–5pm, Sun noon–5pm.
Admission fee, shop, handicapped access.

Yale University Art Gallery
1111 Chapel St (at York St), New Haven, CT.
Tel: 203-432-0600, www.yale.edu/artgallery
Tues–Sat 10am–5pm, Sun 1pm–6pm.
Free admission, handicapped access.

Yale Center for British Art
1080 Chapel St (at High St), New Haven, CT.
Tel: 203-432-2800, www.yale.edu/ycba
Tues–Sat 10am–5pm, Sun noon–5pm.
Free admission, gift shop, handicapped access.

You can kill *three* birds with one stone by heading for Connecticut, getting off I-91 at New Haven, and visiting the campus of Yale University. There you'll find not only the venerable Peabody Museum of Natural History but also a couple of art galleries. But you'd better move fast – it's a lot to see in one day.

The Peabody is famous for its dinosaurs and rich in all other categories, from A/anthropology to Z/zoology. Kids of all ages, as the saying goes, love the place, which is named for George Peabody. He started out life as a grocer's boy early in the 19th century and wound up making millions, only to give much of it away endowing museums and institutions at places like Baltimore, Harvard and Salem, Massachusetts.

One of those places was at Yale. Peabody was prevailed upon by his scientist nephew, Othniel C. Marsh, to bankroll the establishment of a place to store the university's collection, including all the fossils that Marsh was digging up in expeditions out West. (Marsh was America's first full professor of vertebrate paleontology and became a legend in his own right.)

Today the Museum, founded in 1876, has something like 11 million specimens of life as we know it – animal, vegetable and mineral. It's all housed in a massive building that looks something like a Gothic cathedral, with the two-story-tall Great Hall of Dinosaurs – designed to accommodate some of Marsh's own fossils – as a central showcase. One fierce-looking dino is a 67-foot-long (20-meter) *Apatosaurus*. Bigger yet (110 feet/34 meters) is Rudolph Zallinger's great 1947 mural, *The Age of Reptiles*, giving us a kind of panoramic snapshot of 300 million years of life on planet Earth.

There are artifacts of native cultures from the Americas, the Pacific, ancient Egypt and far-flung places. There are wildlife dioramas and specimens of flora and fauna, minerals and meteorites. Many special exhibitions are mounted at the Peabody, both physical and cultural in nature – one such in the latter category, for example, was *The African Roots of the Amistad Rebellion*.

Art attack

You've gotta have art? Then hop over to Chapel Street and stop in at the Yale University Art Gallery. Like so much else of New England pedigree, this is the oldest college art gallery in the country, founded in 1832. Since then it's amassed more than 100,000 items covering a time frame stretching back to ancient Egypt and forward to the present. Most notable is its collection of American paintings and decorative objects, including fine furniture and silver.

There's also art from Africa, Asia, Europe and the Americas of pre- and post-Columbian time. Accommodating it all are a pair of connected buildings, one of Italian Gothic design (1928) and the other modernist in style (1953). A major renovation was completed in 2001 that involved an innovative reinstallation of the American holdings – paintings rehung, sculpture and decorative objects repositioned, all done so as to emphasize their connection aesthetically and otherwise.

The American paintings include works by Winslow Homer, Thomas Eakins, Edward Hopper, Thomas Hart Benton, Charles Sheeler and Marsden Hartley. Europeans are here, too – the French trendsetters Corot and Courbet; the Impressionists Manet, Renoir, Degas; the social realist Millet; the post-Impressionist van Gogh (notably his *Night Cafe*); the modernists Picasso and Matisse; the "crazies" Duchamp, Magritte, Dalí; and others in the avant-garde, including Klee, Kandinsky, Rothko, de Kooning and Stella.

British invasion

Conveniently situated right across the street from the Yale University Art Gallery is the Yale Center for British Art, a haven for Anglophiles and ordinary art lovers. It's the next best thing to being in London, with the most comprehensive collection of British art outside of Britain itself.

All the British worthies are here: the portraitists Gainsborough and Reynolds; the landscapists Turner and Constable, whose work prefigured the Impressionist revolution; Hogarth the realist-

satirist. The collection is housed in skylighted galleries imaginatively designed (1977) by the architect Louis Kahn. The benefactor of it all was Paul Mellon, tycoon and art lover who spent 40 years putting together his collection, which he presented to Yale University in 1966.

Here you get a panoramic account of British life and culture going back at least as far as the reign of Henry VIII in the 16th century. The size of the collection is staggering: 50,000 prints and drawings; 1,400 paintings and sculptures; rare books, maps and graphics. There are paintings by non-English outsiders – the Flemish Peter Paul Rubens, the Venetian master Canaletto, the Americans John Singleton Copley, Benjamin West, James McNeill Whistler. There is a large collection of sporting and animal paintings, of marine paintings, and of travel illustrations, as well as works of sculpture, including pieces by Henry Moore.

Food and drink: The Yale neighborhood is well-known for its eating opportunities. There are snack places such as the Atticus Bookstore Café (1082 Chapel St, 203-776-4040, inexpensive), serving soups, sandwiches and pastries, and pizzerias of outsized legend such as Frank Pepe's (157 Wooster St, 203-865-5762, inexpensive) – was this the first great American pizza-maker? – and Sallie's (237 Wooster St, 203-624-5271, inexpensive). There are also full-fledged restaurants such as Bruxelles (220 College St, 203-777-7752, expensive) and Bangkok Gardens (172 York St, 203-789-8684, moderate).

Horse Attacked by a Lion, ca. 1762, George Stubbs, from the Yale Center for British Art.

The Gallery Scene

Painters, sculptors and dealers rub elbows with prospective buyers, as well as those who are merely curious, at the city's art venues uptown, downtown and wherever creativity is displayed

The Gallery Scene

New York City has more than 500 galleries, from hushed uptown venues dedicated to the Old Masters to impromptu spaces with experimental art.

Most Manhattan galleries are closed Sunday and Monday. For current shows and openings, check listings in New York *magazine,* Time Out New York, The New Yorker, *and the Friday and Sunday Arts sections of the* New York Times. *Exhibit information is also found in the monthly* Gallery Guide *available free at most galleries around town. See pages 218–9 for a partial listing of New York galleries.*

LEFT: The late Leo Castelli, SoHo pioneer and champion of postwar American art.

OPPOSITE: Artist Roberto Juarez at the Robert Miller Gallery.

Y ou could say that New York's contemporary gallery scene was born in the Abstract Expressionist movement of the 1940s. That's when Peggy Guggenheim – niece of Solomon, for whom the world-famous funnel-shaped museum on Fifth Avenue is named – opened a gallery at 30 West 57th Street. Called "Art of This Century," it quickly became the city's most stimulating venue for contemporary art, showcasing her favorite French surrealists as well as edgy new work by a Wyoming-born painter named Jackson Pollock.

As practiced by Pollock, Willem de Kooning, Mark Rothko and others, Abstract Expressionism was a purely American phenomenon, rising from a desire to express ideas and experience through art. Reaching its peak in the 1950s, the movement's geographic center was New York, where the majority of artists lived and worked, often within a block or two of each other's Greenwich Village studios. Manhattan suddenly became the mecca of the international art scene, although its galleries remained firmly uptown on 57th Street, Fifth Avenue and farther up on Madison Avenue.

In the 1960s, driven out by rising rents in the Village, artists began exploring the neighborhood south of Houston Street, where a decline in manufacturing meant that large spaces were virtually going begging. They were perfect for conversion into artists' lofts and studios, and cheap, too. Dealers followed, including the adventurous Paula Cooper, who opened a gallery in what was newly dubbed SoHo – South of Houston – in 1968.

The area's fate was more or less sealed in 1971, when the late Leo Castelli moved his highly successful gallery from the Upper East Side to West Broadway, which soon became SoHo's main drag. Castelli, who helped finance a landmark Greenwich Village show of Abstract Expressionists in 1951, was also the first major dealer to represent Pop Art icons Roy Lichtenstein and Andy Warhol.

By the late 1970s, the gallery scene was in full swing, reaching its zenith in the 1980s, when exhibits by artists like Keith Haring and Jean-Michel Basquiat attracted hordes of black-clad hipsters and well-heeled collectors. By then the neighborhood was overflowing with boutiques and restaurants, a trend that accelerated in the 1990s. As big-name uptown designers opened ever-glossier ateliers on SoHo's cobblestone side streets, galleries closed or moved to cheaper upstairs digs. As early as the 1980s some defected to lower Broadway or followed a new generation of artists to the East Village, which had a brief but intense gallery scene of its own.

The Chelsea exodus

By the mid-1990s, a mass exodus was under way, with a number of important galleries moving to the industrial Chelsea neighborhood of the West 20s, while others migrated uptown in a uniquely New York style art-and-real-estate circle. (The artists themselves – at least those who hadn't snagged rent-controlled lofts in SoHo or adjacent TriBeCa – had long gone in search of greener pastures, including Brooklyn's gritty Williamsburg section.) By 1997, the *New York Times* was calling the far-western block of 22nd Street in Chelsea a "SoHo in miniature." Today, with dozens of galleries stretching from the artist-owned White Columns (320 W. 13th St, 212-924-4212, Wed–Sun noon–5pm) to Robert Miller (524 W. 26th St, 212-366-4774, Tues–Sat 10am–6pm), 22nd Street between Tenth and Eleventh avenues could actually be considered a Chelsea in miniature.

Even some of the trees planted along the block are part of a worldwide installation by the late German conceptual artist Joseph Beuys. Entitled *7000 Oaks* (actually there are only about 23 oaks here; the others are in Kassel, Germany), the work was partly underwritten by the Dia Center for the Arts (548 W. 22nd St, 212-989-5566, Wed–Sun noon–6pm), a Chelsea pioneer that opened a four-story exhibition space near the corner of Eleventh Avenue in 1987. Dia's exhibits of contemporary art, poetry readings, lectures and concerts are well worth seeing. There's also a bookstore and a rooftop espresso bar with views of the Hudson.

Heading back toward Tenth Avenue, works by big-name contemporary American and European artists are shown at the multi-roomed Sonnabend Gallery (536 W. 22nd St, 212-627-1018, Tues–Sat 10am–6pm), once located on West Broadway alongside Leo Castelli – to whom Romanian-born owner Ileana Sonnabend was married from 1933 to 1960.

Nearby, Matthew Marks (522 W. 22nd St, 212-243-1650, and 523 W. 24th St, 212-243-0200, Tues–Sat 10am–6pm) was one of the first major galleries to make the move to Chelsea, in 1995. An influential dealer, he often presents drawings, photographs, prints and other works on paper, as well as contemporary painters such as Lucien Freud and Ellsworth Kelly. Around the corner

and a block south, meanwhile, former SoHo pioneer Paula Cooper (534 W. 21st St, 212-255-1105, Tues–Sat 10am–6pm) offers an intriguing mix of conceptual and minimalist sculpture, paintings, drawings, prints and photography.

At the cusp of the new millennium, a few SoHo stalwarts moved even farther uptown, including the Mary Boone Gallery (745 Fifth Ave, 212-752-2929, Tues–Sat 10am–6pm). Boone, a Castelli protégé who opened a SoHo gallery in 1977, became a major force with shows of 1980s art-world stars like Jean-Michel Basquiat and David Salle, and continues a policy of cutting-edge exhibits both here and at her new Chelsea gallery (541 W. 24th St).

A home for art

At the turn of the 20th century, the National Academy's annual shows at The Art Students League – founded in 1875 and still going strong at 215 57th Street – attracted the crème de la crème of American and European artists. By 1939, the galleries along 57th Street, off Fifth Avenue, were cited for "exhibiting works of virtually every period and phase in the history of art, as well as examples of all contemporary movements."

Such is the case today with the Marlborough Gallery (40 W. 57th St, 212-541-4900, Mon–Sat 10am–5.30pm) showing prominent 20th-century American and European artists, and the George Adams Gallery (50 W. 57th St, 212-644-5665,

Knoedler Gallery.

Tues–Sat 10am–6pm) featuring works of well-known American and Latin American artists.

Back downtown, SoHo's reign as New York's art center may have ended, but there are still enough exhibit spaces to make gallery-hopping a test of endurance. Artists Space (38 Greene St, 3rd floor, 212-226-3970, Tues–Sat 11am–6pm), for instance, is still thriving, though it was founded more than 30 years ago as a showcase for unknown and emerging artists like Robert Mapplethorpe and Cindy Sherman. Other survivors include A.I.R. (40 Wooster St, 2nd floor, 212-966-0799, Tues–Sat 11am–6pm), a non-profit, women's art collective that concentrates on nontraditional and political art, and P.P.O.W. (476 Broome St, 212-941-8642, Tues–Sat 10am–6pm), a former East Village gallery that specializes in works by artists "outside the norm."

There's a plethora of good small galleries, too, especially in the old cast-iron buildings along lower Broadway, including Exit Art (560 and 548 Broadway, 212-966-7745, Tues–Fri 10am–6pm, Sat 11am–6pm), home to innovative works by emerging artists. Also worth seeing, though closed in summer, are a pair of SoHo installations created by Walter de la Maria and maintained by the Dia Center for the Arts: *New York Earth Room* (141 Wooster St, second floor) and *The Broken Kilometer* (393 W. Broadway). The first piece is exactly what it sounds like – a room filled with soil. The other is composed of 500 polished brass rods arranged on a gallery floor.

Village people

When New York's first collective showing of avant-garde art opened in 1913 at the Armory on Lexington Avenue, Marcel Duchamp's *Nude Descending a Staircase* instantly became the cubist catalyst for a generation of American artists. Many of them flocked – along with poets and writers – to the weekly Greenwich Village salons hosted by Mabel Dodge Luhan, a gregarious heiress with radical leanings, who was one of the show's sponsors.

If the romantic image of struggling artists in attic garrets has long been more myth than reality, the Village retains an authentic artistic history that includes the outdoor exhibits held seasonally in Washington Square Park since the early 1930s. On a more important level, it's also home to New York University's Grey Art Gallery (100 Washington Square East, 212-998-6780,

Opening at a SoHo gallery.

Tues–Fri 11am–6pm, Sat 11am–5pm). The Grey has a reputation for being one of the city's most intriguing venues. Its mission to "collect, preserve, study, document, interpret, and exhibit the evidence of human culture" (no small task) means you're likely to see anything from shows of post-Revolution Cuban photography and Japanese cosmetics to police photography and the Czech avant-garde. Exhibits also occasionally draw from NYU's impressive collection of American paintings, which includes several by New York's seminal cadre of Abstract Expressionists – who, in another of the city's art-related circles, had their studios nearby.

Food and drink: The Cedar Tavern (82 University Place, 212-741-9754, inexpensive) is a funky Village bar that, in its original location a block away, was a hangout for local Abstract Expressionist painters in the 1950s. The sleeker Knickerbocker Bar & Grill (33 University Place, 212-228-8490, moderate) serves a menu of American classics, along with nightly jazz. Da Silvano (260 Sixth Ave, 212-982-2343, moderate) is an excellent Northern Italian restaurant (with sidewalk tables) that attracts a celebrity crowd. In SoHo proper, Fanelli Café (94 Prince St, 212-226-9412, moderate) is an artists' hangout that retains a low-key charm, complete with red-checked tablecloths. Jerry's (101 Prince St, 212-966-9464, moderate) is a favorite for basic American food, with a branch in Chelsea (473 W. 23rd St).

Also in Chelsea is the Empire Diner (210 Tenth Ave, 212-243-2736, moderate), a 24-hour spot that gets interesting after midnight. Nearby, Wild Lily Tea Room (511 W. 22nd St, 212-691-2258, inexpensive) is a tiny Zen-like oasis serving snacks and a wide variety of teas. For Irish breakfasts and pub basics, try The Half King (505 W. 23rd St, 212-462-4300, moderate), a "writer's bar" co-owned by Sebastian Junger.

In midtown, the pricey Russian Tea Room (150 W. 57th St, 212-974-2111, expensive) offers vodka, caviar and weekend brunch in opulent surroundings. Le Colonial (149 E. 57th St, 212-752-0808, moderate) serves French-Vietnamese cuisine, and is a good spot for a drink and hors d'oeuvres after gallery-hopping.

Essential Information

Visiting the Museums

CityPass

This pass offers a discount of more than 50 percent on seven attractions – the American Museum of Natural History, Guggenheim Museum, Intrepid Sea Air Space Museum, Museum of Modern Art, Whitney Museum, Empire State Building and Circle Line Harbor Cruise. Buy a CityPass booklet at any of the attractions or online at www.citypass.com. The tickets are good for one admission at each attraction during a nine-day period starting with your first admission. And you won't need to wait in line to buy tickets.

When to Visit

Many museums close on Monday and tend to be most crowded on weekends. If possible, take advantage of evening hours, after schoolchildren and most tourists have left. Many major museums have late hours at least once a week: the Met is open to 9pm on Friday and Saturday; MoMA to 8.15pm on Friday, the Guggenheim to 8pm on Friday and Saturday; and the Whitney to 9pm on Friday.

Admission Fees

Some museums are free, but most charge. This can take the form of a "suggested donation." Technically you can pay whatever you wish, but you will be strongly urged to pay the full amount (or more, if you're feeling generous). Some museums have free admission during off-hours. Nearly all offer reduced rates for children, seniors and students.

People with Disabilities

Most museums are accessible to wheelchairs, although some assistance may be required. Always call for details before visiting. One possible exception is historic buildings that can't be retrofitted without compromising the integrity of the structure.

Disabled travelers can get information about rights, facilities, etc., from the Mayor's Office for People with Disabilities, 52 Chambers St, Room 206, New York, NY 10007, tel: 212-788-2830.

The Society for Accessible Travel & Hospitality (SATH), 212-447-7284, provides extensive educational and resource material to expand travel opportunities in New York and around the world.

Tourist Offices

NYC & Company Visitors Information Center

810 Seventh Ave, New York, NY 10019, tel: 212-397-8222, 1-800-NYCVISIT, www.nycvisit.com. Mon–Fri 8am–6pm, Sat–Sun 9am–5pm.
Maps and information about hotel packages and discount admission programs to various attractions. The *Official NYC Guide* is a comprehensive listing of activities, hotels, tours, restaurants, etc. Walk-in visitors are welcome at the Visitors Information Center.

Times Square Visitors Center

Embassy Theater, 1560 Broadway (between 46th and 47th Sts), New York, NY. Daily 8am–8pm.
A good source of information, featuring a ticket center for Broadway shows, as well as useful facilities like e-mail and currency exchange counters. Free walking tours of Times Square Friday at noon.

Harlem Visitors & Convention Association

219 W. 135th St, New York, NY 10030, tel: 212-862-8497, fax: 212-862-8745. Mon–Fri 10am–6pm.
An essential source of information about tours, events and landmarks in Harlem.

Bronx Council on the Arts

1738 Hone Ave, Bronx, NY 10461, tel: 718-931-9500, www.bronxarts.org.
Offers information about art, music and other events.

Brooklyn Tourism Council

30 Flatbush Ave, Brooklyn, NY 11217, tel: 718-855-7882 www.brooklynX.org.
Information on culture, history, parks and events.

Queens Council on the Arts

79-01 Park Lane South, Woodhaven, NY 11421, tel: 718-291-ARTS, www.queenscouncilarts.org.

Staten Island Tourism Council

1 Edgewater Plaza, Staten Island, NY 10305, tel: 718-442-4356, 1-800-573-7469 www.statenislandusa.com.
Information on events and attractions. Look for a kiosk in the Ferry Terminal at Battery Park.

Tours

Art Horizons International

tel: 212-969-9410
Visits to galleries, museums and artists' studios.

Circle Line

tel: 212-563-3200 or 800-533-3779
Boat trips around Manhattan, as well as harbor cruises from South Street Seaport.

Gallery Tours New York

tel: 212-946-1548
Walking tours of 10 galleries in Chelsea and SoHo.

Gray Line New York

tel: 212-397-2600
Double-decker buses with hop-on, hop-off itineraries.

Joyce Gold History Tours of NY

tel: 212-242-5762
Bus and walking tours of New York history and architecture.

Municipal Art Society

tel: 212-935-3960
History and architecture tours.

Getting Around

Subway

The Metropolitan Transit Authority (718-330-1234, non-English 718-330-4847, www.mta.nyc.ny.us) is the source for route and schedule information for subways and buses throughout the five boroughs. Subways are a fast, easy and inexpensive way to get around the city. Trains run 24 hours a day, with waiting time between trains normally just a few minutes, depending on the time of day.

Routes are identified by letters, numbers and colors. Free subway maps are available in the *Official NYC Guide* and at any subway station booth. The cost is $1.50 per ride, no matter how far or how many times you transfer (as long as you don't pass through the turnstile gate; if you do, another fare must be paid). Purchase either tokens (coins for each ride) or a MetroCard, which can save you money on multiple rides. Options include the $4 one-day Fun Pass; the 7-day ($17) and 30-day ($63) unlimited ride cards; and a pay-per-ride card ($10 for 11 rides, but you may put any amount onto a MetroCard). There are 3,500 MetroCard merchants throughout the city.

If you pay your fare with MetroCard, you may transfer free from bus to subway, subway to bus, or bus to bus within two hours of the time you paid your fare. Unlimited Ride MetroCard includes all transfers, at no charge.

Bus

New York's 3,700 buses operate throughout the five boroughs on more than 200 routes. You are usually within a few blocks of a bus stop. The cost is $1.50 per ride, no matter the distance. You can pay with a MetroCard, a token or exact change in coins. The driver does not give change and fareboxes do not accept dollar bills or pennies. A MetroCard can save money on multiple rides. If you pay your fare with MetroCard, you may transfer free from bus to subway, subway to bus, or bus to bus within two hours of the time you paid your fare.

Routes run uptown/downtown and crosstown from 6am until shortly after midnight, with waiting time between each bus approximately 5–15 minutes, depending on the time of day.

Bus stops have a tall, round sign with a bus emblem and route number; some have bus shelters. Most

also include a "Guide-A-Ride," a rectangular box attached to the bus sign pole that displays a route map and bus schedule.

Artlink

The Queens Artlink (212-708-9750), a courtesy, weekend shuttle service to cultural attractions in Queens, runs from MoMA (53rd St between Fifth and Sixth Aves) to MoMA QNS, P.S. 1 Contemporary Art Center, the Isamu Noguchi Garden Museum, Socrates Sculpture Park and the American Museum of the Moving Image.

Taxi

New York City taxicabs are yellow and may be hailed on the street or found at taxi stands at major hotels and transportation hubs. On the street, stick out your arm to signal a taxi. A taxi is available when its white rooftop number light is lit. The rooftop light also has the words "Off Duty"; when these are lit, the taxi will not pick up passengers.

Taxis have meters. The total cost depends on the distance traveled and time spent in the cab. Taxi fares are $2 for the first ⅕ mile, then 30¢ for each ⅕ of a mile thereafter, and 20¢ per minute when the cab is not moving; a 50¢ night surcharge is in effect between 8pm and 6am. Any bridge or tunnel tolls will be added to the total charge; drivers might ask you to pay the tolls as you go through them. Taxi drivers expect a 15% tip on top of the final metered fare.

Try to hail a taxi in the direction you would like to travel; this saves time going around the block. Only yellow taxis are permitted by law to pick up without prearrangement.

Taxi services are regulated by the Taxi and Limousine Commission; 24-hour hotline 212-692-8294.

Practical Matters

Emergency & Medical Services
Medical services are extremely expensive. Always travel with comprehensive travel insurance to cover

emergencies.
● Police, fire, ambulance, dial: 911
● Deaf Emergency Line, tel: 800-421-1220 or TTY 800-662-1220 (police, fire, ambulance)
● Physicians Home Care, tel: 718-238-2100
● Dental emergency, tel: 212-573-9502
● 24-hour pharmacy, Genovese Drugstore, 68th St and Second Ave, tel: 212-772-0104
● Sex Crimes Report Line, tel: 212-267-7273

Public Holidays
New Year's Day (January 1)
Martin Luther King, Jr. Day (third Mon, Jan)
Presidents Day (third Mon, Feb)
Memorial Day (last Mon, May)
Independence Day (July 4)
Labor Day (first Mon, Sept)
Columbus Day (second Mon, Oct)
Veterans Day (November 11)
Thanksgiving (last Thurs, Nov).
Christmas Day (December 25)

Useful Web Sites

www.newyork.citysearch.com for listings and reviews of current arts and entertainment events, as well as restaurants and shopping. Excellent site.
www.newyorktoday.com from the *New York Times* is filled with details about everything from poetry readings in the Bronx to traffic in Midtown.
www.nypl.org for everything you need to know about the New York Public Library.
www.newyork.citysearch.co for up-to-date information on nightlife, museum exhibitions, restaurants, theater and more.
www.queens.nyc.ny.us for cultural attractions in Queens.
www.bronxmall.com for events in the Bronx and links to various cultural institutions.
www.centralparknyc.org for tours and events in Central Park.
www.galleryguide.org for listings of current museum and gallery exhibitions.

Further Reading

AIA Guide to New York City, Norval White and Elliot Willensky (Three Rivers Press, New York, 2000).

American Anthem: Masterworks from the American Folk Art Museum, Stacy C. Hollander and Brooke Davis Anderson (Henry N. Abrams, New York, 2002).

The American Art Book, Jay Tobler, ed. (Phaidon Press, London, 1999).

The American Century: Arts & Culture, 1900–1950, Barbara Haskell (Whitney Museum of American Art, New York, 1999).

American Visions: The Epic History of Art in America, Robert Hughes (Alfred A. Knopf, New York, 1997).

Dinosaurs in the Attic: An Excursion into the American Museum of Natural History, Douglas J. Preston (St. Martin's Press, New York, 1994).

The Encyclopedia of New York City, Kenneth T. Jackson, ed. (Yale University Press, 1995).

The Metropolitan Museum of Art Guide, Kathleen Howard, ed. (The Metropolitan Museum of Art, New York, 1994).

New York: A Guide to the Metropolis, Gerard R. Wolfe (McGraw-Hill Book Company, New York, 1988).

New York: An Illustrated History, Ric Burns (Knopf, New York, 1999).

New York Art Guide, Deborah Jane Gardner (Robert Silver Associates, 1987).

New York Modern: The Arts and the City, William B. Scott and Peter M. Rutkoff (The John Hopkins University Press, Baltimore, 1999).

The New York Times Guide to New York City Restaurants, William Grimes and Eric Asimov (The New York Times, New York, 2002).

Paintings from the Frick Collection, Bernice Davidson and Nadia Tscherny (Harry N. Abrams, New York, 1991).

Painting the Town: Cityscapes of New York, Jan Seidler Ramirez (Museum of the City of New York, New York, 2000).

Traveler's Guide to Art Museum Exhibitions 2002: The New York Times, Susan Mermelstein, ed. (Harry N. Abrams, New York, 2001).

Other Insight Guides

Insight Guide New York City is the major book in the series covering the entire metropolitan area, with features on food and drink, culture and the arts.

Smaller New York titles include *Insight Pocket Guide, Insight Compact Guide* and *Insight Guide Instant.* The laminated, easily foldable *Insight Fleximap to New York City* is a useful, easy-to-use companion to this guide.

Other cities in the *Museums and Galleries* series include Paris, Florence and London.

Gallery Listings

SoHo

Agora
415 W. Broadway, 5th Fl, New York, NY 10012, 212-226-4151. Tues–Sat noon–6pm.

A.I.R.
40 Wooster St, 2nd Fl, New York, NY 10013, 212-966-0799. Tues–Sat 11am–6pm.

American Indian Community House Gallery
708 Broadway, New York, NY 10012, 212-598-0100. Tues–Sat noon–6pm.

Arcadia Gallery
51 Greene St, New York, NY 10013, 212-965-1387. Mon–Fri 10am–6pm, Sat–Sun 11am–6pm.

Atlantic
40 Wooster St, 4th Fl, New York, NY 10013, 212-219-3183. Tues–Sat noon–6pm.

Axelle Fine Arts Galerie SoHo
148 Spring St, New York, NY 10012, 212-226-2262. Daily 11am–7pm.

Caldwell Snyder
451 W. Broadway, New York, NY 10012, 212-387-0208. Mon–Sat 11am–7pm, Sun 11am–6pm.

CFM
112 Greene St, New York, NY 10012, 212-966-3864. Mon–Sat 11am–6pm, Sun noon–6pm.

The Drawing Center
35 Wooster St, New York, NY 10013, 212-219-2166. Tues–Fri 10am–6pm, Sat 11am–6pm.

Eleanor Ettinger
119 Spring St, New York, NY 10012, 212-925-7474. Mon–Fri 10am–6pm, Sat 11am–6pm, Sun noon–6pm.

Franklin Bowles Gallery
431 W. Broadway, New York, NY 10012, 212-226-1616. Mon–Sun 11am–7pm.

Gallery Revel
96 Spring St, New York, NY 10012, 212-925-0600. Mon–Wed 10am–6pm, Thurs–Fri noon–7pm, Sat 11am–6pm, Sun noon–5pm.

Howard Greenberg/Gallery 292
120 Wooster St, 2nd Fl, New York, NY 10012, 212-334-0010. Tues–Sat 10am–6pm.

Inframundo
106 Spring St, Suite 65, New York, NY 10012, 212-431-7276. Wed–Sat 1pm–6pm.

Kent Gallery
67 Prince St, New York, NY 10012, 212-966-4500. Tues–Sat noon–6pm.

Lehmann Maupin
39 Greene St, New York, NY 10013, 212-965-0753. Tues–Sat 10am–6pm.

Louis K. Meisel
141 Prince St, New York, NY 10012, 212-677-1340. Tues–Sat 10am–6pm.

Montserrat
584 Broadway, New York, NY 10012, 212-941-8899. Tues–Sat noon–6pm.

The Painting Center
52 Greene St, 2nd Fl, New York, NY 10013, 212-343-1060. Tues–Sat 11am–6pm.

Peter Blum
99 Wooster St, New York, NY 10012, 212-343-0441. Tues–Fri 10am–6pm, Sat 11am–6pm.

P.P.O.W.
476 Broome St, 3rd Fl, New York, NY 10013, 212-941-8642. Tues–Sat 10am–6pm.

SoHo Triad Fine Arts
107 Grand St, New York, NY 10013, 212-965-9500. Mon–Fri

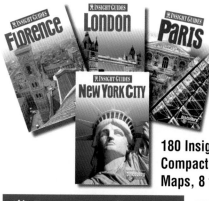

Index